TAKE TO THE UNSCATHED ROAD

Taylor,

Keep adventuring!

Justin Raphaelson

ISBN-13: 978-0-578-64690-9

Cover art by Ariela Paulsen
Cover & book layout by Chameleon Studios, LLC
Edited by Laurel Hecker

For Planet Earth,
the only one we have

Prologue

It all started the summer between my sophomore and junior years of college—the Fourth of July, to be exact. My best friend, Curtis, and I were accompanied by our other best friend, Jason, on the tenth or eleventh iteration of my family's annual vacation to the White Mountains of New Hampshire. It was the third time that Curtis and Jason made the trip with us, something my parents had started to encourage after coming to the realization that there was too much yelling and screaming when it was just our family. Back in those days, my brother and I would sit in the back seat of the car with our headphones on, playing Pokémon while we tried to avoid pissing anyone off. It was a formidable challenge for a confrontational child like me. But all the nonsense ceased once we began to invite friends to join us. For the most part.

On this trip, we planned to tread new ground. For too many years we had idled around the hotel pool, screaming obscenities in the sauna for no apparent reason when we got bored. For three teenagers, this was the only excitement available on vacation aside from the crappy all-you-can-eat Chinese buffet down the street and sleeping in as late as we wanted.

To make amends for our withering adolescence, we wanted to go on a new kind of adventure—one that amalgamated the endurance we had developed as high school cross country and track runners with the common sense we purported to have. Our friend Nel had told us on myriad occasions that we needed to start hiking, and on myriad occasions we had brushed off his advice. Today was different.

* * *

The Franconia Ridge Loop, a hike over Mount Lincoln and Mount Lafayette, is a breeding ground for inspiration. It turns some of the most sedentary people into believers. It's almost impossible to find yourself alone up there. And for good reason. It screams primal beauty—raging waterfalls, calf-burning inclines, winding alpine pathways, and interminable, sweeping vistas—the kind of attraction that has drawn humans to the mountains for millennia.

It wasn't convenient to set up civilization among the frigid slopes of the White Mountains. It was more of a spiritual pilgrimage. Archaeologists have estimated that around twenty-one Native sites existed in what is currently the White Mountain National Forest. People have been in the area for over ten thousand years. We weren't the first posse of explorers to be lured into these mountains. Nor the first posse of idiots.

* * *

"What the hell, Curtis? We're going to die of hypothermia up here!"

I was half-kidding, but the other half was growing steadily more convinced that we were in trouble. The sky was absent as we climbed higher and higher into obscurity. In its stead, thick, leaden clouds swept above us and blanketed the horizon.

We had passed a handful of waterfalls on our way up the seemingly endless and aptly named Falling Waters Trail. Our legs were not prepared for nearly four thousand vertical feet of elevation gain that day. Neither was the rest of us.

At this point in the hike, I had removed my cotton sweatshirt. The material was drenched in moisture from the heavy rainstorm dumping buckets of screw you all over us: *take that you morons, and maybe next time you'll come prepared!*

"Give me that sweatshirt, I'm freezing over here," Curtis replied. Of course, the old adage in the mountains is never wear cotton. We hadn't gotten the memo.

Meanwhile, Jason was only somewhat happier with his moisture-wicking sweatshirt, which was holding up moderately well. Surely though, it was ineffective in comparison to a proper rain jacket. After all, who hikes on a New Hampshire ridgeline in just a hooded sweatshirt, especially with forecasted rain?

Well, a lot of people. Many hikers go into the Whites wearing sneakers, sandals, and even jeans. Comparatively, we weren't *that* unprepared.

As we trudged further up the steep incline to who knows where, the fog insisted on following us. I felt as if we were ever-so-subtly being flipped off by Mother Nature. This bold experiment in the hills was proving to be everything we didn't expect and then some.

"The summit is right there, guys!" Jason yelled over the strengthening wind.

Yes, believe it or not, the dinky White Mountains of New Hampshire can bring with them brutal and tenacious storms. You wouldn't guess it based on their insignificant elevations, with Mount Washington being the highpoint at just under 6,300 feet. But Washington is the proud owner of the second highest ever recorded surface wind speed at 231 miles per hour.

"This is terrible," I muttered, as I found shelter from the gales underneath a rocky platform on the summit of Mount Lafayette.

"Yup," Jason responded. "The wind must be like seventy miles per hour up here!" He plopped down next to me and tried to cuddle with me. I swiftly nudged him away with my shoulder.

"What are you guys talking about, the views are great!" Curtis said, glancing at the dark, opaque skies on either side of him.

"Sure, says the guy who has the sweatshirt," I mumbled. I reached my trembling hands into my backpack and rustled around for something edible. It wasn't even worth the effort to shove Jason away as he inched closer to me. It was too damn cold.

The rain withdrew itself momentarily, but soon came crying back like a clingy Tinder match you should've swiped left on.

"Next time we do this we need to check the weather," I proposed, but quickly reversed course as I began to shiver uncontrollably, and my teeth started to chatter. "Then again . . . w-w-who knows . . . if there will be . . . a next time."

With my body practically inoperable from the cold and wetness, we rose from our perches and began to head down the trail to complete the loop. Typically, one descends the west side of Mount Lafayette, passes the Greenleaf Hut, and finishes on the Old Bridle Path. But we're not typical, and due to an absent-minded effort, we found ourselves on the Greenleaf Trail going north.

It wasn't until we popped out next to I-93 that we realized our mistake.

"Uh, GUYS," I yelled, as I emerged from the forest first.

"What?" Curtis fired back. As soon as he reached me, he gave me an earnest look of defeat.

Jason was the last to grace us with his presence.

"Where the hell are we?" He blurted out.

"I guess we'll have to see if we can hitchhike," Curtis instantly realized. I wasn't so sure.

"We could always call my parents." I looked down at my phone only to discover that we had no cell service.

We began to walk toward the parking lot for Cannon Mountain, which was across the street from where the trail had deposited us. When we reached it, Curtis confronted a couple and asked them if we could hitch a ride to our car, which was several miles south on I-93. Against my better judgment, we shoved our gear into their trunk and hopped into the back seat, unsure if we would make it out alive. Well, *I* was unsure.

* * *

The Quebec license plate should have been an indication that we weren't going to make it home that night in one piece. *Oh Lord, please don't let them take us over the border. Why are we driving north-bound, the car isn't this way!*

Our silent pleas went unanswered, as Hans and Francine sped off into the countryside—well, the mountainside, I suppose. Who cares anyway, we were going to be dinner that night if we didn't do anything quickly.

"Um, Hans, I think you went past the ex—err, went the wrong way," Curtis yelled over the couple who were yelling over the yelling on the French radio talk-show.

"Oui, oui!"

I wondered at the time how stupid three people had to be to get themselves into a situation like this—hitchhiking with random tourists. Well, that's what happens when you don't know how to read a map. One wrong turn is disastrous.

But lucky for us, our gamble to hitchhike, which initially promised only a fifty-fifty rate of survival, turned into a worthy roll of the dice. We made it out relatively unscathed, excepting the temporary loss of hearing invoked by our French-Canadian saviors. Bless their souls for bailing us out of our own stupidity. Contrary to my sarcastic account of the encounter, they were a pleasant couple that instilled in us the concept of "paying it forward."

"Merci!" Curtis yelled, as we frantically removed our belongings from the trunk and escaped toward my car.

"That was a terrible experience," Jason remarked, as we shoved our backpacks in the car and took off back toward the hotel.

"You mean the hike or the hitchhike?" Curtis inquired, as he took off his filthy boots to expose his even filthier feet which began to produce a repugnant smell.

"Both."

"Yeah, it kinda sucked," I responded, "but I'd do it again."

PART 1

Chapter 1

*"There was nowhere to go but everywhere,
so just keep on rolling under the stars."*

—Jack Kerouac, *On the Road*

* * *

The road is a refuge for misfits and wanderers, dreamers and vagabonds. It can be a death trap for imprudent pedestrians, or a throbbing migraine for middle-age commuters. It is a playground for drag racers, yet a profession for their pursuing traffic cops. It is inspiration for countless novels and movies, and an enticing destination for ambitious high school and college grads searching for meaning. Curtis and I are misfits, wanderers, dreamers, and vagabonds. Often, we are imprudent pedestrians, feel like middle-aged commuters, and occasionally engage in a race or two on the local interstate highway. And when we decided to embark upon a coming-of-age storybook adventure, we were sure as hell on a needle-in-a-haystack search for meaning.

What better way to find yourself than to go on a road trip, right? Come up with an impromptu plan, drop what you're doing, embark into a whirlpool of uncertainty, and then eventually return home to resume your former life. But to us, it was more than that. We desired to bolster our passion for adventure and discovery. This wasn't your typical junior year study abroad program. Our intention was not to get drunk to the staccato of foreign dialect in Madrid, Venice, or Paris, but to meet like-minded individuals, visit prominent outdoor locales, and climb big mountains. It was a simple formula, but one that required the proper ingredients. For the trip to succeed, the recipe needed to be impeccable.

We were to leave the following morning on a purportedly divine mission—to embrace our love for the outdoors, but not to forget about the necessity to make friends. To open our eyes to a new outlook, and to embrace it as our own. And to take to the unscathed road, leaving our mark on everyone and everything that we brushed into, and likewise having their mark forever etched into our consciences.

This is the story of two friends who departed and arrived, who came and left, and who loved and were loved. It is a story of restoration—of faith and of friendship. It is a tale of rectification, of redemption, and of reality. It is an attempt to remedy the inadequacies in life, and to replace them with hope and fulfillment. Most importantly, it is the story of me. Of you. Of us. It is an evaluation of the human condition. Namely, that when we are confronted with hardship and adversity, we will come to the aid of others no matter the onus. Whether you're from the East Coast, West Coast, Midwest, South, Canada, or abroad. Because the road does not discriminate; it only welcomes. I welcome you to read my account of this phenomenon in action. So here goes nothing.

* * *

Parked in the left-side breakdown lane of I-290, we panicked. It was day one of our modern bildungsroman—a transformative journey into the mysterious frontier of America. Or something like that. A Massachusetts State Trooper parked a few yards behind Mindy Mariner—my lime green car and one of the few loves of my life.

Mindy had quite the task for the next few months: to lug a roof-top carrier with a few hundred pounds of gear in it. And to endure the foul odor of Curtis's feet. So far, though, we'd only made it a couple of miles from our houses. Curtis and I grew up three doors apart, went to the same elementary and middle schools, but separated for high school and college. Despite our separation, we always maintained an inextricable relationship.

When we were five years old, we went on our first true adventure. We had heard through the grapevine that an older boy had built a treehouse in the woods between both of our backyards. Convinced that all the cool kids in the neighborhood frequented the spot, we made our way into the depths of the forest. For five-year-old children, it was as vast as the Amazon, and getting lost in its complexities was somewhat of a certainty. Eventually, we stumbled upon the structure, but not before rubbing our bare legs against every poison ivy leaf in the vicinity. (Poison ivy and I have a bit of a storied past. When I was a kid, I lived with it for most summers. As I got older, I somehow developed a resistance to it. That is, until the time I inadvertently wiped my butt with it. You know the rest.)

Although it was unfinished and dilapidated, the treehouse became sacred to us that day. We climbed up as high as we could, unable to reach the pinnacle due to its fragmented facade. From our vantage point, we could make out several houses in the neighborhood. It was as if we were the mighty kings of the jungle, concealed from our overprotective parents and immersed in an entirely divergent realm where rules no longer applied.

In the years that followed, we would expand our kingdom westward into the adjacent junkyard behind my house, often spending hours searching for buried treasure. But as all good things come to a screeching halt, so did the existence of the treehouse. Years of decay had rendered it unusable. Similarly, the junkyard was cleared out, and a heinous upper-middle-class house took its place. Despite the untimely demise of our miniature Valhalla, our memories of it remained. Somehow, those adolescent explorations flourished into big-boy adventures in the years that followed. Like the one we were about to embark upon. That is, unless the law had something to say about it.

The officer stepped out of his vehicle and strutted over to us. We were ready for him. After all, we didn't do anything wrong *per se*, we simply made a careless mistake. No, we weren't speeding. We didn't have a taillight out. And we certainly didn't have active warrants for our arrest. Rather, Curtis's belongings were spilled out across all three lanes of the highway. The rooftop carrier had flung wide open on the way to get my inspection sticker for the trip. Prior to the trooper's arrival, we scurried into the interstate picking up whatever we could before it was trampled. Let's just say that crossing the highway wasn't one of our brighter moments, but at least we could put real-life Frogger on our résumés when all was said and done.

Instead of waiting for the officer to approach us, we walked towards him, trying to project confidence. He went through the familiar protocol, taking off his intimidating pair of aviators to reveal a stern facial expression. To our surprise, his seriousness dissipated the moment he opened his mouth.

"What can I do to help?" he asked with a degree of concern.

"Uh ... direct traffic?" Curtis hesitantly responded.

The trooper flipped on his lights and blocked all traffic in the left lane for about a minute while we scavenged for goodies. At the end of our hunt, he told us to be careful next time and sped off into the cityscape of scenic Worcester, Massachusetts.

In the aftermath of our highway spectacle, Curtis's sleeping bag had a minor tear, and an obsolete set of pots and pans had been destroyed by an eighteen-wheeler. But we had no time to dwell over the loss of some useless stainless steel. We had last-second errands to run, and we had already missed our initial departure time of five o'clock that morning.

* * *

As noon crept around, we arrived at the inspection station in Worcester. The day before, I had tried to get my inspection sticker renewed, as it was due to expire while we were on the road. In hindsight, it didn't even matter, since other states don't really chase people down for having an expired sticker from another state. Nonetheless, my grandfather came with me because he said he knew the guy who worked there who would "help me out." When they tried to do the inspection, Mindy couldn't pass because the computer had just been reset after I'd taken her into the shop for repairs. The inspector told me that I had to drive about one hundred miles for the system to reset itself. My eighty-three-year-old grandfather attempted to slip the man some extra cash to get the job done, but to no avail. Needless to say, our departure wasn't working out according to plan, but then again, when does it ever?

Back at home later that day, both of our moms scurried frantically about, concerned that their little babies were going off into the great unknown. At the time, even we didn't know what we were about to get ourselves into. As we packed trekking poles, mountaineering boots, crampons, ice axes, harnesses, rock climbing gear, and other various items, we couldn't quite assure our parents that we would make it out unscathed; for nothing about the prospect of going on an outdoor-oriented road trip promises safety. But we weren't looking for safety. If anything, we wanted to forfeit our familiar lives and embrace a lifestyle far removed from the onerous restraints that held us in one place. Injury—or death for that matter—was a consequence that we contemplated time and again when evaluating our experience levels relative to some of the mountains we planned to climb. Ultimately, we tried to push these concerns to the back burner to free ourselves from any apprehension that would prevent us from going ahead with our ambitious plans for the summer. In the interim, though, packing Mindy was our priority, and by golly did it take a long time.

Since Curtis was already halfway done with his packing despite the interstate scare a few hours earlier, we turned to my own stuff. We threw out what we felt was unnecessary and retained the "essentials." Turned out, everything was essential according to our parents—not the least of which included useless bungee cords that would supposedly keep the rooftop carrier from flying open, cases of bottled water, first aid kits for days, and personal hygiene kits for, you know, hygiene.

As we finished up packing operations and got ready to depart, my dad came up to Curtis and me and handed us each a dollar bill.

"For what?" we both asked.

He said, "Whenever we traveled, your grandfather would give us a lucky dollar. It's a good luck charm." My grandfather has since passed, victim to a devastating form of dementia and bone cancer, but his message prevails, and has taken on an even greater meaning for Curtis and I after our return from the road.

For some, a lucky dollar, penny, rabbit's foot, dreamcatcher, or other token, is perceived as an impermeable shroud that serves as an aegis from all future misfortunes. So long as the shield remains, so does your luck. For me though, that dollar represented home. Whereas my grandfather understood the dollar to be an indicator of luck and fortune while away from home, I saw it as *home* itself.

Location was immaterial. What mattered most was that we never lost our sense of belonging. The dollar, much like the road, was solace. It was a reminder and reassurance. Now framed in my bedroom, it reminds me that what we went through that summer really happened. And it reassures me that *home* knows no bounds for refuge may be found even in a dollar bill.

* * *

It wasn't all sunshine and rainbows, but we were finally on the road at 9 p.m.—ETA to the District of Columbia: 4:30 a.m. Between us and our ultimate destination was an hour-long traffic jam outside of New York City. Summer construction? One open lane? Didn't they know we were coming?

Evidently not. But when we pulled into a gas station in New Jersey after we escaped the congestion, it was as if *they* knew we were coming. As soon as I got out of the car and attempted to insert my credit card, I heard an unexpected yelp.

"Excuse me, sir!"

I turned around to be greeted by an employee who meant business.

"Hi," I timidly answered.

"Get back in the car sir. You can't pump your gas."

What do you mean, I can't pump my gas? I thought to myself. I gave him a quizzical stare.

He quickly glanced at our license plate as he walked over to us.

"A couple of Massachusetts boys, I see," the baby-faced attendant said. His initial out-for-blood attitude seemed to subside, and he let out a chuckle. Glad to know we have a reputation.

I retreated into my vehicle and looked at Curtis, who shrugged at me.

It was after midnight, and I wondered why the hell the gas station was paying someone to work the pumps so late at night.

As soon as the tank was full, I gave my card to the employee and finally asked him: "Why can't we pump?"

He twisted the gas cap and handed me back my card.

"You can't pump your own gas in New Jersey, pal. Have a nice night!"

Despite the relative insignificance of the event, it was at that time that I realized just how much of a culture shock that this trip of ours would be. Each American state is practically as varied and unique as countries with entirely different languages. And that, is what makes the allure of its exploration so desirable.

* * *

In the years leading up to our departure, we called it *the road trip*. Like it was the only one, ever. It was suitably named. Its long-lasting impact has transformed our lives in ways we never contemplated. We drafted the barebones itinerary of our journey in the kitchen of my apartment during the early fall of our senior year of college about nine months prior to our planned departure. All we wanted to do was escape the boredom of the same old Saturday nights where nothing happened, and everyone was out drinking. The banality of routine was crushing on the soul. And so, to the West we would go.

It wasn't at all coincidental that we left on the road trip just a few days after our graduation from college. I suffered from depression for much of my time there because I felt trapped in the college bubble. My experiences were confined to books I seldom read and parties I seldom went to. At the time, I believed the college party scene was a shallow lifestyle and a four-year distraction from reality outside the bubble. I have since learned that everyone's reality is subjective, and everyone's lifestyle is their own. But if it wasn't for my college years, the road trip and its lessons and realizations never would have happened.

* * *

It is in every eighteen-year-old's id to try to fit in. It seems, partially, that this notion is rooted in either their desire to modify the asocial tendencies of their high school years or to maintain their popularity. But the moment that they pack their bags at summer's end and join the melting pot of college is the moment they realize that what has happened in their life thus far means next to nothing—a fresh start is imminent.

The first several weeks of freshman year are some of the most malleable moments of a college-attending human being's existence. Every individual is given the unique opportunity to craft their own fate for the next four years to some extent. Some opt to join every club that solicits new members in the university center during lunch time. Others spend their inaugural days searching for the best place on campus to get high. But with few exceptions, everyone seeks a niche of friends with whom they'll accompany on their quest for a degree. And many of these initial companions are met under the most cliché of circumstances—alcohol-induced revelries.

Driven by an arcane principle stemming from oft-naïve opinions, most of my high school and college years were governed my abstinence from alcohol. When faced with the inevitable inquiries, I could mostly rationalize it, but with a certain degree of inadequacy.

I can't even pinpoint exactly at what point in my life I first proclaimed that I would never voluntarily consume alcohol. I never had the curiosity that most kids develop when their ma and pa are acting like lunatics at the family reunion, Mike's Hard Lemonade in hand. Perhaps this is because my parents were older when they had my brother and myself and had already gotten the irresponsible years out of their system.

They weren't drinkers, and they never gave me a reason to be one. When I was a kid, it always appeared as if drinking was something of a rebellion against your parents because they wouldn't let you stay over your buddy's house on Friday night. Despite the recalcitrant tendencies of most people my age at the time, the thought had never crossed my mind to engage in these habits. Why would I need to? I had a great childhood, great parents, and plenty of hobbies to keep my mind busy. In hindsight, it appears I was looking for an excuse to justify a core principle seemingly innate to my existence. In reality, that principle had been eroding since the very moment of its conception, despite its persistence through my four years in college and beyond.

Growing older, of course, brought with it a whole slew of new ideas about what it was that instigated people to booze and schmooze on the weekends. But I was so far removed from the drinking culture in my high school years that most of these thoughts barely occurred to me. It wasn't until I entered college when I truly realized how oblivious I was.

* * *

We are over-consumers, in every sense of the word. We binge erratically on substances and impulsively consume tangible goods to attach a certain degree of meaning to our corporeal temporariness. Many people, especially in college, measure happiness in the number of "things" they own or the number of drinks or hits from the bong it takes to reverse their unhappiness.

We go off to our respective universities, community colleges, and graduate programs to try and establish a base for our future— but to do so, we suspend reality. We push the pause button on life while we enter a fantasy realm. In college, we have inadvertently constructed a separate society wherein we allow the future scholars of America to experiment—to find themselves, as they say. But how do you learn more about the person you are or the person you want to become while sitting in a classroom for several years?

For myself, and many others, the most profound happenings of my college years came outside of the classroom. Majoring in history was certainly an eye-opening experience that gave me a greater understanding of everything from Jewish scripture to Pol Pot's oppressive regime. But it didn't teach me shit about what I needed to know to strive and survive in this world. My depression all but took care of that lesson—one that was inseparably tied to my once critical perspective on alcohol, which, in turn, was one of the reasons I hit the road in the first place.

The setting is as unoriginal as the beverage of choice. Ten o'clock. Friday night. Thirty-rack of Pabst Blue Ribbon in the closet, door firmly secured with the deadbolt. If the RA walks in, they're certainly not going to notice the beer pong table, the girl passed out on the bed, or the crumpled cans all over the floor.

What better way to chime into your collective subconscious than to alter the mind with invasive substances and commit your-self to a fleeting reality—one that will invariably cease to exist the next morning when your head gives you a good thrashing in retaliation.

This was the proverbial "college living." And I was a spectator to it, unaffected by the pleas of my peers to accompany them in their negligent, albeit voluntary journey toward inebriation.

"Hey Justin, grab me a beer," my roommate Norv called out from the makeshift DJ table across the room. I was on closet duty. I was always on closet duty.

I tossed the lukewarm can across the room through the cluster of scantily clad blondes and wife-beater-and-backwards-hat-wear-ing bros. Norv dropped the beer as it bounced off his outreached hands. It crashed to the floor and spattered all over the tipsy attendants.

"PARTY FOUL!" They all hollered in unison.

"Aww, come on guys," an impaired Norv pled from his throne. To make amends for his ill-timed gaffe, he cued up "Shots" and eve-ryone did one to commemorate the occasion.

I was left searching for a distraction to allow me to forget that I was the only person in the room without a drink in hand. I twiddled my thumbs for a minute, and when that didn't work, I replaced Norv and took over music duties. Maybe if I play something they like, they'll forget about my awkwardness?

I promptly put on some hip-hop from 2003, because who doesn't like Chingy?

"Turn this shit off," one of the backwards-hat bros shouted in a muffled slur.

And with that, my music duties ceased as soon as they commenced. As did my hopes and dreams of fitting in during my freshman year of college.

* * *

This pattern of hopelessness, feeling lost, not fitting in, and the likes, became somewhat run-of-the-mill in the next several years. A part of me wanted to acquiesce to the lifestyles of those around me, not necessarily by drinking myself into a stupor, but by at least tolerating the culture and having a good time. Such attempts proved futile, because I could never quite figure out what was truly bothering me about the weekend culture around me. I was unable to sever my conviction that college drinking culture was stupid, immature, and illegal for those under twenty-one years old. Even condoning the behavior conflicted with my beliefs at the time. I felt as if I had the desire to transcend my confined beliefs and open up to the world—but I was weighed down by the restraint of an irrational perspective. And it bothered the hell out of me.

* * *

At some point during my sophomore year, I gave up. Instead of frequenting shallow parties, where binging was the rule and superficiality the norm, I found myself trapped in my room yearning for better days. In these months of great despair, I had no one to blame but everyone, and that was too broad a constituency to attribute any sort of rational fault.

With several more weekends of solitude notched in my belt of failures, I became cognizant of the fact that I was a victim of my own misfortunes and a product of my own self-pity. But I was still too weak to rise out of bed—that is, until I took a writing class offered in the spring semester that intrigued me. Writing the Beats, as it was called, was a survey of the writers of the Beat Generation, the literary rebels of a past generation. I had heard mention of the marvels of Beat literature in high school, back when I took a class about Bob Dylan.

At the heart of the class's structure was a thorough reading of *On the Road*, the quintessential Jack Kerouac novel, and purported bible of post-adolescent dissidence. As a childhood journal-keeper and "travel writer" who'd barely traveled beyond New Hampshire, I sought inspiration for ways in which I could feasibly leave my dorm room and live to reflect upon it. How far I went was up to me. Smalls steps or large ones, this was the initiation of my wanderlust, my quest for solidarity, and my rectification.

Instead of partying, I had to find my own temporary distractions to make my reality one worth living. I tried desperately to fit in but could not reconcile my undying vitriol toward booze, so I looked for an alternative to get away from everyone and everything that provoked my depression. Kerouac's romantic account of the road, its unscathed beauty, the mountains, and all else, was magnetic. It brought me to a fantasy realm that I could one day make a reality. My reality.

Consequently, I'm not so sure I would have found myself on the road had two factors not been present: my failed acquiescence to the timeworn tradition of college drinking, and Kerouac's magnum opus, *On the Road*. But I did, and I was about to embark on the greatest adventure of my life to date. And I have Norv and Jack to thank for that. Even if they both liked to drink copious amounts of liquor. Oh, the irony.

* * *

It is customary for New Englanders to long for the West at one point or another in their lives. Just the simple thought of escaping the simultaneously stagnant and fast-paced reality of East Coast is liberating. New England is a business-as-usual kind of place, and everyone is always in a hurry.

Many of us who reside in the East are inclined to believe that the West holds infinitely more possibilities and a more laid-back lifestyle. Theoretically, you can have a "West Coast" lifestyle anywhere, but the allure of a new place and new perspectives is practically irresistible. When we left for the road, our perspective was limited to what went on in white suburbia and the college bubble. Clearly, that would change.

* * *

During college, I worked two jobs: one in retail, and one at with my school's Student Safety Services—colloquially referred to as Escort. Yes, the jokes were rampant. Whenever I told people where I worked, they never ceased to bring up the apparent irony of its suggestive name.

Escort is essentially a student transportation service that caters to the needs of those who need a late-night ride home, a lift to the local pharmacy or grocery store, or a drunk shuttle to the closest house party. During my senior year, I worked over thirty-hours-a-week driving people around to fund the road trip. If anything, the job taught me to enjoy long drives, or at least how to tolerate them.

Working 4 p.m. to 4 a.m. shifts a few times a week in Worcester also prepared me for everything we would encounter on the road. According to a study conducted by Allstate Insurance, Worcester is the third-worst city in the country to drive in based on accident rates. I had seen it all to that point, and terrible drivers would be the least of my worries. Hitting animals though, was a real and unfortunate possibility that we would have to be vigilant about.

After our unremarkable seven-hour drive through the Northeast, we arrived at my friend Adalyn's house in a Maryland suburb just outside Washington, D.C. Adalyn was more than happy to welcome us in at an obscene hour. But she didn't seem *happy*.

Over the course of the prior year, Adalyn had become a great friend of mine. She worked with me at Escort and had become a listener whenever I needed to let loose. Through our discussions, I became aware of a controversy that had been plaguing her thoughts for quite a while—whether she was going to return to school for her senior year. We spent the next morning pondering her choice, understanding that it was imperative to be happy above anything else. At the time, she found no satisfaction in the arbitrariness that school often carries along with it. I asked her whether it would be worth it to have gone to school for three years, only to fall short of obtaining a degree. She agreed, but both Curtis and I saw the value of her temporary withdrawal from school, so she could be happy before continuing with her education.

Growing up, we had been conditioned to believe that getting a college degree was a societal norm. Sure, we eventually realized the absolute faultiness in our thoughts. But without external prompting, one's predilections are inextricably tied to their life experience. And we had none. The structure of organized, undergraduate schooling may suffice for some, but ultimately it is more important to find gratification even at the expense of losing the opportunity to obtain a degree.

Appropriately, we decided, what better way to commence our quest for experience and perspective than to go to the government-subsidized National Zoological Park to *ooo* and *ahh* at unjust animal confinement. At least the kids appeared to be having fun. We walked athwart a congested brick road, simultaneously fascinated and nauseated by the sheer number of creatures that the zoo was able to corral and put on display for the public. After thoroughly perusing the travesties that lined the busy park thoroughfare, we returned to our car to attempt to remedy our vomit-inducing experience. A short trip to the National Mall to indulge in American history later, and we were on our way toward Shenandoah National Park, our inaugural experience with nature outside of the Northeast.

* * *

The lush Virginian wilderness was an accelerated step up from the concrete and asphalt that plagued our vision just a day prior. Fanny packs were swapped out for backpacks, sandals for hiking boots, maps and tour guides for intuition. From National Mall to National Park we went.

Nestled among rivers and valleys at the foot of the Blue Ridge Mountains in the northwest corner of Virginia, Shenandoah is home to the renowned Skyline Drive, one of the most scenic byways in the Eastern United States. Unlike the difficult-to-navigate mountain ranges in the Northeast, Skyline Drive winds and weaves directly through the mountains. Ample viewpoints and tourist stops can be found along the road. For this reason, along with its proximity to D.C., Shenandoah has become one of the most popular national parks in the country. But it didn't always look that way.

Nine thousand or so years ago, humans visited the area seasonally to hunt, fish, and gather. When Europeans migrated to the Americas, they started to settle near the area's water sources approximately 250 years ago. As the Great Depression began to plague the country in the early part of the twentieth century, many homes in the area were taken by the government on grounds of eminent domain. It was at this point that the park was assembled, an amalgamation of more than three thousand plots of land, resulting in the displacement of nearly five hundred families.

Alongside the development of the park, engineering firms and the Civilian Conservation Corps assisted in the construction of Skyline Drive. The creation of the 105-mile road helped open the area to the nearly 1.5 million people who visit the park every year. While its creation was controversial, Shenandoah has provided outdoor enthusiasts with scenic views and hiking trails for nearly one hundred years. Though our own visit to the park was brief, it was certainly eventful.

* * *

We had just topped out on Old Rag Mountain, a rocky conglomerate of greenstone, quartzite, sandstone, and limestone. It is known for both its hiking and rock-climbing potential and is one of the most frequented mountains in the area. In his book, *Hiker's Guide to the Geology of Old Rag Mountain*, Paul Hackley relays that the existence of Old Rag is a result of a mountain-building event known as the Greenville orogeny. At one point it was likely as tall as any peak in the Rocky Mountains of the West today, which soar up to fourteen thousand feet. But Old Rag stands at a modest 3,284 feet. SummitPost, a website that Curtis and I frequent, has this to say about Old Rag:

> "Many a Virginian has gotten his or her first real taste of mountaineering on Old Rag, a great mass of exposed granite east of the Blue Ridge crest in Virginia's Shenandoah National Park. . . . Old Rag requires almost three miles of one-way hiking to reach the summit by its shortest route, and elevation gain is anywhere from 2,200 to 3,000 feet depending on the specific route chosen. . . . In fact, one's first hike of Old Rag might inspire a mountaineering lust that may consume great sums of money, time, and family members' patience—you have been warned."

Curtis and I weren't swayed by its beauty like a first time Virginian wannabe mountaineer would be, given our proximity to plenty of larger mountains in New England, but the 8.7-mile loop via Ridge Trail and Saddle Trail was an excellent way to kick off our mountain adventures. On the way to the summit, we ascended

2,300 vertical feet through a cave, a natural staircase, and the occasional class 3 scrambling, which included the use of our hands and feet to navigate the tricky sections.

At the pinnacle, our views were limited because the clouds had started to roll in. As such, we began our descent back to the car to the cadence of silence and footsteps, somewhat disappointed in our viewless quest. About a mile into our journey back down, Curtis finally broke the silence.

"Where do you think we are more likely to see a bear: here, or the White Mountains?" he asked as we scampered down the trail. Neither of us had ever seen one in the flesh.

Only a fleeting moment after Curtis had asked his question, lo and behold, a large mama black bear emerged from the depths of the woods only twenty or so yards in front of us. Behind her were two adorable cubs. Adorable until we realized that we may be their appetizers in a minute or two.

I wanted to tell them that I was sorry for going to the zoo; I didn't even want to anyway—it was Curtis's idea. But I can be a little socially awkward at times, so instead I waved my trekking poles over my head like an idiot and screamed like a banshee. Curtis followed suit, and eventually the bears walked gingerly up the hill, never once taking their eyes off the two buffoons whose protein content now seemed a little less enticing. We breathed a sigh of relief and proceeded onward until we were scared shitless by a snake as long as a garden hose. This was going to be one wild road trip.

* * *

The day was still young, so we made the drive from Shenandoah toward the Great Smoky Mountains National Park in Tennessee.

The Smokies, as the park is colloquially known as, is the most visited national park in the country, with over eleven million visitors per year. Its inception was the result of the National Park Service's desire to have a park in the eastern United States. Much like in Shenandoah, money flowed in, and residents flowed out, victims of eviction. But long before that displacement, the Smokies were home to the Cherokee tribe. Circa the eighteenth century, there were already established footpaths in the area, including a section of the Great Indian Warpath, a system of trails that were used for commerce and war. When Andrew Jackson signed the Indian Removal Act in 1830, the tribespeople were forcefully driven out of their land. They were exiled to Oklahoma and Arkansas initially, but many were forced further westward during what is now known as the Trail of Tears.

Today, things are a bit different, to say the least. As a result of the large-scale eradication of the natives, the tourist-infested towns of Pigeon Forge, Sevierville, and Gatlinburg now reside at the foot of the Smokies. These towns have a bit of reputation among Southerners. In fact, world-famous country singer Dolly Parton is from the area. Notable highlights in the area include Dollywood, Dollywood's Splash Country, Dollywood's DreamMore Resort and Spa, and Dolly Parton's Stampede Dinner Attraction. To add to the allure of the area, a large statue of Dolly herself sits in front of the Sevierville courthouse. For the outdoorsy folk though, there's an endless playground to be experienced.

Unlike many mountains of the Northeast, the Smokies are in a temperate rainforest rather than an alpine zone. Peaks such as Mount Washington and the other mountains of the Presidential Range have maintained their alpine nature due to a combination of wind, clouds, and ice. Brutal storms over thousands of years have prevented vegetation from growing at higher elevations. But in the Smokies, where a more temperate climate exists, these weather and climate patterns are not nearly as vicious.

Case and point: at 6,644 vertical feet, Clingman's Dome stands above all the rest in the state and is the third-tallest mountain east of the Mississippi. It's taller than Washington but doesn't share that alpine character. It does, however, share a common trait with many of the other state highpoints on the East Coast: without any effort at all, you can drive to a parking lot just short of the summit. A travesty against nature, but for our purpose at the time, a convenience.

* * *

State highpointing is a hobby for those who desire to reach the highest point in every state. The hobby itself is a subcategory of what is known as *peak-bagging*. Peak-baggers are people who actively seek to summit as many mountains as possible; it is a sport for those who relish heights and great views. As I have slowly learned in my years as a peak-bagger, the accolade of reaching the top is secondary to the means to getting there. Our ten-minute ascent up a steep, paved road to Clingman's Dome was no exception. In fact, it even invoked an unexpected bout of déjà vu.

To fit in with the handful of tourists who braved the oncoming rain and darkness, we wore sandals and shorts to complement our waterproof jackets. We'd come a long way since our inaugural journey on the Franconia Ridge, I tell you.

As if the day wasn't interesting enough already, we heard terrifying yelps from a woman who was on her way down from the top. As her wailing began to intensify, Curtis and I could make out a facial expression comparable to that of a teenager who just walked in on their parents having sex.

"Honey, it's going to be okay!" her overweight and overly concerned boyfriend or husband or gay best friend emphatically cajoled. It had been three days since we left our homes, but already we were feeling more outgoing, and decided to ask what was wrong.

"There's a BEAR up there!" she exclaimed, fighting back tears as if her child had just been devoured.

"Are you okay?" we responded, genuinely concerned about what may have happened to the two.

"It's still up there somewhere," her companion said, pointing up the concrete hill in front of us, "but it really scared the crap out of her!" He started to laugh as the woman gave him a swift nudge.

"It's NOT FUNNY!" she yelled.

We took a few steps backward up the hill as the argument began to spiral.

"We'll be careful," I shouted, as we turned around and took off, not once looking back. Bear encounter or irrational spousal feud? I'll choose the former.

Since our bizarre screaming ritual had worked oh so well earlier in the day, we decided to emulate it. But this time, we did so in a Southern accent to conform to the community standards.

"ROAR ERRRR UHHHH UNGHHH!" We screamed like disturbed maniacs. If anything, our chances of instant mortality probably increased.

Further up the concrete slope and after our deluded shouting, we encountered another group. A giddy, middle-aged man stumbled down the incline to ask us if we were okay.

Before we could say anything, he whipped out a fancy camera and began to show us up-close-and-personal shots with the infamous bear that we had heard so much about.

"It was awesome," he said, "but you scared him away with your shouting!"

Of course we did. We had missed the opportunity to snap a picture earlier because we were too frightened ourselves, but this time we had been eager to get a glimpse of the scruffy beast. I think Kurt Vonnegut had a saying for that. Oh yes: so it goes.

At the top of the mountain, we walked up to the lookout tower. It was a massive concrete pole with a disc at its apex that bore some resemblance to the Jetson's spaceship. It was one bizarre edifice. After clinging to the top of Clingman's Dome, we were off in a harmonious allegretto toward the Music City herself—Nashville, Tennessee.

* * *

Country music. Irremovable staple of Southern identity. In and around Nashville, you'll be hard pressed to find a bar that doesn't play it. In fact, country is so prevalent in the American South that its undeniable charm will reel in even the most high-profile figures into its local dive bars.

Curtis and I casually trotted along the Lower Broadway strip of town, which was littered with country bars, country museums, and country-style restaurants, all blaring various contemporary country songs. It had been two days or so since our last shower, so we made certain to keep our arms tucked tightly to our sides to prevent any intolerable body odors from escaping our shirts into the public. *Well we're here*, we thought, *so we might as well go see what all the fuss is about.*

Upon entering the bar, we were graced with a truly multifaceted auditory experience. The din of your everyday pub was drowned out by plucked guitar strings, crashing cymbals, and of course, the traditional country baritone heard in just about every Johnny Cash song. On a makeshift stage was a cover band hailing from some Southern state or another, and they certainly had a command of their audience, provoking even the most reticent in attendance to dance like there's no tomorrow.

Curtis approached me sometime during the musical extravaganza to say that he had just spotted our former senator, Scott Brown. Several months prior, Brown had lost his bid for re-election to the U.S. Senate in Massachusetts. It only made sense that he would be scrounging around in bars, reeling from his recent loss.

But rather than pass judgment, we broke out of our shells and approached him and his family, who were now huddled outside the bar.

"Excuse me sir, but we have a question for you. We're from Massachusetts . . ."

Before I could finish my sentence, he extended his hand and said in his most burlesque, political caricature, "Hi, I'm Scott Brown."

What proceeded was a brief discussion about our road trip and school. I wanted to tell him that I voted for him in the last election, but that would have been a bald-faced lie. Not to mention that bringing up his ill fortune probably wouldn't rub him the right way. He wished us good luck, and we went our separate ways. The night was far from over though, if our friend Ted had anything to say about it.

I had only known him for a few months before the road trip commenced, but Ted's first impressions on me certainly weren't short-lived. During my senior year in college, he joined the Model United Nations team that I had been a part of for two years. Model UN is like a debate team, and Ted fittingly strutted into the classroom with a larger-than-life attitude. At six-foot-five, you surely couldn't miss him. He had just a hint of a Southern accent, so you wouldn't immediately know that he hails from just outside of Nashville. One thing was clear though: this guy had confidence. In the months that would pass, Ted would go on to win a Best Delegate award in just his second conference. We had established somewhat of a close relationship over that duration.

We met Ted and his then-girlfriend Charlotte at an unorthodox Southern bar just outside the Nashville city limits. I say unorthodox because there was no country music playing—gasp! At the time, Charlotte was also working toward her degree from a Massachusetts university during the school year, so they weren't too far away from each other year-round.

At first, we were intimidated in our conversation with Ted and Charlotte, mainly because we smelled horrible and were now sitting at a table with a pretty girl who was probably thinking, "I can't believe I consented to this." Not to mention our out-of-town accents weren't very discrete—even Ted, whom I had seen just two weeks prior, seemed to have assimilated a stronger Southern accent since moving back home for the summer. But when we migrated from that first bar to the next, we shed all inhibitions, and learned how to line dance alongside Ted and Charlotte.

At some point in the night while I pretended that I knew the Cotton-Eyed Joe, Ted offered me a drink. I respectfully declined. Ted's gesture was genuine, but I had to politely reject. Up until the road trip, I had never once questioned my steadfast conviction, but only several days into the trip and I was already giving it a second thought. Though I still had a lot of lessons to learn before I could shed my familiar shell in favor of a liquid one, something burned in me that night. Ehh, it was probably just my acid reflux flaring up.

* * *

The fly-over states, as they are known as in East Coast–West Coast parlance, are, for the most part, desolate swathes of farmland outside of the Midwestern cities. It's not uncommon to drive ninety miles into the next town and think that you were just there ninety miles ago. There's not a whole lot of variability in land composition as you roll across I-70 west of Kansas City. Silo, field, field, silo, barn, field, farmhouse, farm, silo, guardrail, state trooper, field, state trooper, silo, errant deer running across the road trying to end its life prematurely—you get the picture. But one of the most glaring and dangerous adversaries in the American Midwest are the birds.

These buggers care not for their life or yours. They dive-bomb your car like pint-sized missiles. And the kicker is they go straight for your windshield. But just before face-planting into it, they quickly divert course, only to leave you their signature white mark. On several occasions I have been shit on with my arm dangling out the window. How they maintain such precision is baffling. In Kansas though, their relentlessness is on another level.

To fill our time on the way out to Colorado, Curtis and I opted to stop at the Kansas state highpoint, Mount Sunflower. It's not really a mountain, but it is the highest field in Kansas. And to get there, you must drive back roads off I-70. Which, if you know Kansas, aren't really roads in the conventional sense. Many aren't paved.

"Which way?" I badgered Curtis, as his attention to the GPS had significantly waned. We had driven through the night from Nashville and were now almost into Colorado, a seventeen-hour drive. We were exhausted.

"All the roads look the same. And I don't have service." He frantically scrolled through the map on his phone. For some reason, our GPS had navigated us to the wrong area, and we were left to our own intuition.

"All I see are dirt and fields. And more dirt and more fields." I sighed. Much of western Kansas and eastern Colorado are comprised of perfectly symmetrical grids that can only be understood when viewed from an airplane.

"Looks to me like you have to take the next road to the left up here and, uh, drive for twenty miles; it should lead right to the parking lot." As soon as he pointed to it in the distance, a bird flung itself into our windshield and left us the undesirable image of guts and blood.

"HOLY SHIT!" I yelled.

Not even a few seconds later, another bird whizzed past us, just missing to the driver's side. I flinched and ducked as the brazen creature brushed by.

"Whaa-a-t in God's name is in their water?" I said, nearly shaking from the deathly encounters.

"They're like kamikaze birds!" Curtis said as he chuckled.

"More like psycho birds," I said.

Seconds later, I ducked again. Wide right this time.

"This is crazy," Curtis remarked, unfazed.

"Ya think?" By the time the next bird zoomed by up and over the roof, I had gotten used to it. At least I had decent car insurance.

After we survived our reenactment of Alfred Hitchcock's *The Birds*, we finally arrived at Mount Sunflower, which proved to be as uneventful an experience as we expected it to be. To make things interesting, we put on our full mountaineering gear and made a silly video to pass the time. We blasted electronic music and danced like buffoons. Dubbed electro-mountaineering, our silly antics lightened the mood after driving through the night. But now it was time to move on, and Colorful Colorado was in our sights. It was ready for us. But were we ready for it?

Chapter 2

Gumby (noun). An inexperienced, unknowledgeable, and oblivious climber. Derogatory.

* * *

Curtis and I were prepped and ready to undertake our first big mountaineering challenge of the trip—Longs Peak in Colorado. Upon reaching the state, we acclimatized to the high altitude by hiking in Rocky Mountain National Park. We got as high as twelve thousand feet or so, but we had set our sights even higher. We wanted to reach the tops of some of the tallest mountains America has to offer. Rising 14,259 feet above sea level and nine thousand feet above the Great Plains, Longs Peak is one of the most coveted summits in Colorado due to its closeness to Denver. However, just because it is accessible doesn't mean it's a walk in the park.

At first glance, a Colorado fourteen-thousand-foot mountain (a fourteener) doesn't look all that imposing from afar. But as you creep closer and closer to the trailhead, you begin to understand. In Colorado, there are over fifty peaks that rise above fourteen thousand feet. The number varies depending on whether you count sub-peaks as true fourteeners. As with most mountain climbing lists, summiting all the fourteeners has become increasingly popular in the last several years. Inexperience and unpreparedness on these mountains have led to severe injury and even death. Nonetheless, with the proper training, one can conquer all the fourteeners without the use of any technical gear.

For the average person, the thought of climbing a mountain is ludicrous. What compels anyone to succumb oneself to hours of agony just so they can say that they topped out on an uneventful, rocky outcropping? It's not normal, they'll say.

The problem is, that none of these people can truly comprehend the sheer magnetism that the mountains emit for people like Curtis and I, despite the potentially grave risks attached. We crave their company with a galvanized vigor, forfeiting the comfort of our beds on a Saturday morning in favor of a few hours of sleep and some fresh air.

In Colorado, any time between midnight and 6 a.m. is the conventional wake-up time to begin your maniacal march to the top of a fourteener. In the summer, this allows you to avoid the afternoon thunderstorms, which are a common occurrence in the Rockies. In the snowy months, getting up early allows you to avoid hiking on unconsolidated snow and melting ice, which severely delays progress and can even cause avalanches. The snowy months could be anywhere from eight to twelve months in the mountains, depending on the snowpack for the year.

In climber parlance, this early rise is known as an *alpine start*. Pioneered by climbers and mountaineers seeking to minimize time spent on the most precarious portions of a mountain, the alpine start has gained popularity with hikers as well. An inordinate number of accidents on peaks such as Everest and K2 have reinforced the notion that the alpine start can be the favorable approach to climbing a big peak, depending on who you ask. We weren't planning on climbing either Everest or K2 on this particular day, but at times it felt like we were.

* * *

At 2 a.m. we were rattled awake by the sound of our phone alarms. Rather than sighing at the unfortunate realization that we had a sixteen-mile round-trip expedition ahead of us, we were anxious to emerge from the sweaty warmth of Mindy and into the chilly trailhead parking lot. Even in late May, you'll be hard-pressed to find a night with above-freezing temperatures in the Rockies.

Oxygen is also scarce in the Rockies, as there is only 60 percent as much of it atop a fourteener as at sea level. To compromise for this deficiency, acclimating your body to the dearth of oxygen is imperative. Especially for lowlanders like us. Hence, we slept in the car at nine thousand feet the night before.

We began in darkness from the trailhead and wove our way up a few thousand feet of switchbacks through an ominous, frigid forest. As we emerged from the trees a few hours later, dawn was imminent. At 5 a.m., the sun crawled up from behind us, above the parapet of the neighboring Twin Sisters. It was a dazzling spectacle for two first-time Colorado climbers.

Further up the trail and fully out of the forest, we saw a sheer vertical wall dead ahead. We later learned that this was the Diamond, one of the most renowned features on the mountain due to its diamond-like shape. It rises a thousand vertical feet and is home to some of the most difficult routes on the mountain. But our objective was a little tamer. Dubbed the Keyhole Route, it is the most popular path to the summit of Longs. To navigate the Keyhole, we would have to utilize our GPS with a pre-mapped route. This was because much of the route was blanketed in snow and all we could rely on was footprints and our own intuition. That is, until I screwed up.

"Hey Curtis, I think I lost the GPS!" I yelled to my partner in crime, as he labored up the rocky trail in front of us. We were fast approaching the snowline and would have to rely on the GPS from now on if we were to succeed.

"Are you serious? Where is it?"

"I'm not sure, I had it earlier."

"Shit."

We agreed that I would have to go back and retrace my steps. I knew I had it in my bag when we had stopped for a snack, so I figured it may be back down the trail. Problem is, that was about twenty minutes ago. If we didn't have it, getting lost on the trail was a certainty. Fortunately, I stumbled across the GPS in the exact spot where I thought I left it and breathed a sigh of relief. As it turns out, finding it made no difference one way or the other.

* * *

"When in doubt, go up" was our East Coast hiking motto. But this was no hike. We had to strap on crampons as soon as we saw the snow at the base of what would ordinarily be a massive boulder field below the Keyhole. Crampons are sharp attachments to your boots that aid in promoting traction. You use them to avoid slipping on icy or snowy slopes. Additionally, you can use the front points of the sharp blades to cut steps into snow or ice.

What makes Longs Peak so hairy is the exposure, even in the months when it is not snow-covered. On the path toward the final summit push, a thousand-foot drop falls off to your immediate right, just waiting for an unwilling participant to break the silence of the mountain. That day, it could have been us. We were lucky.

"I think it's this way," Curtis proclaimed in a seemingly certain tone. He pointed straight up a steep snow slope to our left.

I had no reason to doubt him. He was my climbing partner, through thick and thin. We'd spent the previous year or so preparing ourselves for all the sketchiness that we were inevitably going to encounter over the course of the summer. Even though I had been tracking the exact route on the GPS, it simply did not make sense that we had to circumnavigate the mountain to get to the summit. Ironically, that's exactly what we were supposed to do. It didn't help that we saw not a soul on the entire route all day. Instead, I hesitantly agreed with Curtis' direction and we started uphill.

Our impromptu route to the top commenced with a long snow climb using our axes and crampons. To ascend, we swung the spiked head of our axes into consolidated white, followed by two swift kicks with our sharp metal feet. Every so often we would look behind us to see just how exposed we really were to the probability of death. One small slip would be catastrophic.

Eventually, we came across a portion of the climb where snow and ice turned to rock, swapping our axes for our gloved hands. The walls were not so steep that I would classify them as technical rock climbs, but not so flat that you could skip and chew gum at the same time. But soon enough, as was invariably certain from the start of our blind ascent, we reached an impasse.

"Curtis, we're FUCKED! And NO ONE is coming to save us!"

Hollow words pierced the still air, sending the sky into an unexpected calamity. Storm clouds began to fill in gaps where puffy white had once resided. We had heard about this phenomenon before. The infamous afternoon Colorado thunderstorm.

"Look, we can climb around the side, there's a rock face over there—"

An immense stone tower protruded from a clearing that overlooked the other side of the mountain. As we scurried up to the base of this tower, an impeccable view was all but overshadowed by the realization that we most certainly couldn't climb the face without a rope—or a death wish, neither of which we were carrying with us, though our actions that day suggested otherwise.

Emotions were already volatile at this point, but our present dilemma heightened them into apparent animosity.

"I can't *fucking* believe how *selfish* you were to go off knowing we had a *goddamn* GPS!" Loathing, even hatred, ripped into Curtis's ears.

"Look, you didn't have to follow me!" He shot back in an accusatory fashion.

"I'm not going to leave you behind, I *had* to follow you!"

"What are you talking about, you *always* leave me behind!"

He was right though. Friends for life. Hiking partners for life. Climbing buddies for life. Somehow, these labels were nothing in the face of my impatience. I always felt the need to go at my own pace, disregarding my own best friend's sluggishness in doing so. Curtis was never in as good a shape as I was. That didn't stop me from unconsciously—and sometimes consciously—refusing to accommodate him.

But this was different. This wasn't your traditional saunter up a brightly lit New Hampshire mountain summit. This was the real deal. The Colorado Rockies. And if I was going to maintain my selfish demeanor, Curtis could get in trouble. On Longs Peak that day, I stuck by Curtis, and we were in this together. And we both got in trouble. Go figure.

But I wouldn't have had it any other way. Convinced that we would have to be evacuated by helicopter, we scavenged for our rescue beacon, only to realize that we didn't have it. At that moment, I noticed that I had lost my axe. It had detached from its leash somewhere on the rock climb. No longer did ire fill the air. It had been swept up into the opaque clouds that looked more menacing by the minute. Terror and petrification emerged from the gray skies, taking a seat next to us. This wasn't a joke anymore. We'd pulled a gumby move, and this was our last chance to alleviate it. Our mission was uncomplicated: down or die.

For the next twenty minutes, we played musical chairs with our lives. After each step came reassurance that we would live to see another round. The nearly vertical down-climb would have been almost impossible had I not serendipitously encountered my axe shortly after commencing our descent. The first round was over, the first chair removed.

Prudently placing our crampons into the snow below the rock section that we had just climbed up, we found comfortable footing and searched for a spot to deploy our axes—which proved to be a harrowing prospect. Much of the surface above us was either dirt or rock, not the most conducive locations to dig your axe into.

"Careful down here, we don't have much to work with!" a wind-smothered yell emerged from below me.

"I've got it, don't worry," I hesitantly answered so that only I would hear the words.

Bypassing the crux—the hardest part—of the escape, we found solace in the fact that we could use the previous footholds that we created on the way up to establish traction. The second chair in our theoretical game was gone.

Soon, we made it back to the area where we initially found ourselves perplexed about where to go next. I was sick of playing this game of musical chairs, so I whipped out my GPS and started to follow the pre-tracked route toward the summit. Curtis acquiescently followed at first but started to veer off the path as we began to run out of footprints.

"Curtis, what the FUCK are you doing? Get *back* on the path, you SHITHEAD."

We hurled insults at the top of our lungs, our obscenities often swept away by the tenacious winds.

"SHUT THE FUCK UP. There are footsteps *right here,* ASSHOLE!"

"CURTIS, I have a *goddamn* GPS. If you don't get your ass down here, we're fucking going home RIGHT NOW!"

The last words plunged along the white incline down into the valley below. The wind had hushed itself temporarily, allowing the brutal barrage toward my best friend to sink in. I remember that moment so vividly. How could I forget it? I felt like a revenant, back from a fleeting encounter with purgatory. I had climbed out of the depths of hell and back to the grim reality that our work was far from over. Altitude sickness had begun to take hold. Flushed faces accompanied minor headaches and a hint of nausea—the residual effects of spending an extended period above thirteen thousand feet. Our new physical and mental ailments notwithstanding, we still intended to make it to the top of the mountain. Stupid us. But we were more interested in turning what little energy we had into a vicious vocal onslaught than a final summit push. It had to stop.

"If you weren't so selfish and just looked at the ground—" His voice was drowned out by the intensifying gales, but his message rang as clear as day. We were back on the path.

Little was said in the final two-hour slog to the summit. Our energy had all but depleted. Each subsequent step was more labored than the one before. Even swinging our axe into the snow had become a burden. We topped out on the summit of Longs Peak around 2 p.m., nearly twelve hours after we started.

It was an emotionally charged moment for the both of us, to say the least. There had never been more tension in our friendship. All over a stupid mountain. But in the wake of the great achievement that we had just fulfilled, all bitterness had dissipated. In its place, our attitudes mirrored the now-absent thunder clouds. Stupid mountain or not, our first monumental feat of the road trip had been conquered. We bear-hugged, snapping a picture to commemorate the occasion. The events leading to the top was immaterial. We understood the implications. Our suffering had brought us closer to happiness. In our last moments atop Rocky Mountain National Park, we bellowed a cathartic war cry for the infinitesimal creatures below us, whether they could hear it or not. I'm not sure they would have wanted to anyway.

"FUCK YEAH!"

Chapter 3

*"We are all travelers in the wilderness of this world, and
the best we can find in our travels is an honest friend."*

—Robert Louis Stevenson

* * *

. . . And I ohhhhnlyyyy have eyes for youuuuuuuu.

A delicate, yet powerful cadence rattled through my dysfunctional car speakers. It was bedtime, but you wouldn't have guessed it based upon the implacable fidgeting that filled all corners of the car. After failing to devise a sleeping strategy in the first week of the road trip, we had finally cracked the puzzle. Curtis lay prone in the trunk atop all our gear, which was messily packed into tacky mauve containers. The back seats had been removed and stored into my garage on day one, so there was ample room for his lanky frame to stretch out. I, on the other hand, was quite content with sleeping in Mindy's driver's seat. It took a while getting used to, but by now it had become second nature.

The temperature had taken an expected plunge since the darkness had crawled over the Sangre de Cristo mountain range and into the desert sand dunes of southern Colorado. In the preceding days, we had topped out on the tallest mountain in Colorado, Mount Elbert. It was nothing like the intense struggle on Longs Peak, but the wind chill was below zero at the summit—of all days, on the last of May.

In keeping with our new custom, we parked the car in a free campground, this one just outside the Great Sand Dunes National

Park and planned to sleep in the car rather than go through the minor hassle that is assembling a tent. Given the number of days that we would be spending in the wild for the coming months, it was a necessity. Sleeping outside is such a simple way to connect with the world around you, but we had no intention to desensitize ourselves to it this early in the trip by making it into a routine. Even now, I still prefer to sleep in my car over setting up a tent because I'm just that lazy.

I don't know if we're in a garden, or on a crowded avenue. You are here, so am I.

Frank Sinatra's distinguishable voice hollered at us in a nostalgic furor.

We sought his familiar voice to help alleviate our unsettled minds, which were now encumbered with apathy. But even his lyrics had trouble consoling us.

It had been nearly a week since we had made a meaningful connection with a person other than ourselves. After seeing Ted and Charlotte, we drove from Nashville, stopped for a few minutes in Kansas, headed straight to Denver, spent some time in Denver, acclimatized in Estes Park, hiked around Rocky Mountain National Park, climbed Longs Peak and Mount Elbert, and continued our drive south all in the company of ourselves. Confined in our own mutual thoughts, we were disillusioned by the solitude. Our road-trip mantra had been "to go and keep going," but mental self-destruction seemed imminent without a serious overhaul of that approach.

Why do we travel? Is it to satisfy some carnal desire that yearns for adventure and exploration? Are we discontent with the circadian rhythms stirred up by routine? Or is the strife to go places simply an imperative coming-of-age journey for all willing participants?

I'm apt to say that it's an amalgamation of all those concepts, but ultimately, I believe that travel is all about personal perception. We go because we want to fulfill our objectives or responsibilities, to say that we have been somewhere, to embark upon a meta-philosophical crusade, or to satisfy a divine mission. Each of these rationales are highly personalized, and no two people share the same perspective about why the life of an itinerant compels them. At this point in the trip, we were beginning to realize that we couldn't pinpoint what category we wanted to be a part of.

I turned off the music and shut my eyes.

"Leave it on for a few more minutes," Curtis sighed in response to the sudden pause.

"That was the last song on the playlist. And we don't have service to stream any new songs," I replied, as I switched from laying on my right side to my left, scrunching up into my warm sleeping bag as if I was spooning a significant other.

"Then just put it on repeat."

At the time, it was out of character for Curtis to do anything but repress his thoughts in his head. I, on the other hand, am never too shy to share my emotions out loud. But if body language was any indication, we were both having a hard time drifting into dream world that night.

"I feel empty," he unexpectedly muttered.

"What do you mean?" I inquired, though I had pondered similar sentiments just minutes prior.

Curtis's response was far from unforeseen.

"I feel like Chris McCandless was right. That happiness is best shared."

Of course, what self-respecting traveler can't relate to the quintessence of the college grad turned dirtbagger of *Into the Wild* fame? None, methinks.

"Yeah, I hear you. We need to meet people—friends."

It was in this instance that we decided that, to keep our spirits high, it was imperative to make new friends on the trip—above all else. Even more important than fulfilling any of our ambitious mountain endeavors.

We were done with the exhibition of solitary bravado. This wasn't about us anymore. It was about everyone else. Our own experiences were nothing without the people around us that made them memorable.

We withdrew the dollar bills that we had stashed in the glove box two weeks prior and were immediately reminded of our purpose. To find a home. The only way to properly live life on the road is to find refuge in it. We may have been houseless, but so long as we understood that belonging was an existential rather than physical concept, happiness would fill us, instead of the depression that had begun to consume us.

* * *

The next evening, we met our first new friend, Doc, at the trailhead parking lot for Uncompahgre Peak in the San Juan Mountains. The San Juans are as elegant as they are elusive. Located on the southwestern border of Colorado and Utah, they rise above the desert like prickly cacti—sharp and jagged in appearance, immense in stature. With names like Tower Mountain and Rio Grande Pyramid, these rocky behemoths speak for themselves.

Doc was a Texan, born and raised. During the week, he lived up to his name, fixing the crooked backs his many patients. It was quite ironic that of all the people to meet on our first day of social redemption, we would stumble across a chiropractor. He noticed our poor posture from a mile away.

Because he lived in Northern Texas, he was only able to make the drive up to the Rockies sporadically. It was a seven-hour commute, after all. But for as long as he could remember, the fourteeners would call his name.

Before Doc had taken up mountain climbing as a full-time hobby, he was a borderline professional fencer. In his youth, he was feared and revered as one of the best fencers in the Lone Star State. Eventually, he became an instructor and mentor to up-and-coming fencers across the country.

We were the only people on the mountain the following morning, and we caught up to Doc at some point after our later-than-usual start of 5 a.m. The trail was easy and breezy to the summit plateau, with right around three thousand vertical feet of gain in seven and a half miles. Atop the peak that the Ute natives called *red water spring*, we stared across the San Juans and then began our descent with Doc by our side.

* * *

Later in the day, we sat in a quaint restaurant attached to a gas station in rural Lake City, shooting the shit, as they say, with Doc. It was one of those places that an East Coaster can only imagine, bearing a stark similarity to the old Spaghetti Westerns of the 1960s. I think we even saw Clint Eastwood's doppelganger pumping his gas at one point during our lengthy chat.

While we ate our barbecued Coloradan delicacies, Doc's thick Texan accent filled the air. He had just told us about his climbing career, describing his longtime partner, Cooper, who had recently retired from peak-bagging fourteeners.

"Coop was a real tough guy, a Colorado hardmeat. But it's been nearly five years since I had a real climbing partner, y'know, after Coop had a heart attack and all. I really miss havin' a friend by my side on the trail sometimes. It was nice climbin' with you guys today. I almost forgot what it was like to hike with another person."

"So, you're saying you've been climbing fourteeners alone for the past five years?" Curtis asked.

"Well, every so often my son comes up with me, but he's already deep into his career and doesn't have as much time as I do to get out to the mountains. It's a luxury to have him with me though. I'm nearly sixty-five and my wife is worried sick every time I come out here. But I promised myself that I'd finish all of them before I die. I'm not gettin' any younger, y'know."

"Yeah, that's understandable," I said, truly feeling for Doc in his solitary strife. It's never easy, when you have a goal but no backers. His wife seemed to be supportive, but she never made the trip with him.

"Rut's a Colorado hardmeat by the way?" Curtis inquired as he took a massive bite of his pulled pork sandwich.

"You've ne'er heard of a Colorado hardmeat? Well, I guess you're Boston boys, so I'll forgive ya this time. You ever see a picture of some of the best climbers in the world? Most of 'em have long blond hair, are tanner than all three of us put together, and have muscles like you wouldn't believe! That's a hardmeat, a true Colorado hardmeat."

Curtis and I looked at each other and smiled.

"Tell ya what boys. I'm plannin' on going up to Wetterhorn here tomorrow, and I would love to have yer company. Seems like we can getcha both on the path to becoming honorary hardmeats!"

"What's a Wetterhorn?" I asked, befuddled.

"It's another fourteener right next to Uncompahgre and I sure as hell would love to have friends along fer the ride."

At that point we had to make a tough decision. Our initial plan was to drive to Mount Sneffels, however, Doc made us a proposal that we would have to think hard about. We looked at each other with mopey eyes as we telepathically came to the same conclusion. Despite our new intention to spend our time in good company, we just couldn't pull the trigger.

"Sorry Doc, but we've gotta pass this time. We have to stick to our schedule, you know," I said, hesitantly.

You could tell Doc was upset from the similar mopey look he gave us.

"I understand gents. It was great to have you tag along today. It's people like you that make the seven-hour trek worth it, ya know?"

It sounds so bizarre to say it, but leaving Doc that day was one of the most important decisions of the trip. Had we stuck around an additional day, the very foundation of our journey would have dramatically shifted. We would not have met one of the most important people on our trip. The fabric of our future travels would not have been woven as it was. Sometimes you just need to trust your gut.

We did, and it worked out better than we could have ever imagined. Even to this day, that fateful decision continues to pay dividends.

* * *

To get to our next location we would have to take Engineer Pass, a four-wheel-drive road the apex of which lies at 12,800 feet. The pass, which runs from Lake City, Colorado to Silverton and thereafter Ouray, is not designed for vehicles with low clearance. But apparently, it's the fastest way to go from Uncompahgre Peak to Mount Sneffels, according to the oh-so reliable Google Maps. Whereas the normal route would be around one hundred and sixty miles, taking the pass cuts down the mileage to just thirty-four. But this mileage reduction comes at the expense of your vehicle's well-being.

At some point during our errant journey, we lost cell service, and consequently, our lifeline for getting out of there unscathed. On multiple occasions, I had to drive over mattress-sized boulders that made me cringe every time I heard the loud bangs of Mindy's insides being abused. But the breaking point came when I drove her through a two-foot-deep river and onto an impassable snow-covered slope. Instead of continuing forward on another precarious boulder field, I took a left through the river and onto an apparent path—only to realize that there was nowhere to turn around. What ensued was an expletive-filled occasion where I had to reverse a football field in length along a fifty-foot cliff that dropped into the river I had just driven through. Let's just say that backing up on a narrow stretch of cliff-side road isn't the most soothing of activities, but after improbably surviving it, we were back on the true path.

When we reached the pinnacle of the pass, we were legitimately afraid that we were stuck. We could clearly see our next objective, Mount Sneffels, making fun of us as we desperately tried to get cell phone service so that we could figure out where the hell we were. Realizing it was futile, we continued along another tapering road that appeared as if it descended the other side of the pass. And lo and behold, it did.

Partway down, we fortunately ran into an alpine ranger who gave us a map that would lead us to our salvation. As it turns out, we were driving along the Alpine Loop, a well-known off-roading route that traverses over a hundred years of Colorado mining history. What the map was not clear about was just how treacherous the pass was. It's as if it expected us to know of its rugged reputation, and we obviously did not. All in all, Mindy emerged with a few boo-boos, to say the least.

* * *

From afar, Mount Sneffels is one of the most easily distinguishable fourteeners. Jutting out like an arrowhead, it begs its onlookers to climb it. Known as the Queen of the San Juans, it's one of the most photographed peaks in all of Colorado, rising approximately 7,200 vertical feet above adjacent Ridgway, Colorado. But it certainly does not promise success—especially to those who have no idea what they are doing.

At this point in our trip, we were confident that we knew what we were doing—while climbing mountains, not driving up them. In fact, we were a bit full of ourselves, having climbed three rugged Colorado mountains. So when we stumbled upon a pair of women who appeared to be struggling down the most exposed section of the climb, we offered them words of advice.

"You can put your foot there," Curtis yelled, expecting a thankful answer.

"Are you the ones from Massachusetts? We saw you sleeping in the car this morning," one of them fired back in an accusatory manner.

"Yeah, that was us," I answered, taken aback by the seemingly rude response.

Above us, another climber was also aiding them down. I stood frustratedly at the base of the section and sighed. In my judgmental mind, I thought, *are these people even qualified to be up here?* Seldom do first impressions have any substance or value; this was no exception. And I shouldn't have been talking anyway. Just like my GPS and axe before it, my helmet had fallen off my backpack somewhere earlier in the morning. Go figure.

Atop Sneffels, and not even twenty-four hours after we left Doc, we were greeted by a 360-degree panorama of the great Rocky Mountains. But that wasn't the only welcoming party we had. A furry, brownish-red creature poked its head out from under the rocks that we perched our bottoms on. It gave us an inquisitive glare, as if we were violating its privacy. In retaliation, the mountain gopher, as we decided to call it, spent the next twenty minutes attempting to get as close to our food as possible in order to snatch it away. It was wildly unsuccessful.

"I think he's just looking for attention. I mean, look at how cute he is!" I exclaimed. "We should name him. How about Marvin the Mountain Gopher?"

"Sure," Curtis patronizingly replied.

"You're meaning to tell me that you boys thought that was a gopher on the summit? You really are from Massachusetts!"

The woman with the purple jacket had initiated what seemed to be small talk with us minutes after we slid past her on our glissade down the mountain. What's a glissade, you ask? Picture a ski slope atop a rocky Colorado summit in the heart of June—why sacrifice your knees on the downhill climb when you can just sit on your ass and sled? Well, it turns out that it pisses some people off, especially when you whiz past them at blistering speeds and leave a slippery trail for those ascending.

"I don't know what you call a gopher out here, but that was definitely a gopher," I confidently asserted.

Laughter slid down the treacherous couloir and shook through the valley. My water bottle followed. And I never got it back.

"You boys are funny. It's a marmot!" the quieter woman in the blue said. Her voice was distinct and high pitched.

"It's been a pretty rough week for Justin, so excuse his humor." Curtis laughed.

"Okay Curtis, you're the one who got us lost on Longs to begin with. But whateverrrr."

It really had been an off week. But even an off week while living on the road was at least a worthwhile and meaningful one. Especially when it had the potential to end with a new friend or two.

* * *

Rather than continuing our glissade down the mountain as was customary with us, we opted for our new trend of momentary reflection by slowing down and to chat. We were learning, slowly but surely, the importance of connection on the road.

The more vocal woman with the purple jacket, Abby, set the stage for our two-hour descent. She made it a point to get to know us, for whatever reason. We weren't used to this kind of bonding on a mountain. We always had somewhere to be. There was never any time to talk.

We told her our story, our mission, our vision, or whatever you want to call it. But she had seen it before. Two kids on an ostensibly "life-altering" journey into the great unknown out West. But regardless of its predictability, she saw more in us.

"I think what you guys are doing is just amazing. If I had more time, I would probably be doing the same thing. But I'm forty now, and I don't have the same opportunities as you young kids."

You could tell that she was reeling, although she knew that she had it better than us—what with the Rocky Mountain corridor right smack in the middle of her life. But something screamed that she wanted new experiences distinct from the ones she had in her backyard. Both Abby and Talia—the woman with the blue jacket—were nearing the end of their quest to complete the fourteeners. With the completion of one journey comes the desire to embark upon another one, and it was evident that she wanted something to occupy that impending void.

"So, what's next for you guys?" Talia asked.

"Well we're headed further west and hopefully north before we head home, but the climax of our trip is supposed to be Mount Rainier. Ever heard of it?" Curtis replied.

"Have we heard of it? Do you boys take us for fools?" Abby sarcastically jostled him.

"Abby and I just came back from Rainier only several weeks ago. It wasn't the best trip weather-wise, so we didn't get the chance to summit. Let's just say that the snow had a different plan for us. At least we learned how to build snow caves!"

Talia's tone was playful, carrying with it a tinge of disappointment. Nobody likes to get pushed off a mountain, especially when you fly out just to climb one. But her sadness quickly transitioned into bubbly excitement when we broke her the news.

"We're actually in need of a third partner and we haven't really developed a plan yet, so yeah." Curtis proclaimed.

"Pick me, pick me!" Talia quickly responded.

"Wait, what if I want to go?" Abby added.

"You can both come!"

As it turns out, Abby was mostly joking around when she asked to tag along, but Talia was dead serious. In consideration of our offer, she countered with one of her own: dinner at the local Mexican joint, the first of what would be our many paid-for dinners by people we'd just met. Contrary to popular New England "don't talk to strangers" logic, random kindnesses like these aren't so extraordinary. Life is just full of surprises, ain't it?

Chapter 4

Touron (noun). A tourist who stops but doesn't stare.

* * *

It's been one of those days. No, not one of those days, one of *those* days. You know, the "everything seems to be falling into place" kind of day. We had only left Talia and Abby a few hours prior, and somehow, we found ourselves back in the clutches of sociability—under candlelight, no less. Well, flashlights, to be precise, but it just sounds so much more romantic to be conspiring by a dimly lit flame.

A graying, balding man in his fifties prudently ran his right index finger along an obscure road on our travel atlas.

"If you're going through Crater Lake to Portland, you're going to want to go here." He pointed at a random landmark that was immediately lost in our scrambled heads among the million other places he'd told us to go that evening.

He rose from his seat, climbed into the back of his Ford Expedition, and rummaged through the cabinets under his bed looking for a pen. It's easy to get disorganized after living in your car for fourteen months.

His system, however, was impeccable. A comfortable mattress laid atop a wooden platform that was custom fitted to the trunk of his SUV. Everything he owned was under that piece of wood. *Everything.*

Cole Ariopolous is a man of many faces. For twenty-five years, he worked as an engineer at IBM. He's a second generation American and, though it might come as no surprise, of Greek heritage.

After he gave away his prime years to his profession, it was time for a radical alteration to his lifestyle. It was less of an existential crisis, and more of a personal exodus, if you will. One thing was for sure. He was done settling for settling down.

Returning to our atlas, Cole traced a few paths with the fluorescent highlighter that he had grabbed from under the bed.

"You guys like archeology? There's an awesome dinosaur preserve on your way to Utah. What about hot springs? Volcanoes?"

"All of the above!" Curtis exclaimed.

Cole bombarded us with invaluable information for hours that night. But, notwithstanding our appreciation for his insight, destinations were the least of our concerns. If the last few days had any advice to lend to us, it was that we would end up where we would end up. We hoped that people like Cole would invariably govern the remainder of our experiences, rather than the preplanned objectives.

Our preplanned objective was to hike to the tallest point in the Black Canyon of the Gunnison National Park, an area seldom included in the same discussion as its southern neighbor, the Grand Canyon. But rather than stick to the itinerary, we let Cole take the steering wheel.

The Black Canyon is one of the more underrated and unappreciated parks in our expansive system of nationally protected land. In his book, *Black Canyon of the Gunnison: In Depth*, Wallace Hansen describes the allure of the canyon: "Several western canyons exceed the Black Canyon in overall size. . . . some are longer, some are deeper, some are narrower, and a few have walls as steep. But no other canyon in North America combines the depth, narrowness, sheerness, and somber countenance of the Black Canyon of the

Gunnison." It is truly a magical place. Since we didn't know the area whatsoever, we decided to let Cole show us around.

While following his bulky red Expedition, we were given The Works. Initially, we felt as if we were on a bus tour that stopped at every outlook—tour guide, megaphone, and all.

Ladies and gentlemen, if I can turn your attention to the right side, you can see a big hill. Oh, and the canyon is on the left, if that interests you.

Further into our tour of Disneyland, Cole viciously slammed on his brakes and pulled into a subtle roadcut as we nearly took out his rear bumper. Without so much as a head nod, he rushed across the street toward the canyon and began to speak with a park ranger.

I looked curiously over to Curtis.

"What the—?"

I opened my door, which was nearly taken off by a passing car, looked both ways, and crossed the street, with Curtis not far behind. Cole was already deep into conversation with the ranger as if he had been talking to him all day.

"—so you're saying that we shouldn't go to the vista?"

"I'm not saying you shouldn't, but just because it's the tallest point doesn't mean it's the prettiest."

A gruff, but gentle elderly man in his seventies stood beside Cole with his arms folded in his chest. He had a bushy gray mustache and sported the kind of thick-rimmed glasses that your high school geometry teacher wore before being a hipster was cool. A gold-plated name tag was pinned just above his folded arms and sparkled in the afternoon sunlight. It bore the name Rick. We could tell from the onset that he knew what he was talking about.

"Curecanti Creek is my personal favorite, and it descends all the way to the bottom of the canyon. If you've got time for one hike, that's yours."

Cole withdrew the bright red baseball cap from his head and wiped the sweat off his brows.

"I don't know what you guys are thinking, but I could use a good dip of the feet in the river."

I couldn't make up my mind, so I went to the Great Arbiter.

"Curtis?"

"I guess we can do both if we have enough daylight. Rick, what do you think?"

"I think for a few kids with a Massachusetts license plate, you've got the right idea. What are you doing all the way out here anyway?"

Touché, Ranger Rick. What the *hell* were we doing out in the middle of nowhere on a Saturday afternoon? Why weren't we reveling in our last summer of irresponsibility before grad school? Common practice suggested that we should have been staying up late, drinking copious amounts of alcohol, and passing out, only to repeat the cycle intermittently. Aside from the blatant fact that I wasn't a drinker at the time, I'm not sure we had a good answer.

"We've been on the road for the last two weeks," Curtis offered, "and we have about two months to go."

"Ah, two lost souls on an existential journey trying to find their place in the world."

It seemed that Rick had a better answer than we did.

"Been there, done that," he continued, "Spent twenty years in the military traveling internationally with my wife. Every few years they would station me somewhere new. I decided that I loved the life, so I kept electing to reenlist even though there was the threat of being deployed to more hostile areas. I guess I lucked out in the end. Retired out here in Colorado and got a job as a ranger when all was said and done."

Cole was eager to reply, trying to interject on multiple occasions during Rick's discourse.

"Gee, that sounds like what I did. Quit my job at IBM and took to the road shortly after. I haven't looked back, fourteen months later."

"What a life," I chided—but my jealousy was ever clear. "I'm actually going to law school in the fall," I explained, "and Curtis is going to grad school for engineering. But neither of us really have a clue what's motivating us."

I hadn't worked a day in my life, as my dad would often joke, yet I yearned for a path divergent from the one I had been on before we took to the road. Both Cole and Rick were empathetic to this dissidence and attempted to offer recourse when I outlined my situation.

"It sounds like you're caught between life and work," Cole offered.

Rick stood perplexed, as if he was searching for the right words to say. He stroked his gray moustache and cleared his throat.

"Well, if you ask me, I think you're on the right track."

He reached into his pockets and cleared his throat again.

"I once knew a boy about your age. He was torn between going to medical school and dropping everything so he could build a log cabin in the woods and live off the land. I guess you could say he was sick of it all."

A black sports car suddenly darted past us, nearly taking us out as we straddled the area between the breakdown lane and the road cut.

"God dammit!" Rick bellowed. "I'm sorry gentlemen, but I've got to go. That ruffian has been speeding in the park all week."

He hopped into his truck and turned the ignition.

"Wait, Rick! What happened to the boy?" Curtis shouted over the abrasive engine.

"What do you think? He went to med school. Good luck!" He put the truck in drive and burned rubber onto the road.

* * *

Why do we leave? What motivates people raised in a settled society to pack our cars and head for the nearest airport?

Most jaded workers long for a life removed from the crushing restraint of mortgage, rent, taxes, insurance, car payments, and other obligations. Onerous responsibilities can drive ordinary 9-to-5ers down a path of self-destruction when they stop and think for a minute about how broken and arbitrary the "system" is. For some, these revelations take years to unveil. Others have epiphanies about leaving on a jet plane from the moment they graduate college and realize that what they had just endured was naught but a liaison between thirsty Thursdays in college and sleeping with your boss for a promotion. After all, in its simplest terms, what more is career progression than kissing someone's ass?

We all inevitably yearn for a change of scenery at one point or another in our lives. People are all too familiar with their cars, their office desks, and their couches. Their interpretations of life are limited to the occurrences that transpire each day in these artificial realms. Without a doubt, the writing is on the walls—but to *see* it, to process it, one must transcend the boundaries of the box and read the words from the outside.

* * *

"Cole, about what Rick said—"

"Don't tell me you're going to heed his advice, Justin. Both you and Curtis should drop what you're doing and stay on the road as long as you can until you run out of money."

"The longer I travel, the more I wonder," Curtis said, as he skipped a stone into the river at the base of the Black Canyon. It was so serene, so peaceful, yet so ambivalent. As the rock erratically skipped once, twice, three times, I compared its trajectory to my own.

"I don't mean to say that bluntly. I just think that you two don't fit the lemming mold."

"What do you mean?" I asked, throwing a stone of my own into the creek. It skipped six times and smacked the other side of the canyon, sending a hollow echo through the stony corridor.

"You're not a follower. If you were, you'd be out in some boring tourist trap hanging out with the tourons."

We chuckled at his creativity but were no closer to understanding his perspective.

"Let me put it more clearly. You've got a typical forty-hours-a-week worker who has some vacation time. They decide to go to the Grand Canyon; they fly out to Phoenix and take a pricey shuttle to the South Rim. They stay the night in the ritzy Red Horse Cabin, wake up, walk to the rim, take a quick look at it, snap a million pictures, then go back to their cabin. Rinse and repeat a few more days, then go on home. These are the kind of people that never leave the box."

He took a handful of his trail mix with his right hand, then isolated the raisins into his left palm.

"You see these? These are us. We're unattractive, wrinkly, and discolored. If you saw us with chocolate, peanuts, cashews, and almonds, we'd be the least desirable. But here's the thing."

Grabbing the bag, Cole threw the rest of the concoction, sans the raisins, back where they came from. He proceeded to seal it up and put it back on the ground.

"Let's pretend for our purposes that this bag is a box. Us raisins, we've made it a point to exit the box. Sure, we're shriveled and well-worn, but that just means we've lived our lives. Everyone else? They're still in the box."

He shoveled the raisins in his mouth and swallowed.

"You see, the thing is, despite our weathered exterior, we're still pretty tasty. Our personalities reflect all of the hardships we've gone through to breach the walls of the box so that we have a chance to read the instructions on the outside."

"Like the nutritional facts?" Curtis joked.

"Nutritional facts, ingredients, expiration date—anything and everything. As long as you've given yourself an opportunity to leave the box to read the writing on the outside, you've done your due diligence."

I sat staring out at the Gunnison River for a few moments before I garnered the courage to speak.

"Don't you think education is a prerequisite to being able to read those instructions?"

"Certainly. But you should never forget that there is life outside of the walls that confine you. The greatest experiences you will have will be those that formal education cannot afford you." Cole's tone shifted from that of a wise old man to that of a concerned friend.

"If you're going to go into law, just don't be an ambulance chaser. Do something significant."

But what the hell is significant, anyway? Who sets the ground rules for a balanced and productive existence? Cole's words hit me hard. I mean, I was already on the brink of total discombobulation. Truth is, I had no idea what I was doing with my life. I was following in the footsteps of my father and grandfather before him—to become an advocate and understudy of the law, a malleable human construct with just as much variability as my own convictions.

I wanted to fulfill a legacy or, rather, to continue one. But I wasn't quite sure how, other than to emulate my relatives. I think what bugged me the most about trying to figure out what made me content were my volatile thoughts. Being complacent was tenuous, at best, when I couldn't even make up my mind about what I wanted to do with my life.

For so long, I was divided between two dichotomies. On one hand, I wanted to experience life unswayed and unhindered, with no regard for giving my gift to future generations, whom are almost certain to not heed my advice anyway. On the other hand, I was scared shitless of being forgotten. I worried that I would never accomplish anything substantial. And it was debilitating to constantly ruminate about.

As conventional as it may sound, since then it has become paramount to secure a balance between these two branches, lest I forget my main purpose in life: to be happy. At the time, I still wasn't quite sure what I would ultimately do with a law degree. For the next three years, my plan was fixed, but my passion for it had yet to manifest. Thus, I made it a point to ignore law school's impending grasp on my life while we traveled. But Cole made it impossible to overlook the fact that I could see the progression of my life right in front of me. And that needed to change.

Through Cole's cleverly employed metaphor, I began to understand that the trail I took was my own trail to tread—whether that trail led me along a road of affluence, up a mountain of prosperity, or heaven forbid, down to a flowing river gorge. In the interim, while I still had a thing or two to figure out about myself, I inevitably chose the latter. I dipped my feet into the cold moisture and let my mind rest, finally at ease.

Chapter 5

"The desert takes our dreams from us, and they don't always return. . . Those who don't return become a part of the clouds, a part of the animals that hide in the ravines and of the water that comes from the earth. They become a part of everything."

—Paulo Coelho, *The Alchemist*

* * *

The gas gauge read empty as I coasted in cruise control at a pleasant forty miles per hour on I-70 in Utah. Mindy wasn't feeling well after hours of dashing at a cool ninety miles an hour along the interstate highway with one of the highest speed limits in the country. On numerous occasions, the transmission sputtered, and we were convinced we were going to break down at any moment. To make matters worse, the next exit with a gas station, according to our friend Google Maps, was fifty miles away. Yep, we were screwed yet again.

When I first began researching places to go to while traveling across the country, there was never any doubt that we were going to the Beehive State. We had seen so many pictures of its famous arches, twisting slot canyons, towering cliffs, and perfect crack climbing that it became one of our most sought-after states. Sprinkled throughout its confines is a smattering of national parks, each with its own distinct story and character. From north to south, you can tackle Arches, Canyonlands, Bryce Canyon, and Zion, among others. Our plan was to hit them all. But if our latest debacle was any indication, it wouldn't be an easy task.

Our present dilemma was somewhat reminiscent of the Engineer Pass situation. However, whereas we at least had some control over our fate on the Alpine Loop, our gasoline-starved drive wasn't going to end well if we didn't find fuel—and fast.

"I think it's inevitable at this point. We're royally screwed," I remarked, with next to no nervousness in my tone.

"There has to be a station," Curtis said, as he frantically searched for one on his phone. So far, no luck.

Curtis advised me to drive forty miles per hour despite the study that alleges that the most gas-efficient speed is fifty-five. Every so often I would accelerate up to forty-two just to spite him.

There were almost no cars on the road—a testament to the relative isolation of the area. In fact, I-70 in Utah is home to the longest distance anywhere in the U.S. Interstate Highway System without motorist services—110 miles of desolation, to be precise. Even if we wanted help, the cars we did see were driving twice as fast as us, so our efforts to wave them down would be futile.

At that point, I was starting to settle into our fate as if it had been predetermined. While Curtis desperately called nearby businesses to ascertain whether there were any gas stations not listed on Google Maps, I dreamt of what was going to happen next as my road hypnosis took over.

I began to daydream.

As we sat on the hood of Mindy in a defeated trance after running out of gas, a vintage pick-up truck slowed down and parked behind us. A man and his wife exited their vehicle and started toward us.

The couple, who were clad in overalls, each made an indistinguishable gesture toward us, but we vigorously nodded our heads anyway.

The husband returned to his vehicle and retrieved a gas canister. Hallelujah!

After they filled our tank and we exchanged small talk, they invited us back to their ranch.

"What do you think?" Curtis asked, as we reached the cow farm.

"Let's do it."

And that was the day we became farmers and lived happily ever after.

Back in reality, I swerved Mindy forcefully toward the next exit after Curtis had a successful phone conversation that yielded information about a nearby gas station. By now, the gauge was well below the empty mark, and I wasn't even sure how we were still moving. But alas, all was right in the world on that fateful day, and we rolled into the gas station with no more than a few miles to spare. Moral of the story? Don't trust your GPS. Or just don't go on road trips, period. Soul searching is for stoners and the unemployed. It's a total waste of gas anyways.

* * *

"So there I was, minding my own business, when all of a sudden I hear something hovering over me. It was like a whooshing sound, but I couldn't really tell."

We met Tim at a Bureau of Land Management campsite in the middle of nowhere Utah. He had driven his RV up from Southern California to delve into some time-lapse photography of the celestial dots that flooded the sky on nearly every cloudless evening in Utah's desolate serenity. He was in the middle of telling us a story about a time he heard a phantom aircraft above his house.

"Anyway, my girlfriend and I looked up and there was nothing there."

"Nothing?" I asked.

"Nothing."

"Was it cloudy out?"

"Nope. Clear as day."

"What do you think it was?" Curtis chimed in.

"Aliens. It has to be—it's the only logical explanation."

A foreign voice interjected from the abutting camp site.

"Sounds logical to me."

"What he said!" Tim replied.

It was difficult to make out the man's figure in the blackness of the Utah evening, but the stars afforded us just enough light to see his face.

"I'm Josh. Sorry for interrupting your chat, but I just can't resist to talk about extraterrestrial shit and that kind of stuff."

We rose from our familiar perches outside of Tim's RV and made our way over to Josh. As we got closer, we could make out a few of his most notable features. He was a big guy who appeared to be better suited for a couch than a campsite. But there was something that we saw in him that reminded us of all the others that we had met on our trip.

"You guys want a beer?"

"No thanks," was the consensus among us all.

"Good, I figured I would offer, but that leaves more for me."

We laughed heartily as a baby began to cry in the tent adjacent to us.

"Sorry, Ash. I'm talking to our neighbors."

A hand poked out of the shelter and began to unzip the flap, revealing the face of a young blonde woman no older than thirty-five. In her arms was a baby that was probably not even a year old.

"Hi guys, I'm Ashley. And this is baby Sara. Say hi, sweetie!"

Ashley gently grabbed her daughter's palm and waved it at us. She instinctively began to cry at the sight of three bearded strangers.

"Far from home, huh?" Tim remarked.

"This is Sara's first camping trip," Josh answered, "but we only live up in Salt Lake so it's not too far."

"We got sick of doing nothing at home on weekends," Ashley offered.

We told them our story, and they told us theirs. At home, Josh and Ashley ran a doggy day care of sorts, so they were all too familiar with rearing children so to speak. But like many other people, they became trapped in a never-ending, cyclical rhythm. Their love for dogs became more of a pastime than a profession when they got into financial trouble and had to take up unfulfilling 9-to-5s to supplement their true passion. The upside to their situation was that they became cognizant of its unnerving grasp. And that it wasn't too late to make amends to their routine. They wanted to experience the world just as it was—by living.

"We've got to go back to work on Sunday." Josh took a generous gulp of Bud Light and let out an epic belch. "Shit sucks."

"You guys really make me want to leave my shitty job and travel. But the bills have to be paid somehow." Ashley unzipped her tent and went back in to put Sara to bed.

"Anyone hungry?" Curtis announced. "We've got some freeze-dried spaghetti in the car."

"Now that's the stuff!" Tim exclaimed. "Come cook it up on my stove in the RV."

We obliged by Tim's request and whipped up an entire can for the new crew.

"Not half bad. Better than the crap Ash makes."

"I heard that!"

"Yeah, yeah. Anyway, you guys eat this stuff every night? And sleep in your car?"

"Most of the time," Curtis answered, "but every so often we go out to eat or stay with friends. It's not so bad."

"Not so bad? Man, I can barely sleep a night without my bed. I don't know how you do it. Tim's got the right idea—a memory foam mattress and a stove. I'd be in heaven."

"You got that right brother."

* * *

"Wake up."

I heard a whisper in my right ear as I shifted my limp body away from the source. A few days after leaving Tim and company, we found ourselves on a shuttle bus en route to the trailhead of the renowned Zion Narrows, and I was quite exhausted.

"It's too early," I grumbled. I had forgotten that I was in public, and just as soon as I spoke, the man sitting to my left slowly got up, cavalier to my sleep-deprivation. I curled myself into a ball on the bus seat before summoning the motivation to rise.

"Let's go," the voice murmured. I ignored it as best as I could.

"Go to sleep, Curtis."

* * *

In the preceding week, Curtis and I had made our way from the magnificent arches of their eponymous park, to the phallic structures of Canyonlands, to the peculiar hoodoos of Bryce, and finally found ourselves in the southwestern corner of the state searching for revelation in the land of Zion. I'm not so sure it amounted to that, but it's impossible to leave the park without some sort of reinvigorated spirituality. Especially when you get to relish it in solidarity.

Just a day prior, we had scampered up Zion's signature hike, Angel's Landing. To many, Angel's Landing is the scariest and most difficult hike they will ever do. As many as eight people have died while hiking it. The National Park Service has put forth this description of the hike to detract some from scaling the feature: "Caution— The route to Angel's Landing involves travel along a steep, narrow ridge with support chains anchored intermittently along the route. Footing can be slippery even when the rock is dry. Unevenly surfaced steps are cut into the rock with major cliff drop-offs adjacent."

To us, it wasn't as daunting as most people make it out to be, but I suppose that's the kind of perspective you get when you had a near-death experience on Longs Peak. People gasped and whispered as we went off route and climbed outside of the support chains leading toward the summit perch.

We may not be the best role models in the world, and it's debatable that we will be good parents one day. At least that's what our hike in the Zion Narrows taught us.

Connor and Jamie, a father-son duo who rode the bus with us, were eager to start their day-hike through the Narrows when they got off the shuttle. Rather than wait for the large crowd to disperse toward the narrow trail leading to the river's mouth, they hustled past the trailhead and out of sight before anyone noticed they were gone. Unfortunately for them, two road warriors were looking to follow suit, and before anyone noticed, they were gone too.

* * *

"Daddy, how much longer?" You could barely make out Jamie's nine-year-old frame as he splashed through chest deep water in the shadow of towering sandstone spires.

"Just a little bit more, honey." Connor's tone soothed his son back into sensibility. He stroked his rugged hands through Jamie's fire-red hair, which was soaked from repeated dips in the oft-raging river. We had been traveling both on the banks and in the middle of it for nearly ten miles, often through waist-deep sections—and for a child, nearly neck-deep.

Connor and Jamie were on a weekend getaway from mom and sister. They made the trip up from Phoenix and intended on having some quality father-son bonding in one of the most beautiful locales that the American Southwest has to offer.

As a former ultra-marathoner, Connor found it imperative to bring his children up with an appreciation for the outdoors. He often took off long weekends from his outrageously busy schedule as one of the country's premier endocrinologists to provide his son the outdoor experiences that he had when he was growing up in rural Minnesota, despite his new location in the arid desert.

But it was always Connor's conscious effort to teach his son to work hard so that he could someday be his own man. Throughout the day, that message resonated, not just for Jamie, but for me and Curtis as well.

* * *

Traipsing through the Narrows was hard on the feet, but not on the mind. Curtis and I slipped into our "water shoes" from Wal-Mart when the trail tapered into a full-fledged aqua jog. The only problem was that there were just as many rocks underwater as there were above ground. This was no hotel swimming pool, that's for sure.

But the pain we endured was nothing when juxtaposed with the sights we were afforded. Around every corner, the canyon got narrower and narrower, as its name would suggest. What started as a rock hop across a mundane river became an enchanted wade through lithic paradise.

When observing it from the bottom up, the Narrows are quite possibly the most majestic canyon in North America. I'm obviously biased and there is no reason why anyone should take my assertion as the truth, but I'm willing to bet that anyone who has been there will agree with me. Certainly, the Grand Canyon is unmatched in its splendor when looking from the top down, but when you're at the bottom of the Narrows, the universe seems a whole lot bigger.

The canyon walls shot up like wavelengths, corkscrewing higher and higher into the sky until they repelled all sunlight, capturing their visitors in a claustrophobic cavern entrenched in eerie darkness. In the most attenuated portion of the area, water dripped endlessly into heightening tributaries—a flood prone area, we later learned.

Despite the outwardly eternal darkness and the creepy *je ne sais quoi* of the Narrows, Jamie was a fireball of energy.

"This is so cool, Daddy!"

"Didn't I tell you?" His father responded, "Look over here, son, there's some of those plants I was telling you about."

Connor wrapped his brawny hand around a tiny flower's stem and pulled it gently, so as not to disturb any of the other vegetation growing from the wall. He swabbed his index finger on the tip of the bud and placed it in his mouth. He then proceeded to hand the flower over to Jamie.

"Taste."

Mimicking his father's prudent approach, Jamie delicately handled the fragile plant and tasted the gel-like substance that Connor had advised him to try.

"Mmm, what is it?

"It's honey, dear. These plants grow all over the area. I've just never seen them on rock walls like this. Try it, boys."

He plucked another flower and handed it over to Curtis, and we sampled it for ourselves.

"Pretty cool, huh?" Connor asked.

"I'm surprised that these can thrive down here. It doesn't make sense, with no sunlight and all." Curtis commented.

"Nature is beautiful, isn't it?"

Without warning, a vibrant butterfly perched on the flower that Jamie still clutched in his hand. It fluttered its spotted wings and swiftly rose into a hover, now level with Jamie's freckled face. He smiled and stretched out his free hand. The curious creature descended to an abrupt halt onto his fingertips.

"I think it likes you," I opined.

"Daddy, look!"

The butterfly rose from its outcrop and flapped up into the sky, only to return to Jamie's hand.

"I think it's showing off," Connor countered.

As we continued our hike, the curious creature refused to leave Jamie's side, and only parted ways with us once the water rose further down the river. We didn't know it at the time, but we were going to get used to befriending butterflies that week.

* * *

"You know Jamie, you're a lot different than most kids your age." I reached my hand down to help him get up a tall, rocky hurdle. He grunted as he lifted himself up to a small clearing that only allowed room for one big kid and one little kid. While Curtis and Connor sped ahead of us, Jamie and I conversed about all his adventures with Daddy over the years.

"I know I am! None of my friends like to do the things that I do. It makes me sad."

"Well, what do you like to do that they won't do?"

"Lots of things—" He paused momentarily, as I gave him a lift back down to solid ground—well, water. "Last year, Daddy and I went to Yosemite without Mommy and Julia. They don't like doing fun stuff as much as we do."

He coughed emphatically as he swallowed a mouthful of water from the strengthening river currents.

"Are you okay?"

"I'm fine. Where's Daddy?" He continued to cough, now visibly distressed by the deeper and swifter waters.

"He's over there—Connor, Curtis, wait up!"

Both turned around and stood by as we caught up to them. Jamie was still coughing, so Connor lifted him up on his shoulders and attempted to console him.

"We're getting there, honey. Only a few more miles, I promise. After this we'll go eat pizza and celebrate!"

After hearing his father's familiar voice, it was apparent that Jamie was instantly relieved. He stopped coughing right there and then.

"Okay."

But I wasn't satisfied with his incomplete story just yet.

"So Jamie, what happened at Yosemite?"

"Well—"

His father quickly interrupted him.

"Oh, you're going to tell them about Half Dome?"

"I was going to . . ."

"I'm sorry for cutting you off son, go ahead and tell them. It's a remarkable feat!"

Jamie regained his composure as if nothing had happened.

"Well, Daddy and I went to hike Half Dome together last summer. I was only eight then. It was the biggest hike I've done in my life."

He wrinkled his face into a joyous smirk as he sat atop his father's broad shoulders—whether this was because he was exalted about his accomplishment or because his dad was carrying him through one of the deeper sections is questionable. But no matter the reason, we were all smiles for the rest of our river wade.

* * *

"Connor, we really cannot thank you enough for your hospitality. You really didn't have to buy us pizza," Curtis remarked, as we sat in Connor and Jamie's hotel room just outside of the park later that evening.

"And give us showers," I added.

"You shouldn't even give it a thought. If it wasn't for you guys, it would have been just me and Jamie." The sound of a turning faucet emerged from the closed door next to us, followed by a melodic symphony of sprinkling water droplets. "And he could really use some role models to look up to."

We were somewhat taken aback by his words initially but understood soon thereafter where he was coming from.

"Someday, Jamie is going to be in middle school. He'll go to high school, and presumably get a college degree after that. I want him to see that I'm not the only old guy who does these kinds of things with his kids. Maybe he'll even take a road trip like yours when he finishes school."

The room became still after the water droplets ceased to flow from the shower head in the bathroom.

"The truth is, everyone should leave some day. I think you guys have the right idea. But your adventures are far from over. Don't let anyone tell you otherwise."

We wouldn't.

Chapter 6

"Pin my wings, and I'll fly anyway," she said, whimsically, as if an ethereal being had spoon-fed her the words. "You'll see."

* * *

"YUCCA, YUCCA, YUCCA!"

Our battle cry reverberated into the deep valley below. And when I say deep, I mean *deep*. We had just begun our descent into Arizona's most recognizable and iconic feature—you know, the Grand Canyon—for our epic, fifty-mile, three-day rim-to-rim-to-rim-hike, North to South to North. Unrecognizable, overgrown shrubs lined the switchbacks that we used to descend deeper into the valley. Our humble guide called them yuccas. And the yucca became our rallying call for the remainder of our three days in the hottest goddamn place on Earth. Oh, you want to know who our guide was, don't you?

* * *

It's ten o'clock on a blustery Thursday evening in rural Boulder County, Colorado. A thin, attractive brunette in her early to mid-twenties sits complacently in an armchair in the living room of a humble farmhouse. Her long, sunbaked fingers hold open a copy of *Zen and the Art of Motorcycle Maintenance*.

The last six months have been, for lack of a better word, wild. Dinners with the family in Spokane seem like a thing of the past.

Old friends are naught but an afterthought. And ex-boyfriends? As good as dead.

She hears her phone pulsating vibrations from somewhere in the kitchen. Fumbling stacks of paper on the counter, she finds it wedged in between the cookie jar and the toaster.

"Johnny's gone," an empty voice echoes from the shattered earpiece now lying on the floor.

A half year of adventure quickly dissipates into insignificance, as words of her best friend and former lover's demise sunk deep into her soul. The dereliction sweeping her conscience was overwhelming—incurable, even. It would go on to haunt her for the unforeseeable future.

An unexpected return home and a funeral later, and she knew what her next step was. For twenty-some odd years, she craved destinations. But now, the only thing that mattered was the journey. No more cars, no more deadlines, no more menial responsibilities. All she needed was a backpack, a pan, some extra clothing, a pair of trekking poles, a water bladder, and ten dollars a day. The rest was up to fate to decide. Essentials in tow, she bought a one-way ticket to Denver, and a one-way trip to alleged salvation.

For the next month, she walked. Sometimes, a curious driver would give her a lift a few miles down the road. As a hitchhiker, she had no reservations or anxieties about what she was doing. It was as if this was divinity, and this self-fulfilling prophecy of hers was the only thing left to look forward to.

At the border of Colorado and Arizona, the last willing driver dropped her off during one of the most brutal heat waves that the American Southwest had seen in years. Temperatures eclipsed 110° nearly every day, and with the reflection of the sun on the black rocks, it often felt like 120°. Eighty miles separated her from every-thing that mattered. With only enough water to keep her vitality stable, she busted out twenty-mile days in anticipation of what was to be a search for meditative solitude in the Grand Canyon. She never expected it to instead manifest into an impromptu treasure hunt leading to companionship. To be honest, neither did we.

At the visitor's center of the North Rim of the Grand Canyon, she longed for the opportunity to make a meaningful connection but didn't know where to start. Sitting in the attached cafe for the day and recovering from her desert death march proved to be less enticing than she had dreamt it to be. There were no bearded dirtbags with buns in their hair, no kooky, granola, hippie types strutting around in the rusty desert skyline awaiting a moment of transcend-ence. Just tourists. And us.

"Hi, there! I noticed you writing a travel blog out of the corner of my eye and I figured I would say hi! I'm Butterfly."

I blogged about our trip for its duration, and this was the first time it had directly benefited us.

"Is that your trail name or something?" Curtis inquired. He was dripping sweat from his forehead despite the stale Arizona air-con-ditioning.

"No silly, it's my name! I changed it from Annie—not legally, of course." She was unconventionally playful in her tone, given that we had just met two minutes prior.

Over several hours of getting acquainted, Butterfly told us that she planned to hike the canyon from North Rim to South Rim in two nights. Our initial plan was to hike from North Rim to South Rim to North Rim in just two days and one night. However, Butterfly of-fered us a spot in her campground on the second night so that we didn't have to bear the intolerable heat for fifty miles in just two days. It was settled—we would do it in three days, two nights.

For hours we exchanged poetry, prose, miscellaneous meanderings, and the likes. Dinner was served in the form of quinoa and chicken, a collaborative concoction created from the scraps that each of us had dug out of our diminishing supplies of provisions. And to make matters even more fitting, Butterfly accepted our offer to grace Mindy with the presence of a female traveler—the first such instance of its kind. We slept soundly and stealthily that night in the North Kaibab trailhead parking lot with the gratification of making a new friend.

* * *

The ranger at the visitor's center had told us the day before that there was a heat warning between 10 a.m. and 2 p.m. Being the gumbies we were, we didn't think too much of it, especially since it was a balmy 45° that morning when we got out of the car.

"Chilly, chilly, chilly!" I remarked, as I put my down jacket on.

"Don't get used to it," Butterfly replied.

What the ranger had also told us was that we should wear cotton shirts rather than synthetic. We were perplexed at this suggestion, given that the latter is the so-called industry standard.

"YUCCA, YUCCA, YUCCA!" We shouted in unison.

A tornado of colors swept through the valley below. Hues of red, brown, yellow, gold, black, blue, and orange drew us an incomprehensible landscape. It was an overwhelming experience. Focusing on the beauty was near impossible. There were so many distractions, so many cliff bands, so many colors, so many sights to see along the picturesque horizon. The canyon's vastness was inspiring, but it truly was a sensory overload. At over 270 miles long, up to eighteen miles wide, and roughly a mile deep, it is a natural anomaly and a national treasure.

At Butterfly's first campsite, Cottonwood Campground, about seven miles into the valley, we bid her adieu. The following evening, we planned to meet her at her second campsite, Bright Angel Campground, about fourteen miles from the North Rim.

We had to hike another twelve or so miles to our campsite for the night, Indian Garden Campground, and with temperatures already eclipsing 100°, we knew we would be in for a sufferfest. I'm known to like suffer fests, but this would be the epitome of one.

From the top of the North Rim, we dropped approximately six thousand feet in elevation over the course of several hours. The worst realization we had was that we would have to go right back up on the way back after hiking around forty miles. But at the time it was irrelevant. We were in the Grand freaking Canyon.

As the day wore on, so did we. Our exhaustion was a product of the increasing heat, but one form of relief arose as we continued our trek. Any time we saw water, we dunked our shirts into it so that they were completely drenched. But relief was temporary. Within fifteen minutes, our shirts would dry out due to the intense heat.

This pattern continued for the remainder of the day until we finally reached our camp for the night, about nineteen miles from where we started. Unable to cope with the sweltering heat any longer, we retired to our mesh chambers, indifferent to the dearth of privacy we would have without a rain fly over us. It was that damn hot.

* * *

In the middle of night, which turned out to be only 7:30 p.m., we were jolted awake by the cries of a woman in the adjacent campsite. What was she blabbering about?

"I WANT TO GO HOME!" A painfully obnoxious screech pierced the dry desert air.

"But honey, the rangers said we can't travel during the day. It's too hot." A man whom we perceived to be her husband replied in an attempt to console the audibly distraught woman.

"BUT I WANT TO GO NOW! I WANT TO GO STAY IN A FIVE-STAR HOTEL AND BASK IN THE GLORY OF MY GREATEST ATHLETIC TRIUMPH! I CAN'T STAY HERE ANOTHER NIGHT!"

She actually said that, I kid you not.

"Shut the *hell* up," Curtis mumbled so only I could hear his plea.

To our dismay, the conversation continued for another ten or so minutes, from which we discerned that the group had hiked down five miles from the South Rim to stay the night in the canyon. Five miles. We had just completed a nineteen-mile trek from the opposite rim that same day. And we wanted nothing more than to go to bed but were prevented from doing so by this complainant and her posse of elite athletes. Luckily, the heat was even too much for a bunch of all-star hikers to maintain open eyelids. We thanked the gods of the desert for muffling the annoyances of our next-door tourons, and passed out into a seemingly eternal, alarm-less sleep.

The next morning, we scampered up to the South Rim and "enjoyed" the views in the company of hundreds of people. The splendor was a bit less satisfying since the South Rim is much, much more popular than the North Rim. What was even worse was that Curtis was starting to get painful blisters on his feet because he was wearing light hikers rather than his heavy-duty boots. His suffering became more evident as we made our way back down from the South Rim toward Indian Garden Campground.

We were both struggling at this point. The torrid climate was like a thorn-bush in the side, poking, jutting, and stabbing us with no intent of ceasing. We were brutally dehydrated, exhausted by the heat, and now we had Curtis's blisters to deal with.

It's hard to imagine that the pain from a blister can escalate so immensely in the span of just a few hours. With every step that Curtis took, excruciation was not far behind.

We consulted with the ranger on duty back at Indian Garden Campground, who had his way with Curtis. The result looked like a failed science experiment. Gauze, adhesives, and ointments engulfed his toes and made his feet look unrecognizable. But we were still nineteen miles away from the car, and there was no turning back now. We were fortunate that the Bright Angel Campground, where Butterfly was staying, was only another five or so miles away. It wasn't easy, but we made it. The patch-up of Curtis's feet had made all the difference in the world, but he was still in pain and fell far behind me.

As I rolled into Butterfly's campground, I saw her sitting by a river at the foot of the campground. I ran up from behind her and gave her a hug.

"Hey buddy!" She exclaimed, while craning her head back. "Where's Curtis?"

"He's got some pretty nasty blisters on his feet. He'll be here soon."

"I hope he's okay! He should dip his feet in the river when he gets here. It's magical!"

She gave me a smile and headed up toward her campsite. There was a picnic table and a sleeping bag laid out. She hadn't even bothered to take out her tent due to the intense heat.

That night, we all slept outside and stared at the stars until we fell asleep. If not for Butterfly's example, I would have been too afraid of snakes and scorpions gnawing on us. But her fearlessness and the heat made my apprehension an afterthought. It was still over 80° even after with the sun down. Not to mention fourteen miles still stood between us and our car, and it wouldn't be easy.

* * *

Several miles into our final day, we only felt intense dehydration and borderline heat exhaustion. We had six thousand vertical feet left to climb and, at this point, Curtis's blisters were the least of our worries. The temperature was still hovering around 100° and water and food couldn't even restore our morale.

"Almost . . . there," we would say to ourselves every few minutes. It was the only solace we had left when delirium began to take effect. In fact, we were so sick and disoriented that at times we thought we were hallucinating. I did, at least. At one point when a guided mule tour began to descend toward us, I assumed I was seeing things.

After the most painful hike of our lives to date, we fittingly celebrated with a Gatorade double-fist chug and an enchilada and potato wedge combo at the local gas station. It was only after we gorged on sugar and salt that we finally restored our bodies' natural equilibria. As if we hadn't had enough fun yet, we promised to pick up Butterfly at the South Rim visitor's center. She had found us a place to stay at her friend Alex's house in Phoenix. Problem was, we had to drive 250 miles south to retrieve her from the South Rim. Though the most direct route from North to South is twenty-five miles on foot, the drive is nearly ten times the amount of mileage of the hike. Nonetheless, we scooped up Butterfly from the visitor's center and were en route to Phoenix.

* * *

When we arrived at Alex's house, we were greeted by a guy a few years older than us. He had bright blue eyes, a buzzed head, and a thick, Minnesota accent—you might say it was bordering on Canadian.

He lived alone, although he was once one of three roommates who had moved out of their parents' houses to gain some sort of privacy. Surely, that meant that they could court as many prospective suitors as they wanted to without Peeping Mom looking over their shoulders. Among the droves of people who frequented the house was Butterfly. On her prior road trip, she had spent nearly a month with Alex and the guys.

"So you're the dirtbags that ol' Butterfly was raving about, eh? You know, I'm pretty picky about who I let crash at my house. But when she told me your mission, I had to give in."

"We're very appreciative," I responded.

"How long do you need to crash? Butterfly's one-month stay was kind of rare, but I'm willing to let you guys wander freely for the next few days. Here's a key."

"Alex likes to leave his door unlocked during the day anyway, so you might as well give it back," Butterfly quipped.

"Oh, shut up Annie," he quickly countered.

"It's *Butterfly!*"

"Oh, I forgot you changed it when you went all crunchy and earthy," Alex teased.

Later that night, Curtis and I conversed as Butterfly and Alex retired to their separate quarters.

"He trusts us with his key?" I whispered.

"Probably misses the company. Makes sense, I guess," Curtis answered.

A sudden rattle came from the kitchen, which was conveniently attached to the living room where we slept on couches. Maybe someone had the late-night munchies.

A dark figure emerged from the shadows with a glass of water in each hand. It was Butterfly, and she seemed surprised as she handed us each a glass.

"What are you guys doing sleeping here? I have a big bed all to myself and no company!"

Taken aback, and without much thought, I quickly and politely rejected her request.

"It's cool, we're alright here. But thanks for the offer!"

Curtis gave her a similar response.

"Alright, suit yourself. I'll be in my room if you change your mind!"

Maybe I should have.

* * *

Going outside at 5 a.m. in Phoenix during summer's climax is like stepping into your grandma's house in the dead of winter. For the love of God, someone tell her to turn the damn thermostat down.

Ninety degrees isn't so bad when there is a pool in your back-yard, though. According to Alex, having one is just as common in

Arizona as owning an air conditioning unit. And with such high demand, installing your own piece of paradise is inexpensive.

In all honesty, we needed the relaxation. This was our last day with Butterfly and coping with her departure would be exhausting in and of itself.

"So rut's nerxt?" I asked with a mouthful of eggs in my mouth.

Butterfly handed Curtis a plate of eggs with guacamole and hot sauce on a bagel. We had trouble paying attention to her while we feasted on her heavenly recipe.

"What's next? Wyoming. And then I don't know what. I'll go with the flow, I guess." She headed back to the stove and continued to crack eggs, well aware that she was dealing with two hungry dudes. Make that three. Alex suddenly popped out of his room and announced his presence. He was barefoot and shirtless, but his plaid pajamas really stole the show.

"Good morning sunshines. Annie my dear, what's for breakfast?"

"You know that's not my name anymore. That was another me." She pouted and quickly shifted her attention back to the frying pan.

Alex looked at us and shrugged his shoulders.

"Sorry. Whatever it is, it smells good." He took a seat at the table next to us and pulled out his computer. "By the way, I found a few rides on Craigslist for you last night."

Butterfly turned off the stove and brought Alex his breakfast. "Oh yeah? Where to?"

"They're in Tucson and driving up to the Tetons tomorrow. They seem to be good guys. Appalachian Trail hikers actually."

Curtis sprung up from his culinary visit to heaven.

"What are they doing out here?"

Alex handed Butterfly the laptop and gave her his seat. "I could ask you guys the same question."

"Fair enough," Curtis conceded.

Because the hiking community is so tight-knit even on a national scale, hikers will go out of their way to help another of their kin. This is typically called trail magic. For instance, while we were in the Grand Canyon with Butterfly, a pair of hikers gave us all the food they didn't need because they had too much. They were more than happy to part with it because of the excess weight, but it was this gesture that really got us thinking that maybe this esoteric notion of trail magic actually existed.

Butterfly stared intently at the screen and scrolled furiously through whatever she was looking at.

"They leave at 6 a.m. tomorrow. Can I catch a ride, Alex?"

He doused some more hot sauce on his already covered sandwich.

"If it gets you out of my house, why not?"

Curtis and I couldn't help but laugh out loud. Butterfly scowled at him, but quickly got over it.

"Well, now that the excitement has subsided, let's get to work," Alex called from the dishwasher.

In exchange for his graciousness in letting us crash for a few days, we offered to help dig up his yard so that he could install some new pipes. This feat proved to be more difficult than we expected, what with the sweltering Phoenix heat and aridness. Nevertheless, we made good time, and jumped right into the pool to commemorate our achievement.

"We're gonna miss you guys," I said, as I shot Curtis with my water gun.

"You're free to come back anytime," Alex answered while he jumped off the diving board and made a big splash.

"I'm sure we'll take you up on that offer." Curtis sprayed me back as I dove underwater and grabbed Butterfly by the legs. She let out a piercing screech and threw a bouncy ball at my head as I rose back above water.

"Hey, that's not nice!" I yelled. "I got a concussion once when someone threw a ball at my head in the pool." I happily whipped the ball back at Butterfly.

"Tough luck," Alex shouted from his lawn chair while he dried off, "no one is ever safe in my pool."

We all followed suit and dried ourselves while soaking in the intense heat. In our last hour with Butterfly and Alex, we reflected on our respective journeys in an attempt to find mutual inspiration for our next move. Butterfly began to tell us about where she had been before meeting up with us, and her prospective plans for afterwards.

On her first road trip before returning home for Johnny's funeral, she spent a considerable amount of time in Boulder with two older women whom she referred to as Baby Bear and Goldilocks. As it turned out, they sheltered her, fed her, and allowed her to wander freely around their ranch. She was like the daughter that they never had.

We told Butterfly and Alex the story about when we almost ran out of gas on I-70. We wondered out loud: what if we had run out of gas on that highway? What if some older couple pulled over, filled our tank, and then escorted us to their farm, offering us to stay and work for them, much like the dream that I'd had during my road hypnosis? Would we take the offer in the spirit of spontaneity, or would we carry on with our life plans?

One thing is for sure. Butterfly gave us the chance to see eye to eye with the two purported realities that stood right across from us. We could either be complacent with ordinariness, or dissident to its insidious magnetism. What was *real*, was not what we saw, but what we *perceived*, and what we *lived*. As long as we had people to tell us how to live our lives, we would remember the day that we met our muse and the advice that she inadvertently offered us. We were mad to live before the madness of death by routine swept us under the rug once this trip inevitably ended.

Departures and arrivals are two inseparable components of our fleeting lives. We go, we come back, we leave, or we stay, we wave hello, we wave goodbye. We live. And we die. Seldom do arrivals invoke anything more than a transient bout of excitement. But with every parting, comes catharsis. Sometimes we have to say our final goodbyes to an elderly family member. Other times, we go our separate ways with a significant other due to irreconcilable differences. No matter the implication, emotional release, be it positive or negative, is inevitable.

We drove off into the crimson rays of the departing sun later that evening with heavy hearts, but it was never goodbye. With as little as a whisper, Butterfly was able to lift herself into our consciences with eternal grace. If we were to unshackle the webs that held us in our cocoons, we would need to remember her advice. She taught us patience, spontaneity, openness, and above all else, she taught us how to *live*. She gave us all the direction we needed, and now we just needed to follow the evanescent arrows to where we wanted to be. Wherever that was.

Saying goodbye to Butterfly was both liberating and hampering. In the last few weeks, we had gone from loser anti-socialites, to dirt-bag celebrities. It was as if we had remembered to put our deodorant on, and people were suddenly flocking to our side. And if the friends that we met prior to Butterfly had taught us to smell the roses, she had allowed us to listen to their sway. Before, I'm not so sure we were even looking at them. With this newly acquired skill, we were ready to unleash our new personalities onto the world. But it would come at the expense of losing her for who knows how long. What we failed to recognize, though, is that we would never lose her. Because she had inadvertently woven her way through our DNA, forever synthesizing her unbridled spirit into our chemical makeup.

Chapter 7

"Your amount of passion, fortitude, and entrepreneurial drive is one of a kind. Enjoy the fruits of the challenges and triumphs that come along this journey."

—Shawn

* * *

If you live in Los Angeles, you never get a break. Pollution, traffic, materialism, and traffic are just a few of the repercussions that you must deal with if you live in the City of Angels. Did I mention the traffic?

Sure, any city during rush hour is prone to high volumes of irritable commuters. But LA is not any city. Rush hour, lunchtime, teatime, after midnight—really any time of day—is subject to unyielding bouts of brutal traffic. And don't even get me started with Sunday drivers. I hate Sunday drivers. But what the hell causes all the goddamn congestion?

I gave it some thought, and it's obvious, really. You ever wonder what your retired grandmothers do in their spare time? Every day at around 4 p.m., an ensemble of grannies convenes on the local interstate highways in their Oldsmobiles with the sole objective of wreaking havoc on unassuming commuters. They line up parallel to each other to block all lanes and bar other drivers from passing while they flash toothy grins at each other and laugh uncontrollably. This hobby is not exclusive to LA; for there must be some sort of secret society that they all join—like AARP, but for nonconformists.

For all intents and purposes, rush hour is naught but an old wives' tale. Pun intended.

* * *

Los Angeles isn't all that bad, though. The beaches are pretty, albeit crowded; the people seemingly live a slower-paced life than those on the East Coast; and most of all, it's home to my favorite fast food joint, In N' Out Burger. Which was why eating dinner there with our next host, Shawn, was more than appropriate for our West Coast welcome party. Curtis had only known Shawn as a loose acquaintance in his time at Northeastern University, so it came to us as a surprise that when we reached out to him just several hours prior to convening that he would not only get dinner with us but allow us to crash at his place.

After leaving Butterfly and Alex, we made a quick pit stop in Joshua Tree National Park to indulge in the Dr. Seuss–like sights that the park afforded. The problem was, we had intended on rock climbing there, but with little experience outside of climbing gyms and no local guide, we found ourselves running in circles looking for established routes to try our hands at.

There are two primary rock-climbing disciplines: sport and traditional (or trad) climbing. Sport climbing involves clipping into prebolted routes with quickdraw carabiners, which help to protect a climber's fall. For trad climbers, much of the fall protection comes in the form of protection, or gear, that you fix into cracks in the rock. I could go on for hours explaining these distinctions, but at this point in our climbing career, we had never sport- or trad-climbed outside. We had only top-roped, which involves setting an anchor at the top of the climb and belaying from the bottom So, instead of rock climbing, we screamed at each other for several hours before we realized it was time to move on. Someday, we'll be back—and I'm sure we'll still be screaming.

Raising your voice can be tiresome, so we insisted that Shawn accompany us for our first real fast food experience of the trip. We opted to try the 4x4, animal fries, and a Neapolitan milkshake—all part of the secret menu. Four burger patties stuffed into one bun alongside a tray of fries with thousand-island dressing, and a milkshake was enough to physically incapacitate us. But among a sea of sodium, artificial food coloring, and processed meat, we made a bona fide connection.

While we munched on mostly empty calories, Shawn began to tell us of the true victims of the city's menacing traffic.

"Basically, every night before I go home, I take a two-hour nap in my car so I don't have to deal with it." He tousled his short brown hair with a greasy hand and took a forceful sip of his milkshake.

"Sometimes when it's really bad, I get up at 4 a.m., drive to work, nap, and then start my day. And then after work, I'll nap again for two hours before heading back home."

Our jaws dropped, revealing ketchup, mustard, and ground beef. So much for a more laid-back lifestyle than the East Coast.

"What kind of life is that?" I thought out loud as my acid reflux began to flare up.

"No life at all," Shawn quickly responded, unfazed by the question.

When he first came to LA, Shawn was directionless. Not in the sense that he had nothing going for him, but just the opposite. He had recently finished his degree at Northeastern and needed to shake up his life but figured that the East Coast wasn't the place to do it. With no job, no plan, and substantial debt, he set his sights on La-La Land.

He moved into a miniature, studio apartment forty-five minutes outside of the city, not realizing that forty-five minutes translated into upwards of two hours during rush hour. It took him only two months to realize that it wouldn't be long before he sacrificed his sanity for a meager paycheck and a forgotten dream.

"So where are you going to go after the lease is over?" Curtis asked.

Shawn momentarily looked up from his animal fries.

"It's a month-to-month, so I can leave at any time, really. I don't know, I'm probably going to get a new job somewhere closer before I give up entirely."

Shawn's words echoed the sentiments of recent grads everywhere. Curtis and I still had several more years of schooling, so we were blown away by his revelations. But until you take a moment or two with someone who just spent two hundred grand and four valuable years living a fairy tale, it's impossible to comprehend how truly screwed some people are post-college.

Shawn sighed.

"What do you guys say we go to the beach and forget about this shit?"

Amen to that.

* * *

The three of us enthusiastically strolled around Venice Beach that afternoon. There's so much culture and history to be found in the birthplace of skateboarding, that any number of Jersey Shore wannabes couldn't detract from its amusement. We were fascinated by the outdoor weightlifters and the eight-year-old kids kick-flipping in the skate park. But nothing intrigued us more than that the organized street basketball league that we witnessed, where announcers played rap music and gave politically incorrect nicknames to all the kids.

"And heeeeeereeee's Asian Persuasion taking the ball down the court, with My Mom Dyed My Hair in tow. Wait a second! There goes Old Man Andre Miller with the steal. Old Man Andre Miller takes it to the house and SCORESSSSS!" It felt like we were in that old video game, *NBA Street*.

As we walked further along the boardwalk, we continued to press Shawn about how he ended up here. It turned out that he only had fifteen hundred dollars to his name when he arrived. For months, he survived on peanut butter and cereal, or whatever was the most inexpensive, really. He found ways to get by that one might not attempt except out of desperation.

"Shawn!" Curtis called as we began to lag behind during our stroll on the pier.

He promptly did a one-eighty.

"Yessir?"

"We haven't technically reached the coast yet. We still have to touch the water."

Curtis was right. Caught up in the excitement of everything else around us, we forgot about the fact that we had yet to set foot in the Pacific Ocean. That needed to change.

As I immersed my feet into the warm SoCal water, I looked out into the horizontal sky. From the waterfront, one can see endlessly, creating the illusion that the world is flat. It is befuddling, yet oddly comforting, that thousands of years of human discovery were unable to debunk the naïveté of this theory. Armed with our present understanding that the universe is as interminable as the ocean is to our own eyes, we have frightened our species into galactic irrelevance. I promptly turned around and walked back inland instead of giving it any more thought. I wanted to feel like I was on top of the world, not a mere speck residing in it. Surely, only one place could console me in that moment of powerlessness. As John Muir so aptly said: the mountains are calling. And I must go.

* * *

Most people see California as a haven of opportunity. The landscapes are vast; beaches, plentiful; and experiences, boundless. But there remains an oft-omitted aspect of the Golden State that modestly dwells several hours inland. Away from the congestion and plastic surgery lies the Sierra Nevada—a coveted dreamscape for mountain climbers and world travelers alike. Wedged deep in the heart of the four-hundred-mile chain of peaks is Mount Whitney, the tallest mountain in the lower forty-eight states, at just over 14,500 feet. Conquering Whitney is no easy feat, for the least technical route is a twenty-two-mile round-trip hike via the Mount Whitney Trail. But we weren't interested in spending our entire day in the company of sheep. Our eyes were fixated on the Mountaineer's Route, a much more strenuous, albeit shorter and less crowded hike that gains roughly six thousand vertical feet in 3.8 miles, one-way. After ascending, we would catch the eponymous trail on the way down and join the commotion.

The Mount Whitney Trail is so popular that there is a permit lottery, in which only one in three applications are successful. Fortunately for us, there were walk-in permits for the much less popular Mountaineer's Route. We scooped up a permit right at 8 a.m. when the ranger's office opened, with the intention to complete the hike in one long push the following day.

* * *

At 4:45 a.m., we awoke. There are only two things in this world that can motivate us to wake up so early: mountains and time zone changes. We benefited from both that morning.

Mount Whitney, named after former state geologist Josiah Whitney, resides smack in the middle of Sequoia National Park and Inyo National Forest. Its summit is the southern terminus of the extremely popular John Muir Trail. But before it was officially Whitney, it was Fisherman's Peak. And before that, it was Too-man-i-goo-yah, or "the very old man," according to Judge William B. Wallace, one of the early explorers of the peak. He claims that the Paiute tribe believed a Great Spirit who controlled the fate of their people lived on the mountain. It's easy to see why. The peak is a rugged mass of granite formed during the Cretaceous Age from molten rock and glacial erosion. For early settlers, its existence was akin to the existence of a god. To us, its divine status was still very much evident.

We shared the first mile or so with the Mount Whitney Trail, but quickly turned at the junction with the North Lone Pine Trail, which is part of the Mountaineer's Route. Unlike the well-traveled main trail, we would have to navigate the trail using cairns—rock piles indicating the trail—and our GPS.

Eventually, the North Lone Pine Trail became trail-less, and we emerged at Lower Boy Scout Lake. The lake resides at the floor of a valley wedged between towering cliffs on one side and downtrending, verdant slopes on the other. From the lake, the trail became even fainter, so we took the path of least resistance over loose boulders and damp rock. It eventually led to Upper Boy Scout Lake, which we didn't realize we had passed until we spotted a series of disturbed rocks and gravel that only one person had probably followed before us. Alas, we figured, why the hell not?

Somehow our lackadaisical route yielded desirable results. We were soon at the base of our final climb at 12,261 feet, where the unsuitably named Iceberg Lake resided. It was quite unfrozen.

If we thought the cliffs at the lower lake were towering, the walls that surrounded Iceberg Lake were gargantuan. Adjacent to Whitney were a series of subpeaks—Crooks Peak, Keeler Needle, and Third Needle. Each fiercely prodded upwards toward baby blue skies, uninhibited. From here, we could see our ultimate route to the summit up a steep, loose gully.

* * *

One step forward, two steps back.

"Jesus Christ!" Curtis shouted, as we scampered up the gravelly and unstable talus en route to the summit of Mount Whitney. With every foot we placed, we slipped on the loose rock that lined the Mountaineer's Route.

"We're almost there," I fired back, winded. Altitude sucks, I tell you.

The backdrop of the Sierra Nevada imposed its will upon our mortal eyes when we turned around momentarily to recollect our posture.

"Damn," Curtis collected his breath, as he took in the view.

That's really all that you could say. People often wonder why we do what we do, and Curtis perfectly summed it up in one word.

Much of our ascent up until that point had been exhausting. Sure, the slopes were steep, but it was the altitude that was crushing us. That, and the fact that the freeze-dried spaghetti from the night before wasn't agreeing with us. I guess that's what happens when you go from Mom's homemade American Chop Suey to a pouch holding what barely resembles edible food. Let's just say we had to swap leaders frequently. The brutal stench of preservatives and excess sodium emanating from our bottoms was too much to bear. Which leads me to a related matter, if you can believe it.

As one of the most well-trodden mountains eclipsing fourteen thousand feet in the nation, Mount Whitney is a victim of desecration more often than it should be. From unwarranted trash to ridiculous erosion, she has fallen prey to her own popularity. But what cripples Whitney the most are the carry-in, carry-out human waste bags that every hiker is required to carry along with them. As we made our way onto the main trail toward the summit, we started to notice that people had purposely left the bags all over the trail rather than take them down themselves. An area that was supposed to represent pulchritude and magnificence was obtrusively marred by human malfeasance.

There's a delicate balance between requiring such a policy, and simply allowing people to poop wherever they want. Many forest service policies opt for the latter, but that's because the mountains aren't as crowded or you can dig holes in the sub-alpine areas. But what happens when people start to leave their shit in the plastic bags? The more shit bags on the ground, the more shit bags on the ground. It's common logic. Someone will inevitably propagate the trend until it becomes ritualistic, and in turn, standard practice. It's a heinous affront to one of the most beautiful places in the country.

"Can you believe this shit?" Curtis angrily asked, evidently unaware of his own pun.

"I see it, but I don't believe it," I joked back.

I think it was the first time in our lives that we were pissed off at something other than each other while hiking.

* * *

At the top of the continental United States, we breathed a labored breath and stared down toward infinity. Sharp, needle-like peaks cut gracefully into still, blue air. The nearest clouds were a plane ride away and the sun was blinding, but our overstrained corneas were unfazed. This was true, unbridled serenity.

"Man, my feet are killing me," Curtis remarked, as he shielded his eyes with his hand like a visor.

"Blisters?"

"Yup." He sat down next to the emergency summit shelter, which was built in 1909 after a U.S. Fisheries employee was struck and killed by lightning.

"You bring some of those band aids you got in the Grand Canyon?" I asked. Despite his experience just a week before, we still had forgotten to buy some heavy-duty blister remedies.

"They suck. They keep falling off."

Even if band-aids did have the ability to stay adhesive when you perspire, they would still be no match for Curtis's sweaty extremities.

"You gonna make it? We do have eleven miles between us and the car."

"Is it eleven miles?"

"Yeah, unless you want to descend the Mountaineer's Route."

The 3.8-mile descent of the Mountaineer's Route sounded doable, but not ideal with the atrocious footing. Not to mention we wanted to catch the scenery of the Mount Whitney Trail on the way down.

Curtis got up without hesitation.

"We better get going then, I don't want the adrenaline to wear off."

After a quick snap of the surrounding landscape, we departed the tallest peak in the lower forty-eight—only trees, dirt, rocks, water and some nasty blisters between us and the car.

* * *

"Go ahead and get the car ready so we can leave right when we get back," Curtis said as he winced in pain.

"You sure you'll be alright?"

"Yeah."

Seven miles into our descent, the blisters began to flare up again. At that point, I made the decision that I would retrieve the car. Since we were on the very well-marked Mount Whitney Trail, I figured Curtis would be fine by himself.

I waited nearly an hour in the parking lot before he finally popped around the corner, taking tentative steps and assuring that his trekking poles contacted the ground in sync with his feet. I could tell that he was hurting.

"Thanks for waiting," he frustratingly said.

"I got the car ready, didn't I?" I replied, annoyed.

We stuffed a few cans of Chef Boyardee down our throats and hopped in the car for a six-hour drive to Yosemite after twelve hours on Whitney.

Curtis was fast asleep, relieving some of the tension in the air, as I pounded a Monster to assure that I avoided any wildlife if they decided to attempt vehicular suicide on our way to Yosemite Valley.

I seldom ever drink caffeine, but the post-hike, late-night drives get to you. I just can't imagine being one of the people who need a little something-something to get them out of bed every morning. It seems sinister, that our day-to-day activities necessitate a little pick-me-up so that we can function properly. To me, morning caffeine habits are odious, insofar as they are a representation of all that is wrong with the way we operate—in routine, synchronized to a mechanistic itinerary with no opportunities or desires to stray from the ordinary. Put anyone in any kind of habit and they forget that they're alive. Just like the shit-bag shitheads on Mount Whitney who followed the tutelage of the previous litterer. Unfortunately, many of us never realize our bad habits. It's human nature.

I had no trouble getting to sleep that night despite the excessive amount of caffeine in my system. I thought about my long, caffeinated drive and realized I probably would have crashed into a tree if I hadn't loaded up on artificial sweeteners that night. I was getting used to the road life, fast, much like the morning coffee drinker's prework ritual. I thought—maybe that's the problem with modern society. We adapt too quickly and too efficiently, even to those things that would ordinarily create discomfort. Maybe that's why I wasn't afraid to carry my own waste in my backpack while everyone else was too uncomfortable to do it. Or why I felt the need to rail against the daily coffee drinker. They become habits.

If it was easy to abandon your routines, or to quit your job, or to part with your vices, then life would be so much simpler. What we were doing out on the road had shifted from a personal and spiritual exodus into a habit. Through adaptation to external stimuli, our honeymoon period of unpredictable variability turned into something very different. To me, that was the day that we became residents of the road and, consequently, protectors and defenders of our residence. That day, I'd seen the grave consequences of human nature and negative group habits. The danger of the follow-the-leader mentality was laid out right in front of us. I thought about Cole's explanation of the lemming. We didn't want to be followers, especially not of those who set horrible examples. I thought about my prospective career as a lawyer. I knew that if I was going to protect my current residence from certain destruction, I would have to dedicate my life to it.

Some may think that road trips are not productive—that they do nothing to progress your position in a capitalistic society. What these people fail to understand is that, though our road trip wasn't progress in and of itself, the experiences that we drew from it were. I remember the ire that I felt that day. The uneclipsed sovereign peak of the Sierra Nevada was soiled with bags of shit. To think that there were people out there who would vandalize its slopes was unsettling. But it gave me the perspective I needed to truly understand my place in this world. A classroom or summer internship would have done naught to convince me of my fateful direction in life. Instead, that day on Mount Whitney marked the beginning of my effort for conservation. And may it indelibly flourish onward.

Chapter 8

"Wilderness is not a luxury but a necessity of the human spirit, and as vital to our lives as water and good bread. A civilization which destroys what little remains of the wild, the spare, the original, is cutting itself off from its origins and betraying the principle of civilization itself."

—Edward Abbey, *Desert Solitaire*

* * *

Showering is probably the most overlooked luxury that citizens of developed countries have access to. Indoor plumbing effectively transformed our hygienic habits overnight, and not necessarily for the good. But I'm not here to lecture about the drawbacks of being deluged by scalding hot water; merely to accentuate the fact that my own showering idiosyncrasies had begun to resemble those of a homeless man.

Before the trip, I had been accustomed to using a new towel every night. It was a ritual instilled in me by my mother, who always had roughly fifty clean towels in our bathroom closet. When I was in college, nearly everyone I knew used the same towel for a week straight before washing it, which I found to be bizarre. Ironically, on this trip, my one and only towel was a moisture-wicking facecloth. And I washed it maybe a handful of times during the trip.

Showering is a habit, much like any other, that evolved not out of necessity, but out of repetition. I savor every opportunity to step behind the curtains and relax for a few minutes in solitude with H_2O just as much as the next person. However, a month of sparse and intermittent showers while on the road taught Curtis and me that we didn't need them as much as we previously thought. Sure, it felt gross at first, but we soon became accustomed to having sweaty balls. This, I decided, was not a custom to brag about; but nevertheless, it was more proof of just how easy it is to mold a human's temperament.

Appropriately, we celebrated our arrival to Yosemite Valley by sneaking into the village to "borrow" a shower from their community bathroom. It had been six days since we had left Alex's house, and we couldn't have been happier to clean up. We had a big task in the morning and needed to smell as fresh as a daisy. We looked up at Half Dome from our stealthy camping spot at the trailhead parking lot and retired to our familiar car seats.

* * *

It is an almost effortless task to demarcate an adventurer from a tourist. Tourists are oblivious. They are there for the bucket list. They are visitors, not embracers; they do it for the Instagram photo, not the catharsis. Most of all, they shower—the reason why our national park system is continually losing its natural character. As we continue to "progress," with new developments, we lose our wildness. Is it even progress at all?

Adventurers, on the contrary, are there for any number of reasons, be it spiritual, philosophical, or for training purposes. They live for the experience, not just the summit. Some of them incessantly gripe about tourists. Just like I'm doing right now.

So why do we care so much about the pervasiveness of tourists? And why must we designate them into a separate class outside of our own? Isn't anyone who explores an adventurer? Half Dome, like the Mount Whitney Trail, is capped with a daily limit for foot travel due to its excessive popularity. And what I've sadly noticed over the years is that the more popular a trail becomes, the less gracious its visitors become.

It's a customary practice to say hello to fellow hikers when on a trail. At least that's how it had been for Curtis and me while treading the mountains of New England. But as we continued our pilgrimage to visit some of the country's most revered landmarks, we became increasingly aware of the notion that those around us were no different from the people we would brush by in any old city.

As we passed by person after person, we kept up our familiar practice of greeting our fellow human beings. It seemed as if those around us refused to acknowledge our presence, some going so far as to scowl at us. We're supposed to be empathetic, sentient creatures—yet we often take for granted this most basic of concepts.

"How hard is it to say hi?" I muttered, as we passed by one of the more populated areas of the hike, Vernal Falls.

"There's a lot of people. You can't possibly say hi to everyone," Curtis chided.

He had a point, yes, but it was a strange feeling nonetheless. I had become so accustomed to my "how's it going" refrain on the trail, and even looked forward to getting into impromptu conversations. But I had to accept the reality that there will always be those kinds of trails, where you want to feel welcome but can't get past the fact that you're sharing them with people who aren't used to traditional trail culture.

"It's so damn annoying though. It just makes me mad that these people fly all the way out here to live just like they do back home."

My ire was seemingly irrational, yet to me, these people who abstained from exchanging pleasantries were repressed and depressed, living like shadows. To them, we were no different from the psychopaths and catcallers that said hello on city streets. At that point, our beards were starting to get a little scraggly, so perhaps our appearance gave them the impression that we were raging lunatics prowling through the woods. But a simpler explanation existed: they take the whole "don't talk to strangers" advice a bit too literally. Or even simpler than that: they're just assholes.

Sometimes I walk down the cluttered streets of Boston and imagine what they would have looked like two hundred years ago. Who would I run into? What would they be wearing? One thing is for certain—they would probably stop for a second to say hello.

When I was growing up, my dad used to tell me that in decades past, everyone knew everyone else. Even when he was a kid, he could recite, from memory, where everyone he went to school with lived. But today is different. As we creep closer and closer to technological singularity, we become removed from the solidarity of days past in favor of a distinct and individualized reality where we keep our networks narrow and exclusive. Close-knit communities have been substituted for online ones, where human interaction is naught but binary. Zeroes and ones.

Atop the summit of Half Dome's infamous Cables Route, everyone and their grandmothers were soaking in the views, waiting in line to take a picture on the Diving Board that overlooks scenic Yosemite Valley. On most occasions, I'd sit around for a few minutes and familiarize myself with the people around me. But here, it was futile. That is, until Curtis and I were visited by a new friend.

While sitting down for a relatively uneventful lunch, we saw a small brown creature start to approach us. We were feeling awfully generous, so we let the little fella take a seat next to us.

"Let's call him Rocky," I remarked, referencing Rocky the Squirrel of *Rocky & Bullwinkle* fame.

Rocky wasn't a shy guy, that's for sure. He made it clear to us that he was more interested in our food than in our company right from the onset. But we felt it necessary to give him a chance, since it appeared as if no one else in the vicinity gave two shits about our presence. Indeed, Rocky gave three shits, as he left us a present to dwell upon while we contemplated relocating to a less soiled area.

No matter, we thought to ourselves, as we continued to munch on tuna and watch our friend scamper closer and closer. He was elusive, yet surprisingly social, occasionally stopping for a well-timed candid photo. But he continued to make it clear to us that he merely wanted our sustenance. He even went so far as to attempt to climb atop my boots. Oh well, at least he said hi. That's more than we could say about everyone else.

* * *

As dusk settled in and we crept into our customary sleeping positions, we began to doze off peacefully at the Half Dome trailhead parking lot. Prior to ending up here, I had to bulldoze through a Do Not Enter sign and dodge scores of pedestrians in an attempt to pick up my struggling best friend at the actual trailhead, which is over a mile's walk from the parking lot. Okay, I embellished a bit—but I most certainly ignored the Handicap Parking Only sign en route to Curtis, where I hoped I could minimize his suffering. The blisters were at it again.

Much to my dismay, I was unsurprisingly kicked out by a ranger whose sole job was probably to patrol the handicapped parking area looking for assholes like me. I explained to the ranger that Curtis had horrible blisters and we had just climbed Mount Whitney a day prior. But he wanted nothing of it—although he did mention that he worked in the Whitney Zone prior to being relocated to Yosemite. He let me off scot-free, but poor Curtis had to bear the brunt of his lack of sympathy.

Back in the car that evening, Curtis decided it would be a good idea to leave the light on as he rummaged through the car for who knows what. Not even a half hour later after we had both fallen asleep, the same ranger from earlier tapped on our window. We rolled down the window, pissed.

"Excuse me but you're going to have to leave, RIGHT . . . oh wait, it's you again!"

"We're sorry, sir, we didn't know we couldn't sleep in our car here." Of course, we knew.

Lucky for us, our ranger friend was in an understanding mood, if only because we had just hiked Mount Whitney and Half Dome in successive days. I later heard of horror stories of people getting substantial fines for getting caught camping without a permit in Yosemite. It's one of the strictest parks in the country. Take note. And for the love of God don't leave your food unattended or in your car. If the rangers don't get to you first the bees or the bears will.

"I apologize in advance for this, boys, but rules are rules. If you drive out of the park and just park in one of the dirt lots on the side of the road, you should be fine for the night. Don't tell anyone I told you though."

Forty-five minutes later and sufficiently exhausted, we parked in the first gravel lot that we spotted, apathetic to the fact that it was the site of a sewage disposal plant.

The importance of friendship on the road is paramount, no doubt. Unless you're one of those "better off alone" types, it's one of the make-or-break elements of a successful road trip. In a rare first, Curtis and I had a string of places to crash lined up in the San Francisco area. And we couldn't have been happier. Sure, sleeping in your car is fun, but—yeah, never mind.

Upon arriving in Oakland, we found ourselves in the middle of an important conversation at our high school friend Amelia's house.

"So, how do you guys want to spend your first night in Oaktown?"

We hadn't really given it all that much thought, to be honest. Oakland doesn't necessarily have the most sparkling of reputations among East Coasters. But it unquestionably benefits from being located adjacent to Berkeley, one of the hippest towns on the West Coast.

Although she lived on the Oakland-Berkeley line, the bulk of her time was spent on the campus of UC Berkeley, where she worked in the chemical engineering labs with her roommate and mentor, Kevin. Their specific responsibility in the lab was to study polyelectrolyte membranes, or PEMs. I have no idea what the hell that means, but it sounded important, so I nodded my head vigorously as they chatted about their day-to-day doings while drinking beer and eating plums straight from the trees growing outside their house. After their exhausting day of complicated science experiments, it only made sense to sit on the front steps, kick back, and have a yard beer. I mean, what else is there to do in Greater Oakland?

Turns out, contrary to my initial belief, there's never a dull moment in O-Town.

"Irish frat party, anyone?" Amelia's Russian friend Natalya asked, as we neared hour three of plum-filled socialization.

We were in the middle of preparing dinner, cooking up mole, an Oaxacan delicacy that we'd discovered in Los Angeles with Shawn. It's a type of cocoa paste that gets cooked with tomatoes to create a chocolatey salsa. We had promised Amelia's other friends from the lab, Jose and Tomas, that we would honor their Mexican heritage by sharing the hard-to-find main ingredient with them.

"I'm sticking with mole and yard beers," Kevin remarked, "I'm too old for that shit anyway."

Funny thing is, Kevin was one of the more adventurous guys we had met to date. He was an avid skier and mountaineer, but not an expert at either. His claim to fame was that he was a darn good camp cook. He told us stories about pizzas made from scratch on backpacking trips in the Pacific Northwest. That, and his recent ascent of Mount Shasta, which was our next objective after departing from the metro area. But we had a bit of work to do before that. Irish frat party, anyone?

* * *

It was always so hard to pinpoint what aspects of parties I loathed the most because there were so many—and lucky for me, the entire index of party negatives was on display at the first and last fraternity party that I'll ever attend in my life. Because like Kevin said, I'm too old for that shit. The advantage, though, of attending a party where you know no one is that no one knows you. Gym shorts and a t-shirt are totally acceptable attire. Making an ass out of yourself won't permanently stain your legacy. And finally, wearing a hat of a rival sports team won't get you brownie points, but if it's cool looking, people will flirt with you. At least that's how it worked for Curtis.

Upon arrival, we were greeted by an Irish doorman who appeared as if he had just taken the boat over from the Motherland circa 1845. He possessed an almost-impossible-to-understand accent and we found ourselves struggling to discern his instructions in the loud party atmosphere.

"Et'll be twilv dawluhs," he muttered while scratching his distinct ginger beard.

"Twelve dollars?" Amelia asked, with patience in her tone. "For each of us?"

"Roight." He took a large swig of whiskey amid increasing noise levels that made it even harder to understand him.

Amelia turned her back to the bouncer and whispered loudly to our crew.

"Does anyone have cash?"

We all glanced at each other, shaking our heads. But before disaster struck, another more Americanized Irishman confronted us.

"Billy, whatter yew doin'? Amurikins are free!" He lightly smacked the bouncer on the back of the head in disappointment.

Turns out our little frat party was American themed, and thus natural-born Americans were free—everyone else had to pay twelve dollars. We weren't sure whether it was some sort of sick joke or a token of appreciation of our aid to the Irish during the potato famine. Whatever the rationale, it was well worth the zero dollars.

Entering the building, we were directed to the courtyard in the middle of the first floor. There were hundreds of people, each more inebriated than the next, assembled on what appeared to be a make-shift basketball court. Participants donned their red, white, and blue. There also seemed to be a contest for who could reveal the most without being naked. Then a question dawned on me: what the hell is wrong with these people? I had been traveling across the United States for just over a month, paying literal homage to the land of the free and the home of the brave, only to realize that the only tribute the college masses could honor it with involved themed parties and sensual obliteration.

Beer pong tables scattered the courtyard and screams pierced our ears as the party area became unnavigable. Curtis and I lost Amelia and company immediately, and we spent most of the early evening aimlessly squeezing between groups of people to search for them. And that's when disaster struck. Well, by Irish frat party standards.

To celebrate our arrival in Denver, Curtis and I had purchased hats—him a neon green Rockies hat, and I, a Nuggets hat. They would become our adventure hats from then on, so to speak. Some girl decided it would be funny to snag Curtis's hat right off his head and lead him on a Where's Waldo chase through the entire multi-story building. We were sure of her intentions at the time—she clearly wanted to court Curtis. But as our race through the Hidden Temple persisted, it became apparent that not even a twelve-year-old 90s kid would have a chance against the temple guardians.

"Did you see a girl with a neon Rockies hat run through here?" Curtis frantically asked, repeating the question to at least ten people, all of whom were too plastered to notice.

Eventually, we stumbled across Amelia and the crew down in the kitchen area. They could offer no additional help to our lost cause. Failing to find his hat, Curtis left his name and number with the Americanized Irish bouncer who initially let us in. We all knew that was the last we would see of Curtis's hat. But there was a happy ending to the story after all.

I couldn't bear to see him distraught over the loss of his head-wear, as it had become as essential to him as his three pairs of mois-ture-wicking underwear. As fate would have it, I had also bought the exact same hat, but in a size smaller. Sure, he probably lost a few brain cells while he broke it in, but what's life without a few bruises? Curtis is a tried and true testament of this notion.

Chapter 9

"All paths lead to nowhere, so it is important to choose a path that has heart."

—Carlos Castaneda, from a sign at the Mount Shasta trailhead

* * *

The nearest emergency room was only about twenty minutes from the Mount Shasta trailhead, but I didn't care to take notice during our first stint in the volcano's namesake town, because bad things don't happen to kids in their twenties, right? I anxiously waited in the car while reading *The Hunger Games* to ease my nerves. Something about a badass heroine kicking butt and taking names just seemed so therapeutic at the time. How we got to this point was a culmination of several weeks of bad luck and excessive perspiration. Sure, it was just a foot injury caused by his blisters from the Grand Canyon, but if it was serious, it would hold dire ramifications for the purported climax of our trip. Rainier might have to wait for another year. But goddammit, we weren't going to let a stubborn pinky toe eviscerate our plans to conquer the tallest volcano in the contiguous United States.

* * *

Mount Shasta is a monarch among subservient hills. It boldly towers above everything, only rivaled by Mount Hood some three hundred miles north. It conveniently resides along the Cascade Volcanic Arc, a seven-hundred-mile chain of some of North America's most dangerous natural adversaries—both existential and recreational. Existential because one eruption equals mass destruction. Recreational because who doesn't want to climb a glaciated volcano? It was also the commencement of our acclimatization process for Mount Rainier. But no less enticing a climb, that's for sure.

We awoke from a restful, albeit paranoia-inducing evening wedged between two tractor trailer trucks along a main road in Weed, California. The irony of the name wasn't so apparent at the time we arrived, but it became clear that the police there couldn't care less about what was going on in the town. Dirtbags sleeping in their cars was probably just as tolerable as dirtbags lighting up in honor of the town's name. By now, we had mastered the art of stealth camping, so even if they were actively pursuing fugitives like us, they never would have spotted our lime green car between two vehicular behemoths.

The bulk of our day was spent in our heads. The ranger at the Mount Shasta Ranger Station convinced us that the ninety-mile-per-hour winds on the mountain that evening would prevent us from setting up base camp at Helen Lake, so we heeded her advice. Besides, the forecast was looking optimal for the following day, and as we'd discovered in our mountain wanderings, it's better to be safe than sorry.

We decided to head to the nearest hotel, where we didn't have a reservation, plopped our as-of-late lazy asses on the most comfortable chairs we could find, and rekindled our appreciation for first-world commodities. I tore through three movies in ten hours, savoring every moment until we would have to head up to the Bunny Flat Trailhead and prepare our bags for the next day's ascent. Curtis, on the other hand, was on the phone for hours with his then-girlfriend, a customary occurrence during our down time. At least I wouldn't have to listen to the banter much longer—because it was go time, baby.

* * *

If you think getting dressed in the morning is a hassle, then try readying a pack for a multi-day outing in the wilderness. If you think that's bad, then try doing so while living in your disorganized car.

Because we had spent the last week or so as pseudo-civilized individuals in the Greater San Francisco area, Mindy hadn't been tidied up in quite a while. We had become victims of our own old habits. Given the fact that we were unemployed, you would think that we'd have enough time to compartmentalize our home on wheels. Sure, and pigs can fly.

Our sluggish morning was soon shocked awake by a group that had descended the mountain earlier that day. An overly talkative, guided individual was chatting with a German party about what had just taken place as a helicopter whooshed over our heads and toward the summit.

"One of the guides in our group just fell. It was before we were going to rope up too, so no one could stop his fall," the man said. "We don't exactly know what happened to him because one of our other guides decided to stay back, but it might be a broken leg. I think you should probably stay clear of the mountain, it's too dangerous."

Perhaps it was the only way to justify the fact that he spent money to be guided up a technically easy mountain, or perhaps he felt crippled by failure, but the man continued to preach the dangers of the mountain to numerous other parties who were preparing to head up to base camp.

"The icefall was brutal up there, man. Our friend broke his leg, I don't know if you heard the helicopter going up to get him."

I must say, it was a little concerning to hear that a guide got injured. But then we thought for a moment—the ranger only told us to stay off the mountain until the early afternoon because it was still under a heavy wind advisory. This gave us the reassurance we needed to ignore the nervous juju in the parking lot. Besides, we made it this far, and still needed some snow-climbing experience before tackling Rainier. We didn't drive all the way to the trailhead to succumb to Shasta's imposing beauty by keeling over in a fetal position and whimpering for our mamas. Nothing bad could possibly happen.

* * *

Just a mile and a half from the trailhead lies a conveniently placed cabin called Horse Camp. As the springboard for the many ascents of Mount Shasta's Avalanche Gulch, it sees its fair share of tourists and mountaineers. For those who claim to be mountaineers, Queen Shasta dares them to climb. And climb, we would, but not before we obtained some much-needed advice from the hut caretakers.

Moxie, who was, in her own words, old enough to be our grandmother, got a kick out of our road trip anecdotes. We procrastinated with the help of Moxie and another caretaker named Sue, sharing stories as if we were Tuesday night book club buddies from the local library.

"Boys, you give me faith in the future," Moxie chuckled.

Both Moxie and Sue had silver hair, yet their physiques were astonishingly toned given their age. They appeared to be in their seventies, but you would never have guessed it. Both were dressed head to toe in athletic wear and sported bronze tans that obviously came from natural light. Their faces were worn, but their spirits were not. If their sculpted arms were any indication, they led wholesome lives and couldn't stand to be sedentary.

"I'm trying to convince my grandson to take a trip like yours when he graduates," Sue remarked, "but I don't know if he will."

"Why not?" Curtis asked.

"He's too busy playing those video games to be worried about it. What am I going to do? It's his life."

She sounded sad, and I couldn't blame her. To this day, I continue to spend much of my free time at home playing video games, and it's a hard vice to shake. But I justify it because of the great people I have met over the years online, who, like me, use the chat feature to stay social while enjoying their game. Ironically, many of those friends are more reliable than the people I know in real life. Case and point, just two days prior to starting our Shasta climb, we had met two of my online friends in Redding, California. We got our fast food fix and watched a cheap movie with them. And it turns out they weren't serial killers, contrary to popular belief. Go figure.

Nevertheless, Sue and Moxie gave us something to think about. If we are supposed to be the future of America, yet we would rather spend every waking moment glued to a television screen, then where is the progress? How do we reconcile our itinerant temptations with the need for down-time, for mindless hours spent on social media and video streaming services? Balance, I suppose. But more importantly, awareness and presence. We need to embrace what is in front of us over that which is not.

"Gentlemen, it was a pleasure to meet you. You're going to want to continue up toward the campsites further up the hill and then keep following the path until you see footprints up toward Helen Lake."

The two California hardmeats shook our hands and wished us luck. We then turned our full attention to the path in front of us, heeding the advice of the wise old women who lived in a mountain hut.

* * *

Cities of tents speckled the snowfield at the base of a series of snowy switchbacks where we began our climb. We each lugged forty or so pounds up Her Majesty, our heaviest packs since the Grand Canyon. To be perfectly honest, this would be only the fourth or fifth backpacking trip of our lives. To say we were green would be an understatement. But we were confident in what we were doing—more so than those who resided in the tents near the base, at least.

Like the guy we saw down at the parking lot, most all the people we passed were part of guided multi-day climbs. This was a somewhat intriguing prospect to us at the time because guided trips are not cheap and Mount Shasta is not a technically difficult mountain to climb, at least by the standard route. But if you want to pay for survival assurance and a how-to-set-up-a-tent lesson, it is an option. We weren't interested in parting with our entire road trip budget in one purchase though, so our own intuition would have to do. Besides, we were still riding high from our Longs Peak and Grand Canyon debacles, so the third time must be the charm, right?

After a seemingly endless afternoon slog up slushy snow, we saw the light at the end of the tunnel. The snow gave way to rock, and we crawled up toward what appeared to be a flat section. Indeed, it was a campsite, but we could see no lake. It was too early in the climbing season for Helen Lake to reveal itself, but that was the least of our concerns at the time. We wanted nothing more than to get dinner cooking.

By this point in the trip, our cooking system was nearly flawless. Curtis would light the camp stove, and I would prepare the water to boil. But without the luxury of Helen Lake, we would have to melt snow. As you can probably guess, the process was interminable. While we sat and waited for the first round of snow to boil, we saw a pair of fellow climbers at the tent next door who looked much more competent than us. We decided to take advantage of their knowledge while we could. Our water would have to wait.

"Looks like you boys are having a little trouble cooking over there," a baby-faced Asian man called over to us.

"I'm just having trouble keeping the fire lit with all this wind," Curtis answered.

The man strutted over. He wore a bright red Patagonia jacket and bright yellow La Sportiva mountaineering boots. You could tell he had been doing this for a while.

"Don."

He stuck out his hand and we both gave it a good shake. His grip was like iron, and we suddenly knew that he would have some proper insight.

Curtis attempted to secure our pot to the top of the stove, but it promptly tipped over due to the added weight from the snow.

"Shit."

But his frustration was promptly quelled after Don found a place for us to set up camp out of the wind.

"So what's the plan for tomorrow, guys?" Don asked.

I spoke unconfidently, as if we had never been on a mountain before.

"Well I think we're going to do, uh, Avalanche Gulch—that's what it's called, right? We're not really sure when we're leaving but probably just as the sun rises."

"Better early than late," he responded, nonchalantly. "Gotta keep out of the sun so you're not climbing up a slush rink."

Another man rustled out of Don's tent. He was in typical hiking attire and looked as if he had just taken a nap. He rubbed his eyes as he called toward his partner.

"Hey Don, what time are we leaving in the morning?"

"Three-thirty!" Don yelled over toward the tent.

Three-thirty? Were we starting too late? We knew we had to wake up at 2 a.m. for Longs Peak because we were attempting it in a day, but we figured that the several hour approach to Helen Lake would make up for lost time here on Shasta.

"Why so early?" Curtis remarked. He wasn't nervous, it seemed, but genuinely interested.

Don took a swig out of his thermos and wiped his face before answering.

"Why not? We've got a long drive back to Seattle in the afternoon and have to get back to work."

We had heard so much about the Emerald City and wanted nothing more than to find ourselves sleepless in it. But that dream would have to wait for now.

In the meantime, we asked Don and his partner, Ray, about their experience. Turns out, they had both been climbing for years and had summited Mount Rainier only a few weeks back. We were ecstatic to hear of their exploits, as we would soon try to find ourselves in a similar position.

"The thing about Rainier is you don't want to camp at Camp Muir at ten thousand feet or so. You're better off climbing another thousandish feet up to Ingraham Flats. And from there, mostly everything is marked by boot prints and wands. Even the crevasses are easy to spot."

Don was helpful in his explanation, but we still worried.

"Are the crevasses easy to get across?" I inquired. We had never seen a crevasse in the flesh, so we were terrified by what we were getting ourselves into.

"Not a problem at all," Ray answered. "You guys will be fine, assuming you can get up Shasta here."

Don was quick to counter. "Oh, they're a little treacherous, at least if you've never traveled on a glacier. Which I'm assuming you guys haven't, right?"

"Yeah," Curtis responded, "but we've done a few fourteeners in Colorado, Whitney, and a few other big peaks."

They weren't sold.

"Rainier is a completely different beast if you don't have perfect weather, though. Just pray for blue skies. You guys seem competent enough. Just remember to follow the boot path."

Although night was approaching, it did so slowly. Don and Ray retired to their tent for an early start while we contemplated their message and cooked up our dinner. Amelia's roommate Kevin had donated a carton of hash browns to our cause and boy did they hit the spot. We grew up eating home-cooked meals nearly every night, but tonight was a luxury compared to the typical peanut butter and Nutella or jelly or marshmallow fluff that we were accustomed to lately. You really don't know what you have until it's gone.

We hopped in our sleeping bags at 8 p.m. and watched the sun begin to set, only to realize that it was at least two hours from fully doing so. The longest days of the year in Northern California are a lot longer than those we're used to, so when the crimson sun refused to set, we were frustrated, yet content. We wanted some shut eye, but this would do for now.

"I could get used to this," I said, as I munched on the remainder of our golden hash browns.

"I'm afraid about Rainier though," Curtis answered while he tucked himself in his sleeping bag.

"Why?"

"It's my feet. They're still hurting from the Grand Canyon."

"Even after all that rest we got?"

"Yeah."

I worried about him, but I figured he had been through a lot worse than that. What's a few blisters anyway? I guess we would find out in the morning if he was just making a big deal out of nothing.

* * *

It was still dark when we roused ourselves out of the faux-comfort of our sleeping bags. Even now, after all these years of sleeping in tents, I want nothing more than to get out of them as soon as possible, knowing that it comes at the expense of sleep. And that's saying a lot—because I'm known to get eleven hours a night when I don't set an alarm.

But when I unzipped the tent fly and glanced out toward the horizon, I saw a kaleidoscope of colors in the sky. Light blues, dark blues, oranges, yellows, and black shadows filled our vision. It was a portrait worth painting a thousand times over and immortalizing within our own minds. Somewhat ironically, this was a moment we would celebrate by turning our backs on the view and heading up nearly four thousand vertical feet to the top of Northern California.

We were one of the last groups out of camp. At 5:15 a.m. sharp, we started along the path with crampons attached to our feet. In the distance, we could see the light from headlamps scattered across the snowfield. This would make our path toward the top much easier, at least until the sun was fully out.

Rather than plow our way straight up the hill, we decided to forge our own path. Since it was so early, and the sun had yet to bake the snow into slushiness, we opted to walk up, switchback style, which would minimize the effort we needed to climb vertically. Although this would technically add more steps to our journey, it would come with the added benefit of increased endurance.

This turned out to be one of the more intelligent moves we had made so far on our trip—within an hour, we began to catch up to those who had started much earlier than us. Although many of these people looked more experienced than us, we immediately noted that they did not seem to be using our switchback technique.

As Curtis explained to me, your body is like an automobile. If you rev the engine too high, you might go faster, but you'll run out of gas much sooner. You may be traversing less distance if you go straight up, but your body will become tired much sooner. There's a reason I keep him around.

We plowed our way up the route fuel-efficiently, and eventually reached an impasse. A few groups, including Don and Ray, were nestled below The Heart, a section of the climb notorious for its ice-fall, and the site where the guide broke his leg just a day prior. To our left was the Left Chute of Red Banks, the standard route to the top. To the right was Thumb Rock, a longer, but safer approach to the ridgeline. We could see that there was an inordinate amount of ice at the bottom of the chute, but most of the shards were smaller than a golf ball. We decided to consult with Don and Ray and the guided group that stood like statues beside us.

"Good to see you guys," Don shouted. "I'm surprised you caught up."

"We're no slouches," I reassured him.

"What's going on?" Curtis asked. But we knew the answer.

"That's where the guide was evacuated yesterday. So this guy here thinks it's best to go up to Thumb Rock and go from there." Don seemed to be dissuaded by the guide's advice, but likely didn't want to take any grave risks either.

"Well I think we'll try the chute," Curtis said, confidently.

"Wait, what?" I asked. I was not about to get my legs severed by car-sized icicles.

"It doesn't look too bad. Let's just go for it."

After swearing to never trust Curtis's discretion again after the Longs Peak debacle, I was quick to acquiesce to his suggestion. I don't know what came over me, but I think it was pride. I wanted to prove to Don and Ray that we had what it took to conquer Rainier, even though we seemed like gumbies from New England. No matter what I convinced myself of that day, we were still gumbies from New England.

Turning away from the hesitant groups below, we headed left and up into the icy gully. Curtis took the lead. Without warning, the ice began to rain down on my helmet as I followed him up toward certain death.

"CURTIS!"

"SORRY."

He began to be more careful where he put his feet, and I consequently stayed as far to the other side as possible. Nevertheless, small pellets of ice would every so often rain down on me—clearly the wrath of Mother Nature revolting against us for attempting to challenge her. She thought that we had learned from the guide's broken leg, but evidently, we hadn't.

The chute started out about ten to fifteen feet wide, but it eventually narrowed out and was no longer big enough for the both of us. Carefully manipulating our ice axes and crampons, we swung our way to the top without further incident. I was pleasantly surprised that it had gone so well. But we had a long way to go to the top from there.

As we continued our climb, Curtis began to complain of some hot spots on his foot. Thinking nothing of it, we pressed on to the summit, where we reveled in the experience of being on top of the highest glaciated peak in California.

* * *

At some point during our descent, after we glissaded roughly two thousand vertical feet but before we reached Horse Camp, I heard a scream.

"Curtis?"

He took a seat on a nearby rock and removed his right boot. We were no more than five minutes away from Moxie and Sue's lean-to, so I presumed that he would be fine to make it there without issue.

"I'm gonna head down to the camp. Will you be alright?"

"I'm not sure." He grimaced in pain as he removed his sock.

"Is it the blisters?"

"Yeah."

"Okay, well I'll go see what they have down there for them."

Without so much as a nod, I turned my back on my faithful friend and booked it down to the cabin. When I arrived, I saw Sue mingling with some hikers, and inappropriately interrupted them.

"Sorry to bother you, Sue, but Curtis is hurt."

"Is he okay?" She appeared unconcerned that I had disrupted her but concerned about my message.

"I don't know. But he has some bad blisters that have been bothering him since the Grand Canyon."

"I'll get him some extra-strength aspirin and bandages."

Over half an hour passed, and there was no sign of Curtis. I was worried, but it seemed unrealistic that something bad would happen given how well-traveled the trail was. I decided to start back up toward the mountain, but quickly ran into another climber who was descending. He told me that Curtis was still sitting down further up the trail but had another climber with him. This eased my mind enough to make the descent back to the car, only stopping to tell Sue of my intentions.

There was something seriously wrong about my conduct that day that has resonated with me ever since. And I didn't even realize it until two hours later, when Curtis's backpack finally appeared in the parking lot.

"Are you Meester Justin?"

A tall Hispanic climber who had a minimal grasp on English dropped my best friend's pack on the ground by my car.

"He is okay, will be down."

I wanted to ask him more, but he was gone before I even had the chance.

A short time later, the lanky, awkward-looking guy who had set out on this trip with me finally appeared through the trees. He took fragile steps, clutching his two trekking poles like an elderly man holds a walker. He had the appearance of defeat and grimaced in pain with every stride. He was physically *wasted*.

"I'm sorry for running ahead," I said, somewhat remorsefully, "but I needed to get the car ready." In reality, I just wanted to be done. I didn't think twice about leaving Curtis behind.

He could sense the bullshit exuding from my tone, but he was just happy to be down.

"Let's just go. I need to go to the ER to check out my foot." He screamed in pain as he took off his boot and the adrenaline began to subside.

"Why do we need to go to the ER?" I selfishly asked.

"So we can see if I can climb Rainier."

"You'll be fine!" I raised my voice.

"What's wrong with you? I think my toe is broken."

What was wrong with me? What the hell was his problem? He would dare injure himself before Rainier, our biggest challenge of the trip? Indeed, his problem was graver than I thought. He was on the verge of tears as he poked around on his foot to test his pain while I sped toward the nearest emergency room. He told me about how he spent the last mile and a half from Horse Camp contemplating Rainier. By this point, the heavy-duty aspirin had come into full force, and there was no pain, only numbness—both physical and emotional. But it was his anesthetized emotions that were cause for concern, because he couldn't bear the thought of not going through with our plans to conquer the tallest volcano in the lower forty-eight states. He reasoned with himself that he could potentially climb it in snowshoes or custom orthotics which would take the pressure off his injured toe. But such a proposition seemed unlikely, at best.

I had never seen my best friend so visibly shaken in my life. He wanted Rainier, it seemed, even more than I did. I thought back to the summer before, when we climbed Mount Washington with Jason. On the way back down, he sprinted ahead of us as we hastily followed, dodging rock after rock as we blew past people on the overly crowded Tuckerman Ravine Trail. The other hikers on the trail weren't too pleased with us, but Curtis told us once we reached the bottom that he felt as if he had something to prove to us. Curtis was never known for his athletic prowess, whereas Jason and I had always been athletes.

I wondered if Curtis was willing to sacrifice his pride in exchange for a possible rescue, if that's what it came down to. To be perfectly honest, I was more than willing to take that chance, perhaps somewhat imprudently. But my perception was skewed by the belief that it wasn't my toe that was hurting. And it seemed as if at this point in the trip, I was forgetting about what brought us here in the first place.

We were becoming far too driven by personal gain and had forgotten about the importance of being there for each other. I know I was, at least. I had ditched my best friend in his time of need because I was too impatient to wait up for him, knowing that I had nowhere else to be. And he had to depend on the goodness of others to make it back that day—from the miracle man from Mexico City who brought his pack down; to Don and Ray, who gave us valuable advice; to Sue and Moxie, the courteous caretakers who shared laughs with us and provided Curtis with the medicine he needed.

But where was I during all of this? What the hell was I thinking when I left him on the mountain? It didn't matter that he was only a few hundred yards from Horse Camp. I failed in my one and only job and instead had to rely on complete strangers to perform it for me. Yes, I was selfish. Yes, I was juvenile. But did I make the wrong choice? Any sane human being would say that I did. But I'm far from sane. And in hindsight, while I know that I made the wrong choice, there was a silver lining that made that bad decision worth making.

Everything in life is luck and circumstance, or so I've told myself over the years. But this road trip of ours was becoming the anomaly that we needed to shake the foundation of our world. Closed off in a suburban lifestyle, we were raised on the virtues of avoiding strangers and trusting no one but ourselves. But if my desertion of Curtis in his time of need taught me anything, it was that there are people who are willing to fill the void when all hope is seemingly lost. Sure, it may only be one person out of a hundred—but they're out there, and especially so on the trails.

I may have failed my duties that day, but I learned an invaluable lesson that may not have manifested if not for my self-centeredness. But for the kindness of complete strangers, Curtis likely would not have made it to the hospital that night to learn of the favorable diagnosis of a simple toe infection. It looked like we would be climbing Rainier after all, and we were both elated. However, we needed a little time to rejuvenate and reflect on what had just taken place.

After a quick stop at beautiful Crater Lake, we set out for Seal Rock, Oregon, where we planned to stay with Curtis's uncle and get a feel for what it was like to live in the middle of nowhere by the ocean—something we weren't too familiar with on the East Coast. Not only that, but we hoped to rediscover some of the magic that we had experienced earlier with Abby, Talia, Cole, Connor, Jamie, Alex, Butterfly, Shawn, and everyone else. We had no interest whatsoever in revisiting the empty feelings that we had endured in the Great Sand Dunes.

Chapter 10

"Expectations were like fine pottery. The harder you held them, the more likely they were to crack."

—Brandon Sanderson, *The Way of Kings*

* * *

The No Trespassing signs strewn across the property immediately gave us a pretty good idea about what we were getting ourselves into. I had it solved: Curtis's uncle had to be an anti-government, militant nut job who would hold us hostage for the next twenty-four hours while he grilled us on our political beliefs. The only solace we had was the quaint setting.

Coastal Oregon is nothing like anywhere on the East Coast south of Maine. The beaches are rocky and mostly desolate of humans, and wildlife thrives. En route to our secluded destination, we spotted thousands of birds floating among the clouds. Like us, they were unhindered by the crushing onus of a full-time job. But unlike us, that would be their permanent situation. Shucks.

I was convinced that Uncle Al and Aunt Betsy were as free as the birds. I posited that they were tax evaders whom the government gave up on, leaving them to absent-mindedly reside in a deeply wooded area a few minutes from the ocean. But how long could they hold out before the IRS came in with the big guns and knocked down their door?

We rolled Mindy slowly across harsh gravel and parked her alongside a beaten-up truck. There was tension in the air, and I wasn't ready to sacrifice my life for one night of comfortable rest.

"What are you doing?" Curtis asked, as he rummaged through the trunk for his belongings.

"Nothing," I replied, as I anxiously bit my nails, still in the driver's seat with my seatbelt on.

No matter my trepidation, I needed to give them a chance. Our motto was to embrace experiences with an open mind, and I had to at least offer Al and Betsy that.

I edged toward the door while I contemplated what my last words would be. "Hi" seemed too passive, and I wanted to go out swinging before I was executed. It was settled then—I would beg for mercy all the while screaming "YOU CAN'T MAKE ME!"

But my hysterical musings were swiftly dispelled when a pleasant, middle-aged woman opened the door and greeted us with a beaming smile.

"Hello gentlemen! We're so glad you made the trip!"

I'm telling you; you can't make this stuff up.

* * *

Famished from many weeks without a home-cooked meal, we gorged on steak, shrimp, corn, potatoes, and a decadent chocolate cream pie as our bellies started to emit obscene rumbles from within. Al and Betsy had just gotten through telling us about their jobs as climate scientists, and I had just gotten through eating my preconceptions. Turns out these Oregon hillbillies were a little more socially conscious than I imagined—and boy, was I pleasantly surprised.

Betsy, a strong-willed, strong-bodied woman, spent years in a research lab before she finally decided to obtain a PhD, because, according to her, you need one to be taken seriously in the field of climate study.

"Your uncle Al and I don't have any kids together. But we share a passion for the world around us. And we need to protect it."

Uncle Al was much more timid than his wife, but behind his tired eyes, I could see ages of wisdom. Confined to a walker, he sported a Santa Claus beard and a weathered face. Notwithstanding his handicap, Al was a larger than life figure.

Born and raised in Connecticut, he got the hell out of there when he realized he needed to start over. Liberating himself from the fast-paced East Coast culture was his idea of a fresh start, and so he began his new life some forty years ago. And we couldn't blame him. They lived in a paradise beside the ocean with no neighbors and reputable jobs in the local lab to boot.

"Research isn't the worst job in the world," Betsy proclaimed, as she shoveled more pie onto our plates. "Al and I have been doing it our whole life."

Betsy made it clear that she would do it even for pennies—because she felt its worth and reward even absent a paycheck. To me, Betsy's passion for her work was everything that I ever wanted. And I dreamed that maybe, one day, I would help the world and its people and find meaning in doing so. But in the meantime, I still had to figure out what the hell I was doing in the here and now.

Near the end of our dinner, we were introduced to Betsy's son's friend, GC. If his name wasn't any indication already, George Carl was something of a character. Twenty or so years ago while Betsy was with her ex-husband in North Carolina, she basically raised both her own son and GC—that best friend you grew up with whom your mom fed and housed on the regular. Essentially, GC and

Betsy's son were the equivalent of Curtis and me—inseparable, and practically siblings.

Al and Betsy had taken GC in at the beginning of the summer after he decided it was time to escape the East Coast for a little while. He had free rent and food just so long as he held up his end of the bargain—which was to help redesign the second floor of their home. He had learned the construction trade back home under the wing of his father, whom he referred to as Bummie. Bummie had been in a bad accident when he was younger and much of his body and face became disfigured as a result. But as GC explained it, it made their family more renowned than anything. Or notorious, if you will.

"Bummie and me ne'er liked the attintion that they gave us back home. That's why I decided it was time to get outta there fir a bit." He stood poised and proud adjacent to the table, like the local celebrity that he was.

"I kirn see how that would be anroying," I replied, with a mouthful of whipped cream.

He continued, "Another reason I left is cuz I had to lay low."

"From rut?" Curtis interjected as he took the last bites of his pie.

"Well, them cops out home were on our side mosta the time. But this time they were a little worried."

What in tarnation was he talking about? Were Al and Betsy harboring a fugitive?

"He likes to embellish sometimes," Betsy said, as she chuckled nervously. She rose from her seat and escorted Al out of the room and into the kitchen.

GC instinctively raised his voice. "I'm tellin' you, it's a true story!"

"Go on, we're listening." I folded my arms and sat back on two chair legs while I made a subtle movement toward my fly and unzipped it, relieving some of the pressure from our scrumptious feast.

"Well, my pa and uncle were out at the townie bar one day and the owner was makin' advances on mah aunt. Bummie n' Uncle Pete were pissed, so they came back that night with their dump trucks n' completely demolished the bar."

Curtis and I looked at each other in awe. So much for surviving our visit to Seal Rock. I was just about to scream "YOU CAN'T MAKE ME" when I realized that he might be kidding. But as soon as he spoke up again, I knew that GC was a man of his word.

"The coppers like our family, so we didn't think nothin' of it. Most people know not to mess with us."

"But you think this time is different?" Curtis asked.

"Dunno, guess we'll have to see what them policemen say."

I got the feeling during our bizarre chat with GC that his family had bought off the town police, that he was a compulsive liar, or both. They essentially bulldozed a guy's bar with no repercussions to speak of. Something smelled fishy here. And then I realized it was the lone shrimp that sat on my plate uneaten.

* * *

Surprisingly, we made it through the night. The next day, Betsy fixed us an early lunch of burgers topped with cottage cheese. As if our stay in Seal Rock couldn't have been any more unique.

"Where's GC?" Curtis asked.

Oh God Curtis, please no. You can't make me.

"He's probably still sleeping," Al remarked. He was reading the newspaper in the corner of the living room where we sat and ate our brunch. It was the first thing that I'd heard out of his mouth since he said hello when we first arrived. I wanted to pick his brain about his job and his life, but I couldn't get over the semi-awkwardness of asking him a question.

Instead, my jaw dropped when GC stormed down the stairs screaming like a banshee.

"Helloooooo boys n' girls. So whatter we doin' today?"

Going deaf, apparently.

Betsy gave him a plate with a cottage cheese burger and he demolished it within thirty seconds. Despite my unreasonable fear of him, GC was growing on me, if only incidentally. Maybe we just got off on the wrong foot. It's not like he was a psychotic criminal or anything.

"I'd like to go check out the beach."

That's my Curtis. Always filling the silent void with relevant conversation.

"You boys better head down there soon because the low tide is in a half hour."

Betsy suggested a few places for us to go, and we settled for a spot several miles down the road. GC offered to drive, and Curtis graciously accepted on behalf of both of us. It was at that exact moment that I realized that death was in fact inevitable, and that I should just suck it up. Even if I ended the day in a body bag.

* * *

As we parked at the beach and got out of the car, we were impressed by the spectacle in front of us. Imposing rocky structures protruded out of the water, rising like spires above the light fog that danced along the shoreline. We could see tiny pools of water at the edge of the sea. On our ride over, we learned that these tide pools were home to a diverse ecosystem of marine species that only revealed itself during low tide. At all other times, the ocean would obscure the pools, which is why Betsy urged us to hurry.

Curtis and I scampered down a sandy hill toward the Pacific while GC lagged far behind, as if he hadn't gotten any exercise since he left the military almost ten years ago. Now woefully out of shape and on the heavier side, GC still paid homage to his days in the military through his gun ownership. We're not exactly sure how many he had, but it had to be dozens based on Curtis's lengthy conversation with him on the beach. I was just about ready to assume the fetal position when he suddenly pointed out a large animal sitting on a rock about a football field away from us in the ocean.

"Y'all ever seen a seal in the flesh?" He shouted, as the waves rushed gleefully toward our bare feet.

A massive white creature lay prone on a flattened rock in the middle of the ocean. It was statuesque and appeared as much a part of the landscape as the cliffs that towered to its right. That is, until another seal crept up from underwater and jumped on top of it, effectively knocking it down and stealing its spot. A loud splash ensued.

"Are they always here?" Curtis asked, as he laughed off what he had just seen.

"Yep, just bout ev'ry day we see 'em when we drive by."

"I didn't think they would be so receptive to humans."

"You kin blame them tourists who leave food on the beach fir that."

GC's comment immediately reminded me that despite our sentience, humans aren't the most sensible creatures in the animal kingdom sometimes. Don't feed the birds, people.

We had yet to see the tide pools, but GC was already out of sight when we were about to ask him where the best place to start would be.

"O'er here fellas!"

From the residue of the higher tides, a series of small waterways wrapped around a bite-sized, rocky peninsula. Beneath this peninsula, puddles of water formed below dark miniature caves where a battalion of sea creatures resided. There were green sea anemones, orange and purple starfish, hermit crabs, other types of small crabs, and oysters. It looked quite cramped in there, to say the least.

Curtis reached his hands into the puddle as if he was going to grab one of the starfish but withdrew when he heard an ill-timed screech coming from the direction of GC.

"NO!"

I had no idea a grown man of his stature could hit such a high note.

"Get yer hands outta there. Them sea anemones will kill ya if you ain't too careful."

"Kill me?" Curtis said, exasperated.

"They're poisonous. An' they'll paralyze ya."

GC further explained to us that sea anemones are predatory creatures that will open to a large diameter and reveal toxic tentacles. Upon first glance, they look like sea flowers. But if a small fish or crab decides to crawl into its open "mouth," it will immediately close, snagging its victims with its tentacles and releasing a powerful neurotoxin that can cause fever or paralysis in humans. Appropriately, Curtis reached his right index finger into the fray and proceeded to prod at the toxic beast of the tide pool.

"They're squishy!"

GC and I looked at each other and shrugged our shoulders. I felt as if we were having a moment. No, we were definitely having a moment. He put his arm around my shoulder and huddled me close like he was going to give me a noogie, but just held me tight. At that point, I knew we were totally bros. It didn't matter that he came from a family of alleged criminals. That is, until he started squeezing me harder.

"You boys are the best thin' that's happinta me since I got here!"

"Glad to hear it," I said, as I gasped for air.

He finally let go and I said a Hail Mary in my head to thank the universe for its mercy on my depraved soul.

"Time to go home?" I asked, but it was not so much a question as it was a demand.

"Aww man, ahlright." GC said.

Curtis was too busy poking the sea anemones to give it any thought. So I walked back to the car without turning once, and a few minutes later we were gone, all limbs surprisingly intact.

When we arrived back at Al and Betsy's, Curtis could tell that I was ready to move on. With a simple head nod and a few goodbyes, we were back in our familiar car seats, far, far away from all the irrational dangers of Seal Rock, Oregon.

* * *

Hood River is a magical place. It sits smack dab in the middle of its namesake peak, Mount Hood, and an equally worthy massif,

Mount Adams. The former dominates the Portland skyline and the latter unassumingly resides in the middle of nowhere but is just as pleasing a sight for the aspiring mountaineer.

We'd spent the previous day in Portland, touring Portland State, the five-dollar food carts, and of course, its famous bookstore, Powell's. By night, we waited in line for forty-five minutes to get our hands on some Voodoo Donuts. It was worth it. If you like dough and you like sugar, then it's the place to be, offering an endless selection of diabetes-inducing delicacies, not the least of which includes a mango-filled mango donut, a Fruity Pebbles donut, an M&M-covered donut, an Oreo crumble donut, and a maple bacon donut. We bought a dozen.

From there, we spent the night with a guy from Alaska named Tom. We had to do some last-minute scrambling for a couch with the help of Talia, who not only renewed her promise to join us in a week on Mount Rainier, but also pledged to provide us with contacts in any state where we needed them.

Tom was the archetype of Alaska. In my eyes, at least. He was like a tough-as-nails Colorado hardmeat on steroids. He told us of his daily morning commutes in the winter: ten miles on his bike, with temperatures often reaching negative forty degrees Fahrenheit. No, that was not a typo. I didn't even ask if that included the wind chill, for fear of coming off as a weak New Englander. So I quickly retreated to my pull-out couch and scrunched up in my blanket just a wee bit tighter that night, anticipating that at any moment the air conditioner would be jacked up to full-blast.

We left Tom the next morning to satisfy our touristy desires along the Columbia River Gorge, the line of demarcation between Oregon and Washington. The guy who we were going to be staying with in Hood River suggested that we check out Multnomah Falls, which, even on a Monday afternoon, was completely jammed with fanny-pack-clad, camera-wielding sightseers. It was evident why— the falls are a two-tiered, six-hundred-plus-foot monster that sit directly off I-84, which travels from Portland to Boise, Idaho. We came, we saw, we conquered, and we moved right on to Hood River.

Outside of a McDonald's just down the street from the town's namesake river, we met up with Abby's brother's good friend Barry. Maybe it's just me, but there's always at least one token lunatic that you meet while traveling for an extended period. It's probably just me. But if only you were there. If only you'd met Barry, you would really understand. He had just gotten through kite-boarding, a popular hobby in the area, and was already on fire not two minutes into our conversation.

"Hey boys, nice to meet you! Glad you decided to come to our wonderful town. Picked a bad time though, there's a lot of a-holes crampin' my style and taking up all the parking. Damn idiots!"

Barry was about five-foot-six and looked like a career lifeguard. Blond, tanned, and a bit pompous, he made us feel perfectly awkward right from the get-go.

"Doesn't matter to us, Barry, we're just here for the ride," Curtis remarked.

"What are you boys here for anyway? Abby tells me you're on a road trip. You trying to get smashed tonight? I can show you some great places to park your car. C'mon, follow me!"

Rather than engage him, we looked at each other in mutual bewilderment and just let him do his thing. We hopped in Mindy and followed him on a weave through downtown Hood River.

Our first stop on the Barry Takes Us to Town Tour was at the top of the hill just a few blocks down from the main drag. He parked his car, got out, and gave us the rundown.

"Now, you can park right along this road here for the night if you wanna get hammered and just walk back. You definitely won't be making it back to my place tonight—I can see it in your eyes!" His intuition was a tad bit off, but we appreciated the ensuing internal laughter that his miscalculation provided us.

Next stop on the tour was the marina, where we were shown the seventy-five-cent showers.

"If you plan on vomiting on yourselves, you can get a good wash down here first thing in the morning. Just make sure you bring your own towel."

Thank goodness for Barry's esteemed wisdom. I'm not sure we could have survived the night without him.

After parking adjacent to the river proper, we were introduced to Babs, Barry's purported girlfriend—a relationship that would become even more unclear as the night progressed. We were also greeted with a moist lick on the face by their pug, Jazz, who, ironically, was probably the sanest in the family.

Notwithstanding the big talk about getting hammered and sleeping in our car, Barry ended up inviting us to his house anyway. It was another few blocks up the street from the bars, and very much within walking distance despite previous indications to the contrary. Before exploring his home, he led us on a short walk through the neighborhood where on one side we saw Mount Hood rise sharply like a pyramid; on the other, Mount Adams gradually painted its snowy slopes from valley to sky. It was an impeccable

360-degree panorama of everything that made me drive so far away from home in the first place.

"Too bad you boys didn't get to climb Hood over there. Perfect mountain, just perfect. A buddy o' mine paraglided down the whole goddamn thing!"

"That's impressive!" Curtis replied. "We were planning on hiking it until that guy died a few days ago and bad weather was forecasted."

Indeed, a man had gotten lost on a solo climb of Mount Hood during one of the nastiest storms they've had during the summer climbing months in years. They found his body a week later. He had succumbed to his injuries during a fatal fall. Without a witness, it is impossible to speculate as to how it happened. The mountains can be awfully unforgiving sometimes.

Back at Barry's abode, we toured the small but quaint residence, where all types of wonders awaited us. The garage was stacked to the ceiling with gear for kite-boarding and windsurfing, which, believe it or not, are entirely different sports. In kite-boarding, participants use the wind and handheld kites to propel themselves across the water while riding a small board similar to a snowboard. Windsurfing, on the other hand, utilizes a sail and surfboard not so different from those used by the people who catch waves in SoCal and Hawaii. The emphasis on the latter is to glide on the water like a sailboard with nothing attached to you.

Behind the house was Babs's most prized possession, her garden. In it were myriad raspberry bushes, various vegetables, and an eight-foot-tall sunflower. We stuffed our faces with berries until our bellies fattened and our faces took on the appearance of blood-sucking vampires.

Much to our surprise, Babs invited us to stay for dinner. I guess our initial encounter with Barry made it seem like he wanted nothing to do with us. Perhaps it was the suggestion of voluntary over-intoxication that paved our impression. The smell of avocado chicken sausage and the sounds of an episode of Antiques Roadshow circa 1998 made us forget about the whole ordeal—at least temporarily.

But then it was time for boozing. I was the designated driver for the night, as I always was back then. Although we had little to no room in the car, we stuffed Barry's small frame behind the passenger seat on the floor. The drive was no more than a few minutes anyway, and we were soon thereafter on our way to the bar.

As expected, Barry was quickly sloshed. He was pounding free tasters and following them up with brews of 10 percent alcohol by volume. It became quickly apparent that he was a regular at the first bar after we were introduced to what seemed like a dozen people in the span of a few minutes. Then the same thing happened at the next bar. This trend would continue as we hopped from bar to bar for the next several hours. Hood River was full of characters: a professional snowboarder who had just won a gold medal at the X Games, a plastered group of twenty-somethings, myriad flies and bugs, a tall old guy who looked like he should probably quit drinking, and an overly inebriated, short-haired blonde woman with a pink dress and a massive gash on her leg. She immediately took a liking to Barry.

"You are soooooooooooooooooooooooooooo pretty! You know-www that?"

Stunner Barry couldn't help but be flattered.

"What's with the leg, honey?"

"Ohhhhh, this?" She pointed to her disgusting open sore, flaunting it as if it were some sort of bragging right. "I got it on my board, duuuude."

"What kind of board?" Curtis asked, as he tried to make the bizarre conversation into a somewhat more normal one.

"Looooooooooonnnnnnggg board. Just like that. Looooooonnnnnggggggggggggggg board."

"Barry here is a kite boarder," I said, deviously, as I jokingly tried to play matchmaker.

"Reaaaally? You are soooooooooo prettyyyyy."

Just as soon as the words exited her mouth, Barry and the mystery lady began dancing like a middle school couple.

"Those two are the sloppiest looking drunks I've ever seen," I whispered to Curtis.

"Yup."

The gash-lady spectacle left us questioning the whole Babs-Barry relationship. To be perfectly honest, I had assumed Babs was Barry's mom when we first met her. Maybe she was. But this is a book about adventure, not Barry's perplexing relationships. So, I leave you with the pleasant image of Jazz licking my face at two in the morning after Curtis and I passed out in Barry's backyard later that night.

Chapter 11

"Here in the corner attic of America, two hours' drive from a rain forest, a desert, a foreign country, an empty island, a hidden fjord, a raging river, a glacier, and a volcano is a place where the inhabitants sense they can do no better, nor do they want to."

—Timothy Egan, *The Good Rain: Across Time & Terrain in the Pacific Northwest*

* * *

At some junction or another during any long trip, everyone longs for home. It's clichéd, I know. But every dose of wanderlust comes with an equal dose of homesickness.

We had just finished a tour of scenic Crater Lake, one of the bluest I've seen in the United States. Additionally, we climbed what has become one of my favorite mountains—Mount Adams, which we first laid eyes upon in Hood River. What separates Adams from so many other mountains is its legendary descent trail. Every summer, glissade chutes form so perfectly that one can comfortably butt slide down over two thousand vertical feet at blistering speeds. To put it in perspective, it took roughly two hours to get up the mountain from base camp, but just over thirty minutes to get back down.

From the trailhead for Adams, we took the backroads toward Seattle, ready to experience one last bout of rest and companionship before we would attempt Rainier. Because despite the imminence of our daunting goal, we were a tad bit homesick.

* * *

When I was a freshman in college, I lived in a dorm hall with a guy named Mark. Mark and I always got along, but I knew next to nothing about him during college. Many people from the hall would frequent my room to play video games while they were stoned, but Mark was not usually among them. I figured that he was an introvert like me, and thus I didn't bother engaging him past the occasional head nod or hello.

Sophomore year brought a lot more Mark into my life, but just as little conversation. He was a good friend of one of my roommates, and they often cooked dinner together at my apartment. Since I was more often found moping in my room than engaging in substantive conversation, or even idle chit-chat, that was more or less the last time I regularly saw Mark for the remainder of my college years.

But that all changed when I decided to message him out of the blue after I remembered that he lived in Seattle. He was more than happy to accommodate us, with the caveat that we wouldn't see him on the first night that we arrived. So, it was initially a bit awkward when Mark's mom asked us how we knew him.

"Well, to be honest Sally, I don't think I've seen him in almost a year, but I've known him since freshman year."

I anticipated that she would scowl at us like we were some mooches trying to get out of paying for a night at a hotel. Quite the opposite ensued.

"Well I hope that you two can reconnect with him on this trip! He hasn't stopped talking about how much he has been looking forward to this day. He's had a long summer bussing at the steakhouse down the street."

Sally had a beaming smile as she opened the fridge and started shoveling out excessive amounts of meat. We could tell she was a damn good mother and presumably as good a cook.

"Pot roast is for dinner; I hope you boys are hungry!"

We were given the tour of the house and our living quarters. We were staying in the basement, where a bed and a couch gave us a lot more space than our usual sleeping arrangements. The room was prim and proper with fresh towels and sheets galore. It was as if Sally had been waiting all summer for us too.

At some point during our preliminary conversation with Sally in their outdoor "dining room," her husband, Malcolm, arrived home from work. He wore khaki shorts and loafers and reminded me a lot of my dad. But he soon altered my initial impression once he started delving into his lavish travel lifestyle. My dad is not really a vacation person (and he'd be the first to admit it).

Malcolm spoke of his life as a young man in Israel during the Yom Kippur War, barely old enough to have a drink. He had moved there from New York to do what many Jews felt was their calling and their birthright. He told us a wild story about being in a field and witnessing a plane zip overhead and crash nearby. It was like a scene out of a bad Spaghetti Western, but in real life.

As the evening progressed, Malcolm told us of how he lived in a cave in California for two months shortly after returning from Israel. But he didn't stop there, and Sally would often butt in with a story of her own. They spoke of their travels to Guatemala, Thailand, and Calcutta, India, where they were intrigued by the dichotomy between life above and below ground. In the subways of Calcutta, the platforms were inundated with middle-class businesspeople and other prosperous commuters. It was like any other major city in America. But as soon as you entered the fray of the over-world, things were starkly different. Poverty was rampant—shanties were the majority of buildings; beggars lined the street corners. It was a perfect paradigm of leaving the undesirables behind, not unlike what goes on in our own country. In Calcutta, though, they put their poverty on display. We conceal it with subdivisions and gentrification.

By that point, we were sufficiently bloated from Sally's feast of Thanksgiving proportions. It was nearing 10 p.m., but in Seattle around the Fourth of July it never really does get dark until you're ready to go to bed.

Mark arrived home only a few minutes before we turned the lights off at 11 p.m. There was a bit of awkwardness in our initial encounter. I mean, I hadn't seen the guy much in the last few years, and even then, we weren't terribly close. The most absurd part of the whole ordeal was that I could confidently say I had spoken more to Mark's parents in just several hours than I had to Mark in all my four years in college. That would change quickly.

* * *

I've never been much of a city person. To me, there isn't much more to do than hopelessly search for parking or ride a twice-delayed train, walk a few blocks, grab a bite to eat, get sloppily intoxicated, and then do touristy stuff, I guess. By the time it's all said and done, you're down a few hundred bucks and a few liver cells. I don't know how he did it, but Mark made our first trip to the city of Seattle into something akin to a kid's first exploration of a playground or a candy store. It was that damn good.

It only seemed fitting that Mark would commence our day's revelries at Pike Place. When we got there, we made the rounds outside of the actual marketplace, seeing notable areas such as the gum wall, the bronze pig, and the first Starbucks. (Mark later told us it wasn't actually the original—wouldn't be the first time Starbucks screwed with the hearts and minds of the American people. Like the time they "killed Christmas" with their plain red cups.)

We followed our opening act with a little appetizer in the form of a barbecue chicken hum bao, a strange but delicious dough-based Chinese delicacy. Already, I was feeling as if I had been left in the dark for my whole life. The only Chinese food I'd had to date was the kind that failed to keep you satiated, caused at least one horrible bathroom experience, and left you wanting more after it was all gone.

Moving on to the main attraction, we entered the actual marketplace, which was simply amazing. The first sight you see is the fish market, which sits under an enormous neon sign, proclaiming Public Market with a 1930s vibe, like something out of an early Alfred Hitchcock movie. From our perspective as tourists, it was somewhat overwhelming, akin to a busy sidewalk in Boston or New York City where you constantly bump into people. But the congestion became more tolerable as we made our way from the top level, which mostly consisted of food and clothing, to the bottom floor, which was mostly gift shops.

We perused the many eclectic stores between the nostalgic walls of neon signs and old-time pictures. Included among these shops was one of the oldest comic book stores in the country, a magic shop, a Tibetan gift shop, and a paper store that sold old posters in keeping with the market's theme. There's no doubt we could have spent all day wasting our time and money, but Mark had better plans for us.

One Indian buffet and a miserable bloating later, we found ourselves at the local disc golf field.

"Gentlemen, this here is the sport of the future," Mark proudly told us.

What is disc golf, you ask? I had heard a bit about it here and there, but honestly had no clue until our introductory lesson with Mark. The field itself was in a public park. Instead of cups in the ground, disc golf "holes" are cages with a basket in the middle. The goal is the same as in golf: get the disc in the hole. Each hole is par three, but we had a hard time believing that, especially given the length of some of them. According to Mark, some pros can score birdies on nearly every hole, a baffling concept given the fact that we found ourselves bogeying and double-bogeying on the regular. But I guess that's what separates the pros from the amateurs. Or in our case, the newbies.

By hole 16, we were just about done getting our asses kicked. It was around that time that Mark focused our attention toward something that made us really feel like we sucked.

"Guys, look behind you, you're in for a real treat today." He didn't have to rub it in. Our inadequacy was already wholly apparent on the score sheet, where we trailed Mark by more than I am willing to disclose.

"Are you kidding me?" I exclaimed, as I watched a disc fly nearly the length of a football field and land just a few feet away from the hole 15 basket.

A somewhat overweight dude in a visor slowly strutted toward us with what appeared to be a wheelie suitcase in tow. Mark exchanged a few words with him as I threw my disc into the woods for the umpteenth time. After I spent the better part of the next ten minutes searching for it, Mark reappeared. It only took him ten seconds to locate my lost disc. Golfing of any type is just not my forte.

"Who was that guy?" Curtis asked, a little more interested in the answer than me. I didn't give a crap who he was. What little ego I had left slowly dissolved into nothingness.

"Oh, him? He's just a local pro." Mark lined up for his next throw and winged his disc into a tree. That made me feel just a tad bit better about myself.

"What the hell was that stupid rolly backpack he had with him?" I sharply inquired.

"He custom built his own disc-bag. He even has a caddy with him."

"What a loser," I muttered under my breath. But the only real loser that day was me. At thirty-five above par, I had probably broken a record for the worst disc golf performance of all time. Even the caddy would have beaten me.

* * *

That Fourth of July was the first one spent with a family other than my own. As it turned out, Sally and Malcolm have the whole family over at their place for a massive barbecue every year. When we arrived back at Mark's house, we acquainted ourselves with his extensive family—his brother, cousins, cousins' families, and his aunt, to be specific. There was his brother Neil, his cousins Ron and Tina and their kid, Sarah; Mosley, Jen, and their kids, Larry and Heather; Ellen, Sam, and their kids, Leah and Alex; and Aunt Susie.

There was also Sarah's friend, whom everyone called Gator. We never did figure out why. She didn't even look like an alligator.

Much of our dinner was spent in conversation, or at least in between bites of burgers, sausages, salmon, and other foods. Aside from the standard, boilerplate introduction we gave them about our trip, we learned quite a lot about Mark's diverse family. For instance, Mosley is a world-renowned architect who helped design the Australia island in Dubai's World Project, and Ron is a virtuosic carpenter, artist, and jack of all trades who has designed displays in museums.

But the highlight of the evening was a welcome return to our childhoods. Curtis, Mark, Neil, and I played with the little kids for over an hour, running after each other with blow up bowling pins. After tiring ourselves out, Mark gave us all dime-store poppers, smoke bombs, and sparklers. We went a little crazy, to say the least.

At the end of the night, as everyone left or went to bed, we mentioned to Mark just how important it was to have shared our Independence Day with his family. Especially with the climax of our trip commencing in under twenty-four hours.

"We loved having you," he remarked, with a grin on his face.

"We never would have expected that so many people would come to our aid," Curtis spoke, reflecting the exact thought I had in my head.

"I'm glad to have spent the time with you. You guys better be careful and come back to celebrate your triumph!"

To be honest, we had no idea what to expect of Mount Rainier. But this was it. Second and goal from the one-yard line, under a minute to go on the game clock. Were we going to pass up on this chance to succeed, or run it right down the middle? We weren't going to make the same mistake twice. We were going to go full Beast Mode straight from Seattle to the summit of Mount Rainier. Pete Carroll couldn't have drawn it up better.

Chapter 12

"Mount Rainier is the most luxuriant and the most
extravagantly beautiful of all the alpine gardens I
ever beheld in all of my mountain-top wanderings."
—John Muir

* * *

Rainier, Rainier, Rainier. She who eluded us for so long, waiting patiently for two amateurs to tread her slopes. A beast of a mountain, glaciated on the outside, volcanic to her core, an impeccable dichotomy of fire and ice—blazing infernos below; frigid, snowy paradise above. She towers above the Seattle skyline and captures the hearts of all who witness her majesty. A modest giant, she resides peacefully among snow-capped mountains in a quaint, isolated town in Washington state. She creates a symphonious equilibrium in a state full of beauty and diversity—blissful beaches, lonely lakes, verdant forests, skyscraper mountains, majestic meadows, raging rivers, vibrant flora, and elegant fauna.

In our month and a half of travel so far, America had made quite an impression on us. But that all paled in comparison to the wonder, amazement, curiosity, and exuberance that Rainier had stirred up in our inquisitive minds. What was it about the mountain that was so captivating?

Rainier is the undisputed queen of glaciated peaks in the United States (outside of Alaska), and undoubtedly the most attractive mountain we had laid our eyes upon to date. It is an active stratovolcano—one of the most dangerous in the world, in fact. It is a mammoth among mammoths, the cream of the crop, the Incredible Hulk, the Odin of Asgard, the Zeus of Greek mythology, and the target practice for an ascent of Denali. Put simply, Mount Rainier is the proving ground for any aspiring mountaineer. It is one of the most prominent mountains in the world. It can be seen with ease from Seattle, which sits at sea level, though Rainier is over 14,400 feet tall. It looks like a monstrous behemoth from the city. And it is. But that still doesn't answer the question. Plenty of people who live nearby never have any desire to scale its treacherous flanks. So what made it so special to us?

To me, it all stems back to that fateful day on the Franconia Ridge when we froze our asses off and took pleasure in it when it was all said and done. That's the short story. But bear with me while I elaborate extensively and somewhat controversially. I guess it all starts with a word that many people dread. Privilege.

* * *

In 1943, Abraham Maslow penned a paper titled "A Theory of Human Motivation." In it, the now renowned "Hierarchy of Needs" was conceived. Imagine a pyramid, where at the bottom lie your most basic of needs, and as the pyramid climbs to its apex, your needs become more and more elaborate. Physiologically speaking, air, water, shelter, warmth, and food are required by everyone. If you struggle to obtain enough of those necessities, you care little about the upper echelons of the pyramid.

As the layers become more complex, so too do your human desires. Safety and love, the next two tiers above physiology, often go together. Many unprivileged people remain within these two tiers for most of their life, where their biggest strife is to breach into the self-esteem category, the second-highest tier. Self-esteem encompasses the desire to achieve, to be recognized, and to be respected. But the constant struggle to achieve these goals can often be defeating even to those who work the hardest. Some people will just never have the same opportunities as others, either due to economic or biological restraints, or both. I had plenty of opportunities, and thus, plenty of free time to think about how I would occupy the rest of my time. I chose to play in the mountains.

It sounds quite ludicrous when you tell someone that you enjoy putting yourself in life-or-death scenarios where your fate is subject to several uncontrollable factors. I don't mean embarking on suicide missions, merely placing oneself in a mortally challenging situation akin to what our ancestors had to endure daily. Some of us have an unexplained craving for the visceral.

For comparison purposes, unprivileged people need not seek out visceral experiences—for they are constantly struggling just to get by. Food, water, and shelter are always at the top of the list. Then you must factor in transportation, clothing, household items, and all other essentials. By the time the monthly budget has been exhausted, many of these people become riddled in debt, or simply can't afford necessities. It becomes a never-ending cycle, and often carries over from generation to generation. Every day is a struggle to survive.

On the contrary, you have privileged people like me—and I will be the first to admit it. I was born into a family of lawyers, my grandfather was a judge, I was guaranteed a job right out of law school, and I would graduate with very little student debt. My life is hardly a sob story, but what was missing from my purported fairytale was happiness and purpose. How could I not be happy, you ask, when I was afforded such a head start in life? It became apparent to me that always getting what I wanted with no struggle wasn't a meaningful life at all. In fact, as I stumbled through four years of college with little ability to cope with my depression, I wondered how other people did it. Obviously, for many, alcohol was that crutch. For me, it was writing—creating fantasy worlds to quench my desire for adventure and variability.

When writing began to lose some of its swagger, I longed to get away. I took a class about Jack Kerouac and the Beat Generation and discovered what I wanted to do when I left college's restraining fortifications. As I toiled to pass my classes over the next three years, I also religiously researched mountains and other beautiful, isolated places scattered across the country. I was sick of being in a bubble, confined to my depressive thoughts. I needed something *real*, rather than the artificial constructs that society creates. My societally constructed depression created the need for the mountains. And only by realizing my privilege was I able to reach that conclusion.

So where does that leave me in the Hierarchy of Needs, and why the hell is it even relevant to my lust for climbing Mount Rainier? The top tier of the pyramid is self-actualization, or the pursuit of inner talents, creativity, and fulfillment. To me, my navigation of the pyramid mirrors that of my formative years of life. As a baby, all I cared about were physiological needs. As a kid, I was afraid of ghosts and bad guys, and so safety was my desire. In high school, I wanted nothing more than to be loved. In college, I wanted to be loved and do well and impress others. And as I reached the latter years of college, I desired a monumental change that would challenge my very existence and bring me toward some sort of salvation-like feeling. I wanted to transcend whatever shortcomings that life had presented me with—to reach this elusive state of self-actu-alization, if that was even possible.

And so, Mount Rainier seemed like the perfect challenge to ad-dress my own personal shortcomings. No matter how entitled and gimmicky the whole psychological spiel sounds, that was at least part of my rationale, but even to this day I can't fully grasp it all. I doubt I ever will.

* * *

We picked up Talia at Sea-Tac Airport, did a little reconnais-sance mission to scope out the start of our route and secure our per-mits, and settled down on Skate Creek Road, a common camping area for cheapskates like us. Driving an hour out of the park to save a few bucks was worth it at the time. I guess the whole unemploy-ment thing was catching up to us.

"Do you guys remember your glacier travel basics?" Talia asked in a seemingly rhetorical manner.

"Uhhhhh, yeah!" I remarked, albeit with a bit of subterfuge to make it seem like I was being serious. To be honest though, just three months of not tying elaborate knots and manufacturing com-plicated pulley systems had pushed snow travel skills right out of my mind.

After our quick refresher course with Talia, we were in high spirits. The weather forecast was prime, calling for bluebird condi-tions and no precipitation during our two-day window. And the best part about it all? Talia had offered to pay for all our gas, food, and climbing passes. Had we not come along to tackle Rainier with her, she would likely have hired a guide as she had a few months earlier, when she was pushed off the summit due to a crazy snowstorm. I'm not exactly sure why she and Abby chose to ascend Rainier in May, but that was the price they paid, and trust me, it isn't cheap for a mountain guide.

It was a bit surreal that we were less than twenty-four hours from Ingraham Flats, a heavily crevassed base camp at 11,100 feet where we planned to pitch our tents for the first night. Typically, parties spend the night at Camp Muir, which is located at approximately 10,800 feet. We wanted to get an extra hour of sleep and a head start on those mostly guided groups. Our alarms were set for 5:30 a.m., and Curtis and I were both giddy and anxious as we settled into our car beds.

"Well, we're here," I said, as I plopped my body into my sleeping bag and reclined my car seat.

"I'm nervous," Curtis replied from the back of the car, as he removed his smelly socks to reveal his heinous blisters.

I tried to reassure him. "They don't look too bad."

"They're better, at least."

Who would have thought that such a seemingly inconsequential foot ailment would cause us so much grief and uncertainty?

"They'll hold up. They did on Adams. And you've had almost a week of rest." I closed my eyes and shuffled my head toward the driver's-side window to avoid inhaling foot sweat.

"I know. I'm still worried. Not just about that but also just everything else."

"Afraid you're going to fall in a crevasse, are ya?" I joked.

"I guess so. I'm sure once we wake up and get on the mountain, I'll be alright."

Curtis's anxiety wasn't any different from my own, but I tried to conceal mine lest we both lose sleep that night. Pre-climb jitters, much like those you would get before any other high-performance activity, can be onerous for your mental well-being. Contemplating what can go wrong is not uncommon. Nor is the prospect of death or grave injury. Suffice it to say, we had our doubts as we dozed off that night.

Although your imagination and subconscious thoughts cannot be controlled, when you're there on the mountain, it's a whole different ball game. The butterflies go away. Your thoughts are replaced with the primal instinct for success and survival. Pain becomes secondary to your objective. The desire for self-actualization is suddenly transformed into a simple game of survival. Everything in the Hierarchy of Needs comes full circle. Our experiences in the mountains provide psychological and physiological sustenance. Undoubtedly, Rainier was the ultimate encapsulation of that notion, and of two clueless college graduates' journeys toward redemption from their once mundane lives. Or something like that.

* * *

"Boys, keep your eyes peeled, the crevasses are coming up."

Without Talia, we likely would have found ourselves barreling down a hundred-foot hole until it narrowed enough for our bodies to become permanently lodged in both the mountain's interior and its long history of casualties. Some day when oil greed and factory farms finish destroying the planet, our skeletons would thaw out and be nibbled on by post-apocalyptic cockroaches. Better than being buried in some stinkin' casket, I suppose.

All jokes aside, Rainier is a crevasse-ridden volcano with around a 44 percent success rate for non-guided climbing parties. Part of that failure rate is attributed to weather, which is unpredictable and unforgiving. The other failures primarily come from altitude-related sickness or general fatigue, but there have been around one hundred fatalities on the mountain since statistics have been tracked. That doesn't include the many, many injuries that have occurred on Rainier's icy ramps.

So, from the get-go, it seemed the odds were stacked against us. To somewhat ensure that we would remain injury-free, we roped ourselves together as a three-person team. It is good practice to climb crevassed peaks in such teams to avoid deadly falls if a snow-bridge collapses. If one person falls into a crevasse, the other two are trained to catch that person by self-arresting. This is a method akin to the stop, drop, and roll. The roll, however, is replaced by jabbing your ice axe into the ground, lying forward on it, and digging deep into the ground to slow down and stop. It's easiest to catch the person in the front when hiking uphill, and the opposite for going downhill, for reasons called gravity. The person in the middle often has the hardest job—assuming they do not fall in themselves—since they must catch the victim first. Falling in a crevasse isn't an ideal situation and should be avoided at all costs. Obviously.

From the Paradise trailhead, we followed a well-worn, easy-to-navigate trail that leads up to Camp Muir. I fought back tears of joy as I stared gleefully up the mountain of my many dreams over the course of several impatient years. It truly took my breath away. Or was that the altitude?

At the camp, we encountered what seemed to be a hundred people lounging around in their tents and showing off their brand-new gear to each other. Most of these parties seemed to be accompanied by a guiding service; in every tent colony there was one person demonstrating how to properly tie a figure-eight knot to a group of people. At the time I barely knew how to put my harness on properly, let alone tie a perfect figure-eight, which is the most common knot to secure yourself to the rope. Nonetheless, we continued past these apparent gumbies and found ourselves crossing over our first crevasse with Talia at the helm.

"Holy crap, that's *deep*!" I exclaimed, as I nearly toppled over my own feet and into it. I'm a bit uncoordinated when I wear crampons.

"Jeeeesus, be careful," Curtis said, as I watched him cross the crevasse. It took not more than a simple hop to clear the width of the hole.

In the distance, we could see hundreds of massive cracks in the surface of the Ingraham Glacier. As we looked more closely, it appeared as if these crevasses lay just to the right of our intended route, the Disappointment Cleaver, suitably named for its reputation for failure. There was something so serene, yet so dismaying about witnessing these gaping craters. They're getting larger and larger each year, and no one in their right mind is disputing that. As the glaciers recede, so too will our ability to scale the mountains that house them.

Aside from a few simple jumps, we didn't run into too many crevasses on our way up to base camp at Ingraham Flats. Even though we were just at sea level a few days prior, the altitude was treating us well. Training in the Rockies was certainly the reason for this.

As we neared our campsite for the evening, we looked ahead with awe. A labyrinth of crevasses complicated the only evident path to the top of the mountain. It was a vast field of seasonal wounds and allergic reactions that only emerged during the warmer months of the year. It really looked as if some snarky higher power had gotten a little stab-happy with a holy pocketknife.

Behind us, an equally exceptional scene: three familiar friends, Adams, Saint Helens, and Hood bashfully poked out from the valley below. Together with Rainier, they complete the quadrangle of Pacific Northwest volcanoes—a quadrumvirate of infinite beauty. Speaking in Legend of Zelda terms, we were in the presence of the Quadforce. In anatomical terms, they would mold the quadriceps of North America. And if they were dinosaurs, they would create the mighty Quadrosaurus! RAWRRRR!!

We were just as silly and giddy in the moment, too. Once our tents were set up at Ingraham Flats—among a much smaller congregation than at Camp Muir—we lounged and soaked in the vistas. Just a few hundred yards away, one of Rainier's subsidiary cones, Little Tahoma, jutted abruptly into the Washington skyline. It was quite dissimilar from its parent peak, in the sense that it was not snow or ice covered and appeared to require a slog up loose scree to get to the top. Some climbers do make the trip up there—but we had more important endeavors that weekend.

At 6 p.m., we held our game-plan conversation for the next morning over freeze-dried chili macaroni and beef. We clearly hadn't learned our lesson.

"I'm so happy you boys let me come with you," Talia said, as she rustled through her tent for a headlamp. Although it was nowhere near dark, we had proposed a start time of 1:30 a.m. and needed to make sure we were well-equipped.

"We might not have been here without you," I remarked. I pulled my liner gloves over my now freezing hands.

"Well I certainly wouldn't have been here either!" She plucked some batteries out of a zip-lock bag in her pack and put them in her headlamp.

"How are the blisters?" I asked Curtis, who had just returned from taking a crap next to a massive crevasse about a hundred feet from our campsite.

"Fine surprisingly. But I'm having some shortness of breath."

"What else is new," I frustratedly responded.

"Hey, cut it out you two." Talia had noticed the tension between us not two minutes into the start of our climb. It was obvious given how non-confrontational we were when we'd first met her on Sneffels about a month prior. That was a different time in our lives—one when we were mutually depressed with how our trip was unfolding. Now, we were just sick of sharing the same tent and recycled air with each other, nearly forty-five days on the road. Not to mention the stench of his damn feet was getting more and more filthy.

"I'll be fine," Curtis assured us. We retired to bed on his somewhat unconvincing reassurance.

* * *

When natives settled in the basin of the mountain formerly known as Tacoma, they were convinced that the mountain housed powerful spirits at its summit. In the 1800s, a native guide named Sluiskin led a handful of European settlers up the cursed peak as far as he was comfortable. Going anywhere near the summit was out of the question—for a fiery demon resided in an infernal lake atop the peak. Against Sluiskin's better judgment, the colonists made the brazen decision to scale the blazing beast now known as Rainier.

A few days after their separation, Sluiskin was confronted by three men whom he believed were revenants returning to inform him of the white man's inevitable failure. On the contrary, the climbers had arrived with news of their success—ending the supposed demonic curse in the process.

Nearly a century and a half later, the supposed curse of Tacoma still exists for nearly 50 percent of the people who attempt to conquer her glacial stairs. Where the spirit of magma once resided, clouds of leaden gray have filled the void. And unlike the spirit, these wispy nightmares will mercilessly trap their victims, thwarting any chance to prevail.

We knew not of the native folklore as we emerged from our tents at 1 a.m. to the tune of crunchy footsteps and flashing headlamp lights. The climbers from Camp Muir had already beaten us to the chase. But it didn't quite matter. The stars were as bright and ethereal as any we had ever seen. No puny headlamp light or ominous cloud would even think about compromising our impeccable, celestial moment.

Despite the bright stars, darkness still swept over old Tacoma. Navigating the crevasse fields would be a daunting undertaking. Nonetheless, the perfect, ebony sky had subdued our nerves—what we couldn't see couldn't hurt us.

The going was steady after we roped up and started heading for the unknown. To our surprise, a series of flags were placed along the route indicating the locations of hidden crevasses. We later learned that it is customary for the guiding companies to mark the route. While we were fortunate for this practice, it certainly took away some of the serendipity that we expected to encounter on Rainier. But where adventure was stymied it was also stirred up. Because we were relying on the flags as our beacons, when we began to stop seeing them, we collectively became disoriented.

"THIS WAY!" I shouted to my team of explorers. I had no idea if I was right.

A steep scree field appeared as a promising alternative to a crevasse field that may or may not have been our only other option. Still dark out, it was difficult to make sense of our surroundings.

"ARE YOU SURE?" Talia countered. Clearly, she had a better understanding of our route than I did.

"WHERE ELSE WOULD IT BE?"

When we encountered a seemingly insurmountable cliff band, it was apparent that we were well off our bearings. We weren't good role models either, as two other groups behind us had followed our errant path.

"OVER HERE!"

Talia had gone from the back of the team to the front simply due to our unexpected turnaround. She would assume leadership duties for the foreseeable future. Apparently, our lives depended on it.

As dawn neared, navigation became less of a problem. Headlamps were off in due time, and the altitude began its assault on our respiratory systems. But in the wake of our increased struggle, we were appropriately compensated for our adversity.

A bold, blood-orange orb abruptly peered out from behind the undercast clouds on the distant horizon. Its face was familiar, but we had never seen it present itself with such poise and splendor. With our breaths already taken away by the exertion, there was nothing left to steal from us. Instead, the moment became forever enshrined in our memories.

Now that our visions were restored by the natural light, we could see the remainder of our path uphill. And it was damn steep. In keeping with our switchback strategy that we had employed on Shasta, we forged our own path up the unforgiving incline. The going was brutal, and we were all exhausted from the altitude. Abruptly, Curtis yelled up at us to stop.

"HOLD ON," He belted out.

"Oh great," I mumbled, so only Talia could hear me.

"Oh, leave him be," she admonished.

He began to fumble through his bag for something. Minutes went by and I became increasingly impatient. I began to walk down toward him to figure out what was going on.

"What the hell are you doing?" I called out to my faithful friend.

"Try-ing . . . . . . to find—my . . . . . . inhaler," he said, gasping between words.

"Don't tell me we're going to have to go back."

"N-no."

"We'd better not."

I strolled back up the hill with my hands above my head and shrugged with Talia looking on. We were less than a thousand vertical feet from the summit, and goddammit I wasn't about to turn around. But I couldn't leave Curtis behind. Not again.

His inhaler nowhere to be found, we continued up at a snail's pace, which was still too fast for Curtis.

"STOP TUGGING THE DAMN ROPE," I screamed back at him. He had already done so four times before I decided I couldn't take it anymore. Between us, the rope was fully extended, and we were a good sixty feet away from each other. I couldn't hear a word he said as he attempted to shout toward me.

Not wanting to stir up any more animosity between us, Talia stood expressionless a few feet ahead of me with her arms folded. It was almost as if she was telling me I was better than that—that for just one second, I could stop being so damn impatient. I decided I would suck it up and just roll with the punches. Or the tugs, rather.

A half-dozen more incidents later without any verbal assaults, and we were atop the crater rim. We quickly unroped and threw our packs down, but our task was not yet complete—another half mile or so stood between us and the most coveted summit of our trip.

Curtis was not doing well at all. Even after we shed all the excess weight from our bodies, he was on all fours with his head down, hyperventilating.

"Are you okay?" Talia said, as she rubbed Curtis's back.

"I'll . . . be fine."

We decided to give him the benefit of the doubt and wait around for a few more minutes before we made the brief trek across the rim. It was a vast and marvelous sight to see and left me wondering if this is what the craters of the moon look like. Snow-covered and perfectly flat, it was easy to forget that just thousands of feet under us was a bubbling pool of lava that will one day destroy everything within a hundred miles of it.

"I'm . . . good . . . to go," Curtis said, unconvincingly, as I uselessly contemplated places to hide if the volcano got angry.

"You've got this! We're so close!" Talia encouraged. She began to hum the theme to *Rocky* and got us all in a triumphant mood. No dysfunctional lungs or thoughts of Armageddon were going to halt our most adventurous achievement to date.

We three bold alpinauts traversed the longer-than-advertised crater rim over to the base of a rock band that led up to the summit proper.

"This is it!" Talia exclaimed. We continued humming all the way up as we scrambled along easy ledges.

"DUH NUH NUH, DUH NUH NUH!" we all shouted in unison.

Chills crept down my spine as we took the last few steps toward the true summit. I was overwhelmed with emotion, and not just because of the sensational view of the Pacific Northwest that confronted us when we got there. This was it. This was what we trained for. This was what we longed for. Three interminable years in the making. It brought back instant memories of the psychological struggles I faced leading up to our moment on top, including the countless lonely nights provoked by my own self-pity. They were merely an afterthought in that moment. I had driven nearly ten thousand miles with my best friend for some sort of closure to my college years, but I knew that this was just the beginning of a lifetime of adventures. In the interim though, this was a feeling I wouldn't soon forget.

Talia, Curtis, and I embraced in one big bear hug. We knew Rainier wasn't the biggest or the baddest mountain in the land, but it was our Everest. Sluiskin would have been surprised. The poor, superstitious son of a gun. His beliefs were not that different from those of the people who tried so hard to convince Curtis and I to stay home. But we just couldn't live in fear of the unknown any longer. To us, it was better to live life running like hell than to struggle just to crawl. And Rainier, well, Rainier was just the beginning of our new directive—to forsake our inspiration-deficient past lives and transcend *reality*.

Chapter 13

"Canada is like a loft apartment over a really great party.
Like, 'Keep it down, eh?'"

—The late, great Robin Williams

* * *

We were back with Mark before we knew it, happy to be reunited with our road family in Seattle after a whopping success on Rainier. Our itinerary showed Olympic National Park and Mount Baker on the list, but we weren't particularly interested in the former after Mark told us he was itching to go to the San Juan Islands for the first time in years. Our desire for social interaction now trumped our prewritten list, and once we convinced Mark to skip work to come along with us, he happily obliged.

Our destination was Moran State Park, located on Orcas Island. The area is part of the greater San Juan Islands, which are prime ocean vacation destinations for Pacific Northwesterners and only accessible by ferry. Mark referred to this location as the Garden of Eden Within Shangri-La, boldly calling it the most beautiful place on Earth.

At 5 a.m., we boarded a ferry from Anacortes. The three hours of shut-eye the night before wasn't ideal, but when you get to have Jack in the Box for breakfast while you are still experiencing acid reflux from the night before, sleep deprivation isn't so bad after all. The taste of imitation sausage coming up your throat all morning is a little burdensome, but you get used to it after a while.

Our ferry ride was spent listening to an NPR broadcast about a kid from Philadelphia who got laid off and spontaneously decided to walk four-thousand miles across the country. He brought an audio recorder with him and wore a sign that said, "Walking to Listen." Every time someone inquired about it, he would ask them what they would do differently if they were twenty-three again. The responses, as you would imagine, included a whole host of regrets. From these interactions, he gleaned a number of life lessons that only the road could afford him—trusting strangers, seeing the good in people no matter how bad they are, and believing that people you don't know will go out of their way to give you a meal or place to stay when you are in need.

These lessons were not exclusive to him, and with two-thirds of our trip behind us, we could relate on so many levels. We didn't pack our car and hit the road with the intention to emerge with newfound wisdom. Destinations were the priority but experiences became the byproduct.

The next few days on the island were spent in good company with Mark. At our campsite, Mark taught us how to throw a knife against a tree stump, identify stinging nettles and a nearby plant used to counteract their effect, and even how to make a homemade bow and arrow out of the string from our bundle of firewood.

Later that morning, we thoroughly explored Mark's Garden of Eden Within Shangri-La. We hiked on a trail alongside Cascade Lake, which was surrounded by several bonsai-esque trees. One such tree had a rope swing attached to it, and I decided it would be a good idea to Tarzan into the lake. At the peak of the swing, though, I was too afraid to jump. In the process of sliding down, I tore my hands up with rope burn. It wasn't a pleasant experience, to say the least.

From there, we drove to the island high point, Mount Constitution, where we got an amazing vista of Mount Baker. We then escaped to the bay and hung out with crabs and starfish.

"Hey Mark, come look at this!" Curtis shouted as he wandered off trail. We had just finished our photoshoot with the sea life and were on our way back to the campsite to retire to our quarters. To get to this particular area, we had hiked about a mile downhill to the shore.

"Oh brother," I muttered under my breath, as Mark bushwhacked his way over to Curtis.

"Justin, come look!" Curtis shouted in my direction.

I decided to walk a few feet into the thick brush so that my two loons for friends were in view.

Curtis had his hands around a massive dead tree that was precariously held up by a few thin branches.

"OH NO YOU'RE NOT!" I yelled.

"WHY NOT?" Mark yelled back.

"Idiots," I mumbled.

Before I could even respond, Curtis and Mark ripped the forty-foot giant from its delicate perch and felled the tree.

"HOLY SHIT!" I shouted, more startled than I've probably ever been in my life.

The immense tree ripped through adjacent branches on its way down in the opposite direction of Curtis and Mark. It crashed as loudly as if a bulldozer had just decimated a forest.

"YOU GUYS ARE MORONS!" I shouted. Mark and Curtis were laughing hysterically at their dastardly deed.

"Life's short, fell a tree!" Mark yipped as he and Curtis sauntered back to the trail in front of me.

To cap off our day of questionable decisions, we created a makeshift Ouija board and talked to a woman named Ava who died in 1927 in Leningrad because she was having an affair with a man named Vladimir.

The next morning, I rolled out of the car, still angry about listening to Mark snore all night. To make amends, he introduced us to Tim's Cascade jalapeño potato chips, which were just as good as they sound. We sadly left him back in Seattle later that day, content with our direction as of late, but still craving more mountains despite our recent success on Rainier. Mount Baker seemed like the ideal glaciated giant to conquer. But the mountain gods put a handful of roadblocks in our way to stall our attempt from the get-go.

Mount Baker is a massive peak in the North Cascades that sits majestically adjacent to Mount Shuksan, an equally enormous and highly photogenic peak. Known to the indigenous people of the Pacific Northwest as "Koma Kulshan" or "Kulshan," (roughly translated to, "White Sentinel" or "puncture wounds") Baker was first discovered by colonists in the late eighteenth century. It is, of course, one of the most heavily glaciated peaks in the lower forty-eight states. With an annual snowfall of approximately fifty-seven feet a year, Baker is a snowy giant that just begs to be climbed. What better way to follow up Rainier than to add to our brief climbing resume with another volcanic, arctic mammoth.

We found ourselves in Glacier, Washington, a few hours after dropping Mark off and leaving Seattle. Along the way, we saw trees, trees, and more trees. In Glacier, we parked our car downtown, where there was an emergency services building, a gas station, and the town watering hole, which was our destination. We hoped to obtain some beta on Mount Baker, but instead we came out with the realization that it is indeed a small world, after all.

Both of the waitresses hailed from the East Coast, one from Vermont and the other Plymouth, New Hampshire—one of the first towns in the White Mountains, and a place I spend most of my nights prior to any of my hiking adventures. As for the girl from Vermont, her dad went to my high school many moons ago. How these two women ended up in Glacier is your typical "I'm sick of this place, get me out of here" narrative. We were not exactly sure how they selected Glacier, but to each their own, I suppose.

Our new friends gave us advice for what we could do the next day, none of which included an ascent of Mount Baker. They warned us that the road to the trailhead was still closed, despite it being nearly mid-July. Our summit fever was on hold in the interim.

The next morning, we understood why the waitresses cautioned us. We drove up to a mountain viewpoint where we were graced with snowy walls over fifteen feet tall at the top parking lot. One wall completely engulfed the parking lot bathroom, which inevitably led to several dissatisfied tourists who had also made the drive to the top. Turning snow yellow was our specialty, so we couldn't have cared less, but some people just didn't get the memo, and one man was so angry that he attempted to dig out the port-o-potty while frantically screaming like a maniac.

"WHY THE HELL DON'T THESE PEOPLE DO SOMETHING!? I'M A TAXPAYER FOR GOD SAKES!!!"

His embarrassed wife began to walk in the other direction, presumably hoping that no one would know that they were related.

"Reminds me of that woman from the Grand Canyon," I whispered to Curtis.

"Maybe worse." He chuckled, as he zipped his fly.

"There's plenty of white snow over here for the squatting."

Modern plumbing can turn people crazy; I tell you. Sometimes I think it's an American thing. But if Canada had anything to say, well, they're just as insane as we are—in their own Canadian way.

* * *

Crossing the border for the first time was like an out-of-body experience. Well, an out-of-car one, at least. No one really knows what the border patrol people do in their spare time, but most of it probably includes sharpening up their death stares and practicing the art of the rhetorical question. The Canadian agents do their best to sound as Canadian as possible to remind you that you are indeed crossing an imaginary border into an entirely different country.

"What's in the trunk, eh?"

"Oh, well we made a homemade bow and arrow while we were camping the other day," Curtis said.

Out of all the obscure items that littered our smelly car, he had to bring up the homemade weapon we made to fend off grizzly bears and marmots who decided to get too close.

"Sorey fellas, but you've gotta pull up your vehicle over there." He pointed to a parking lot just over the border and had one of his cronies follow us.

"Unlock the doors please. Give me your passports. Go sit in there while you wait." He pointed to a waiting room area that looked more like purgatory.

We took our seats across the counter from a menacing looking border patrol agent with an imposing moustache. Everyone at the border probably figured we were smuggling drugs or harboring fugitives in our tire storage space. No innocent people would be crossing the border with a shithole of a car like ours unless they were up to no good.

We twiddled our thumbs and tapped our feet while we waited for the bad news. If this was the end of the line, well, so be it. We had a good run. But then I remembered: we hadn't had poutine yet. God almighty, if you hear our pleas, just give us this one last chance to stuff ourselves with French fries, cheese curds, copious amounts of meat, and gravy, and we'll voluntarily turn ourselves in for whatever deeds we may have done afterward.

As if our prayers were heard, an agent barged into the waiting room with our passports and our final judgment. He went over to the mustached man behind the counter and began loudly whispering something in French. He turned around and started to strut over toward us with as stern a face as you would expect from a border patrol agent. Yep, we were doomed.

"Curtis, Justin," he barked.

We flung ourselves out of the chairs and stood up as straight as arrows.

"Yes sir," Curtis nervously said, as if he was answering to his sergeant.

The agent handed us our passports and gave us a big grin.

"Welcome to Canada! Enjoy your stay."

"Oh, Mercy!" I remarked. "I mean, merci!"

After years of indomitable yearning, we had finally done it. We had crossed the border into the promised land. Hans and Francine would have been so proud.

* * *

Kilometers? Liters? Tim Hortons!? Where the hell were we?

"I thought people here drove on the left side of the road," I stated, obliviously.

"That's only in Europe and some other countries." Curtis quickly dispelled my ignorant theory.

We made it to Vancouver after about an hour and a half drive from the border and I was struggling to get used to my foreign surroundings. It was my first time out of the country, and it was oh so apparent.

"I owe you a loonie."

"What's a loonie?" I quizzed the clerk at Little Caesers as I exchanged money for a pizza. At least they had some familiar places.

"Sorey, you must be an American. It's a dollar coin. The toonie is a two-dollar coin. Clever, eh?" He handed me a loonie and a couple quarters back.

"Hey, wait a second!" I exclaimed. "You owe me two pennies!"

"We don't have pennies anymore. They started getting rid of them earlier this year."

I gave him a death stare much like the one our border patrol friends had given me earlier in the day.

I decided it wasn't worth my effort to fight over two cents, but I couldn't help but think to myself, what kind of drugs were these people on that would compel them to eliminate the penny? First, they came for the pennies, and I was silent. What would they come for next?

I forgot all about my present dilemma not two minutes later, when Curtis and I trotted toward the adjacent 7-Eleven and a ragged-looking guy told us they were handing out free slurpees in honor of July 11th.

"This is my third one today," the man stated. He was wearing a dirty Nirvana shirt and tattered jeans and had a greasy, disheveled brown hair.

We heeded the stranger's advice and came back out to thank him.

"Any time, boys. I noticed you were from Massachusetts. I went to school out there for a little bit before dropping out. The name's Moses."

We chatted for a few minutes with Moses, telling him this was our first time in Canada. He certainly didn't look like a Moses, but it seemed like he had a good heart. Which is why we hesitantly accepted his offer to go "hang out" at his place.

"Why did we agree to this again?" I whispered to Curtis, as we followed Moses across the street in our car to his apartment complex. As soon as we parked and got out of the car, he broke us some positive news.

"I hope that rooftop carrier is locked. We've had a lot of daytime car break-ins lately."

"Oh great," I muttered under my breath.

He led us into a dumpy apartment that smelled like death. Lo and behold, as soon as we crossed through the kitchen and into the living room, a man of indiscernible age was lying in bed, unconscious, with a lit cigarette in an ashtray lying on his stomach.

"DONNY! YOU'RE GONNA BURN THE FUCKING HOUSE DOWN."

Donny remained unresponsive despite Moses's angry outburst. It was hard to tell whether he was on his way to the morgue or he did a damn good job emulating a corpse.

"Is he gonna be okay?" Curtis asked.

"Oh sure, he'll be alright." Moses went over to the kitchen and filled a glass of water. He walked back over to Donny's seemingly lifeless body and dumped the water directly onto his face. His posture remained unchanged.

"Is he dead?" I asked, nervously.

"Naw, he gets like this every once and a while."

I glanced at Donny's stomach for any sort of movement. He seemed to be breathing, to my relief. Last thing we wanted to do was be part of a police investigation during our first day in Canada.

"Let's just head over to the kitchen, don't worry about him."

I had never seen a man die before, but today seemed like as good a day as any. All because I wanted a free slurpee.

Moses put on some 90s alt-rock to ease the mood. Something about listening to Pearl Jam's "Alive" just seemed so fitting.

Curtis attempted to divert our attention from our impending court summons to a more pleasant subject.

"So how did you end up in Vancouver, Moses?"

"Well, that's a long story, really." He lit up a smoke and reclined back in his chair. "After I dropped out, I hopped from place to place. Thailand, Hungary, Ontario, Florida, Massachusetts, you name it, I lived there. When my pops died, I packed my bags and headed for Budapest. Married a pretty girl and settled down a few years."

"That's really cool, I've always wanted to go to Budapest," Curtis said. How could he socialize at a dire time like this?

"You boys want to get another slurpee?"

"Absolutely!" I exclaimed. We finally had our exit strategy.

"Shouldn't you check on Donny?" Curtis asked.

Heeding Curtis's advice, Moses walked back over to Donny and gave him a good shake. In an unexpected turn of events, Donny began to cough, but it further affirmed the fact that this man was in horrible shape.

"What's wrong with him?" I asked.

"Oh, he'll be fine, I told ya. He smokes like a chimney. Hey, Donny, this is Justin and Curtis."

Donny gently lifted his frail face toward us.

"WHO?" He followed up his question with a nasty cough.

"Oh, don't worry about it," Moses replied.

Before Donny could worry, my hand was on the doorknob.

"Free slurpees, anyone?"

* * *

If our encounters at the border and with Moses and Donny weren't bizarre enough, my first day outside of America was about to get even more wild.

Much like Talia was able to get us a place to stay with Tom, Abby was also able to make a few phone calls and get us a place to stay in Vancouver with a girl named Elise. She had recently moved out from Toronto to, in her words, "try and make something happen." She worked as a card dealer at the local casino, often working as late as 4 a.m., and seldom went to bed before six.

We offered to pick Elise up at work at the fairly reasonable hour of 8:30 p.m. Not even two minutes into our car ride, she asked us if we wanted to go to her friend's birthday party. Curtis happily obliged, and I hesitantly acquiesced, as always.

Not long thereafter, we rolled up into a suburban neighborhood that looked pleasant enough. Maybe this would be the moment when Canada finally became normal. We were greeted at the door by Leah and John, two twenty-something-year-old siblings who resided at the house. We had barely been introduced when John asked us if we wanted to see "the stain."

"Oh, come on, Johnny. Why do you have to do this with every guest?"

"Calm down, Leah!" He yelled back at her, as we followed him into one of the bedrooms. It was a total cesspool, much like my car. It was clear that no one had done any upkeep in months.

John snickered as he headed toward the back of the room. He lifted a carpet only slightly, turning around right before he unveiled the big surprise of the evening.

"Are you ready?"

Curtis and I looked at each other and we shrugged our shoulders in agreement.

John unveiled his surprise, pulling the rug out to reveal a heinous looking black stain. It was shaped like a human silhouette. Turns out, it was, in fact, a human silhouette.

"What is this, a crime scene?" Curtis joked.

The smell was horrendous, and I could only stand it for a few seconds before my shirt was over my face.

"Oh no, we didn't kill him," John remarked, as if to allude that someone did.

"Blood money?" Curtis continued with the joke, not yet realizing that it wasn't.

Leah rushed into the room in a panic and walked directly toward John, slapping his hand down so the rug returned to its previous spot.

"What did I tell you?"

"Alright! Alright!" John replied as he rubbed his now reddened right hand.

As Leah stormed toward us, we retreated from the room, not wanting to cause any more animosity. Who the hell were these people?

It was at that point that the mumblings began among our hosts. What did they have planned for us? Leah and John retreated into the basement, presumably to mull ideas about our fate. With so many close calls already, our mortality seemed like a foregone conclusion.

Another guest at the house, Hal, confronted us as we started munching on the poutine pizza that had just been delivered, a perfect decoy while the murder weapons were sharpened downstairs. At least we would elapse with a belly full of unpasteurized goodness.

"You guys know that's a real stain, right?

Curtis and I both looked at each other in bewilderment. Or wonder. Or disgust. Maybe all three.

"For real?" Curtis asked.

Blood money. No question.

"They're basically house sitting for their great uncle who used to own this place."

"Uh, what happened?"

"He had a massive heart attack and just collapsed in that bedroom. No one found him for over two weeks. He just started decomposing. Freaky shit, eh?"

Phew, we thought to ourselves. Maybe we'd make it out alright after all. Can't say the same thing about their great uncle though. Poor guy. His life investment was going to go down the shitter not even a few months after he passed away. Well, that's the thought I had later that night when the calamity commenced. At least there was one slice of pizza left.

We had ice cream cake for breakfast the next morning and played video games with Hal until 1 p.m., when Elise decided to roll out of bed and take us to a local nude beach, because Canada.

Not much more needs to be said about our adventures in Vancouver. Curtis and I needlessly fought with each other about staying another two nights in town, but I was over it. It was time to go back to the mountains.

Chapter 14

*"The alpinist is attracted to the high peaks, compelled
by the opportunity to grow in the face of adversity and
by the uncertainty of success. For some, the reward lies
in the fulfillment of childhood dreams, for others who
venture into these wild places, the power of the mountains stirs the imagination."*

—On alpinism, from the Grand Teton National Park
Visitor's Center

* * *

"Don't waste your time in the Canadian Rockies," the sign read,
a fitting double entendre only understood by those who have actually "wasted their time" there.

We found ourselves at the visitor's center for Mount Robson
Provincial Park, but not before an action-packed eight-hour drive
until three in the morning in a downpour through windy backroads
with abundant deer-in-the-headlights moments. Let's just say if it
wasn't for Red Bull, we would have been seeing red.

Our near-death experiences were nothing compared to our bank
accounts'. On average, it cost sixty to seventy U.S. dollars to fill our
gas tank in Canada. During this particular summer, the conversion
rate favored the Canadian dollar, and our college savings were bearing the brunt of it. But if you saw Mount Robson, if you laid just one
eye on it—no dollar sign could emulate that experience.

Robson, or the Emperor, as I like to call it, gracefully weaves
rocky cliffs athwart ancient glaciers that form an impenetrable
shield for nearly ten thousand vertical feet to its lofty summit of

12,972 feet. Known to the Shuswap First Nations people as Yoh-hai-has-kuh, or "Mountain of the Spiral Road," it is the tallest mountain in the Canadian Rockies, and the most prominent mountain in the North American Rockies. As geologist Arthur P. Coleman describes it: "Its effect is of a monstrous wall of masonry, heavily buttressed, with a ridged roof lifting to a pyramid."

What is most impressive about it aside from its dramatic vertical relief is its elusiveness. The success rate for parties attempting to scale Robson is something like 10 percent, due to an amalgamation of its technical difficulty and the horrendous weather it sees year-round.

Our objective was not to climb it. We had neither the drive nor the experience at the time. But the Berg Lake Trail, its approach trail, was just as worthy. The Robson River, the first point of interest on our twenty-five-mile backpack, was fed directly from the glacier waters off the slopes of the mountain. It glowed a bluish-gray, reminiscent of heavily chlorinated pool water. Further along the trail we encountered Kinney Lake, which took on a somewhat darker blue than the river, and the Valley of a Thousand Falls, which, as its name suggests, contains myriad waterfalls that crash down to the valley floor. As we would soon find out, we had barely scratched the surface of the infinite beauty that resided here.

Emperor Falls was next. Aptly named, the falls fantastically tumble several times over, raging toward the comparatively slow Robson River below. The first level of water smashes against rocks and produces a large outcropping of white water and spray. One might call it the Emperor's Hand. Not even the Emperor, though, could prepare us for what would come next.

Just prior to arriving at Berg Lake proper, divinity ensued. As we meandered along a flat portion of trail that hugged the imposing canyon walls to our left, our eyes became fixated on the most inspiring vista of our lives to date. The walls to our left, likely carved by ancient glaciers, were flanked by icy, soaring monoliths. To our right, the familiar Robson River gently snaked through a vale shaped by a larger tributary long ago. It glowed a prismatic glow, a brilliant foreground for the best sight of them all: The Emperor, an obelisk that pierces the sky, uninterrupted, resembling a natural pyramid. It commands the entire valley below, occupied by a massive army of glaciers, bursting outward, as if to shield their Emperor from peril. To remind all observers of their subservience, the Emperor put on its wispy crown, allowing a cloud to sit atop its apex. It was a spectacle reserved only for us, and we graciously accepted our reservation.

We strutted along, unable to take our eyes off our new Garden of Eden Within Shangri-La. Sorry Mark, but this was the real deal. And our opinion was further bolstered as we reached Berg Lake and saw the cleanest, most pristine, turquoise water. The lake was supplied with fresh ice melt from Robson's immense glaciers. You can only imagine how elated we were when we set up our tent next to the lake and closed our eyes in paradise.

* * *

For some bizarre reason unbeknown to us, we find ourselves lost quite often. Whether deliberately, by mistake, or a combination of the two, we consistently end up in dire predicaments. Think Engineer's Path and Longs Peak, to name a few.

Waking up in the Garden of Eden Within Shangri-La, we readied ourselves for the day, stopping to eat breakfast on a log conveniently placed along the lakeshore. The water soaked in the mountain, reflecting an impeccable emulation of the pyramidal massif above.

After thoroughly exhausting all the beauty around us, the wow factor began to fade away a little bit and we knew it was time to depart. As we scurried back down the trail, Curtis saw a steep slope below the foot of Robson's glaciers to our left.

"I bet you a million bucks there's another lake over that hill," he said, determined to find out.

"Seriously?" I said, impatiently. "I'll meet you at the car."

I watched Curtis cross the Robson River as I angrily chugged along the trail. I saw him nearly take a dive on at least three occasions and chuckled to myself.

After finally crossing the river, he began to scamper up a crumbly talus field until he disappeared.

"This was a bad idea," I mumbled to myself. What if he got lost? No one would know where he was. His corpse would be unlocatable.

Second thoughts began to rush through my head. Do I head back to the car without him? Or do I follow him into the abyss of the great unknown?

"Screw it."

I rolled up my pants just a smidge and began my descent into the Robson River. Contrary to our initial belief, it wasn't as still as it looked. I had to plant my feet with every step I took, lest I get knocked over and swept away downstream.

At some point, the river became a complex series of conjoining streams. I was knee deep in the water, and crossing became no simple task. Bundles of sticks became my best friend, and I thanked whatever creature had the foresight to dam the river.

Not long thereafter, I came to the foot of the crumbly hill that Curtis had disappeared over. It was at this point that I began to frantically blow the whistle on my backpack like a madman. I blew so forcefully that I was out of breath not long after I started. My efforts were futile though, as the current drowned out all my pleas.

It was at that point I decided I had no other choice but to climb up the talus field and see if I could spot Curtis. I half expected to be sucked into a deadly wormhole as soon as I reached the pinnacle, but much to my satisfaction, I was greeted with more surprises.

Below me, an unexpectedly massive body of glacier water resided, unscathed and unseen by the prying passersby on the trail. Based on the sheer amount of effort required to even reach this lake, it's unlikely that many people have ever seen it in the flesh. Its solitude made it a sight even more Edenic than the formerly proclaimed Garden of Eden Within Shangri-La. The glaciers that we had seen from a distance before were now up close and personal. A smattering of waterfalls sprinkled untapped resources that have likely only started to seep in the last hundred years or so. Of course, I thought nothing of it at the time. I was too wrapped up in the fact that Curtis was nowhere to be found.

Well, now we were in trouble. What if Curtis had fallen into a crevasse while exploring the glaciers? No, he's not that stupid—but he could have easily drowned in the lake. Never mind. His body would have been floating by now. Maybe he decided that the city life was no longer his thing and decided to peace out into the wilderness? And forego paying off college debt? Yeah, right. There was only one explanation left. A grizzly bear had eaten him. That couldn't be right either—I would have already spotted his half-eaten rotting corpse nearby.

But alas, one farfetched, albeit perfectly logical explanation remained. The lake had to have swallowed him. Whole. Like in the movies when you see a whirlpool converge upon a helpless individual and proceed to spin them from the outside in, until the aqua tornado pulls them straight to the middle and there's nothing left but a calm body of water. That had to be it. Poseidon was pissed off that someone had disturbed him in his secluded lake and as a form of punishment, he unleashed his wrath upon an innocent Curtis, turquoise trident in hand, flowing serpents protruding from his skull.

About fifteen minutes after conceiving this perfectly sane explanation, I found myself back on the trail. Curtis had left his backpack when he decided to skirt up to the hidden lake, but now it was gone. As fate would have it, a hiker coming up toward Berg Lake strolled onto the scene.

"Are you Justin?"

Welp. I was done for.

"That's me," I nervously stated.

"Your friend Curtis is about ten minutes down the trail."

All's well that ends well, I suppose.

* * *

We used to visit the local middle school on warm summer nights with the whole crew during our college summers. Lisa, the soft-spoken coordinator of our group, had assembled a list of her favorite adventure spots in the state, and wanted nothing more than to share them with her good friends. Atop the list was a hastily scratched insignia that bore resemblance to the roof of a house:

Λ

But this didn't symbolize any house—it was sacred government property, an institution dedicated to the transmission of the knowledge of our elders to the future generations who were supposed to mend the problems that their forebears could not alleviate. You could say that this was our conscious affront to all that our upbringing stood for.

You would be wrong.

We were just bored.

I fondly remember the first time that I ascended the drainpipe to the pinnacle of the school and looked down at Suburbia below. It will forever be etched in my mind—an exhilarating effort that got me thinking. Well sure, it was fun to be a bad-ass and climb to the top of a school roof, but what do we climb next?

* * *

Disclaimer: Don't try this at home.

"Dorian, you're on belay!"

Curtis's voice echoed along the narrow corridor leading toward the summit of the Grand Teton. It was his first time trad climbing, but you wouldn't have presumed it based on his tranquil composure while ascending the classic Upper Exum Route. The Upper Exum Ridge Route is a 1,700-foot climb with twelve pitches of climbing graded at 5.5 YDS (Yosemite Decimal System). The roughly 5,300-foot vertical approach is arduous, but the climbing is among the best in the country at the grade. For perspective, a 5.5 is typically seen as an easy climb on the scale. But for us, it would be all but easy.

It was evident that we were in over our heads, but we hadn't realized it at that time. Two idiots, wet behind the ears, attempting a technical route with no technical skills. Our only saving grace was Dorian, a fifty-three-year-old chain-smoker who once graced the covers of climbing magazines in the eighties. At least that's what he told us.

Prior to finding ourselves suspended from a cliff, we had driven through Alberta's Jasper and Banff National Parks, hung out with bighorn sheep and mountain goats at Glacier National Park in Montana, explored the geysers of Yellowstone, and trotted into the Tetons.

The Tetons are an aesthetic, rugged mountain range adjacent to Yellowstone National Park that abruptly springs above Jackson Hole. Once called Teewinot, or "many pinnacles," by the local Shoshone people, their modern name derives from early French explorers, who thought they looked like breasts.

In all seriousness though, what were we doing at the foot of the first pitch, or section, of the technical crux of the Grand Teton, aptly named Wall Street? Investing in our future—albeit at the expense of potentially not having one. We were losing our "real mountain" virginity in the foolhardiest of ways. Without knowledge about how to use protection.

Sparing you as much detail as possible, in climber parlance, protection refers to the mechanism by which you protect yourself if you fall while climbing, hence why it's called protection. If you are sport climbing, you use fixed bolts, clipping onto them as you go with a quickdraw carabiner. The same process goes for traditional climbing; however, instead of using fixed bolts, you place your own equipment: cams, nuts, hexes, tri-cams, and so forth. What separates you from your early grave is your ability to safely squeeze these apparatuses into small cracks in the wall. And until we found ourselves dumbfoundedly staring at Wall Street, some 12,800 feet above sea level, we had yet to put our gear-placement skills to test.

Dorian may or may not have known this small little detail at the time, but it became wholly apparent when we let him take the lead for the first few pitches, reluctant to expose ourselves to the prospect of falling off a two-thousand-foot cliff. That is, until Curtis volunteered to take one of the earlier pitches of the climb—The Wind Tunnel.

"YOU'RE HAULIN' BOTH OF US UP CURTIS!" Morris shouted in a thick Southern accent, unable to reach our fearless leader.

"WHAT?"

Although Curtis couldn't hear us, we heard him loud and clear. Surely, the name of this pitch was no irony.

"BOTH ROPES!"

I wondered if he knew what he was doing. I sure didn't. His responsibility was simple yet challenging. He needed to get us up to where he had climbed to without dropping us if we fell. But to do so, he needed some sort of an anchor system at the top to belay us from. Many people who climb outdoors do so on a fixed anchor that was built directly above their route. Once assembled, the rope is fed through the anchor so that the climber is belayed from the bottom of the route, and subsequently lowered to the ground when they've finished it. On the contrary, trad climbers on multi-pitch routes must belay from the top after they have led a pitch.

"OKAY, YOU'RE ON BELAY JUSTIN!"

I was entirely unrelieved by this proclamation, but I assured myself that it was easy climbing and I didn't have anything to worry about. Dorian climbed ahead of me, while I followed shortly thereafter.

With each vertical movement came relief, yet the higher I went, the more fatal a fall would have been if Curtis had indeed done something wrong. I wasn't going to wait to find out. I climbed out of fear, yet confidence quickly bloomed after each movement upward. My motions lacked method; they were born out of survival instinct. I clung to those rocks for dear life, petrified by the thought of what lay below. And when I finally reached Curtis and Dorian above, relief swept over me. For now, at least.

"Good job there, buddy," Dorian remarked, as he took a drag from his cigarette. It was his fourth that day, yet he had the stamina of an ox. Pernicious habits sometimes do yield paradoxical results.

Curtis and Dorian took the next few leads, and the higher we went, the more poised I became. I was ready for my first trad lead: 13,500 feet above sea level.

"You sure you got this?" Curtis asked, as he removed his rack of gear from his chest to hand off to me.

"I think so," I replied, anxious, yet simultaneously convinced that I was fated to lead my fellow comrades to victory.

"Well, it looks to me like we might be off-route," Dorian said, as he looked at a photo of the Upper Exum Route on Curtis's phone.

"What do you mean, off-route?" I asked nervously.

"I mean I don't know where we are. I don't remember this part of the climb."

The wind picked up. Or maybe it didn't. But for dramatic effect, let's say it did.

What I can tell you, though, with certainty is that we were running out of daylight, fast. Although we began our ascent from high camp at 5 a.m., we were understandably progressing about as fast as a pair of newbie climbers and a middle-aged smoker typically would. It was almost 6 p.m., and the sun was due to set in just over an hour. We were out of lifelines. This was closing time—and the moon made sure we understood this. It stared at us from afar, waiting to rise higher.

Dorian scrambled around for a few minutes looking for the path of least resistance toward the summit. He was convinced that we were in trouble, but Curtis reassured us all when he found a faint boot path over to the last true pitch of the climb. It appeared to traverse along an extremely exposed section where a fall would indeed be death-inducing. Fittingly, they saved me the best for last.

I begrudgingly looked back at my partners as I proceeded onward through the sedimentary jungle of the Grand's uppermost ridge.

"I don't like the looks of this," I yelled back, as I neared the first vertical section.

"You'll be fine!" Dorian convinced me, pocketing the remnants of his butt in true conservationist fashion.

I spent a good five minutes in a struggle with the hastily placed sling of equipment that rested on my shoulder. Something like a hundred pieces of gear were clipped to the sling in a manner that made no sense to the layperson. In this case, I was the layperson.

After what seemed like a lifetime of *hmm*s, I removed a cam from my rack and abrasively shoved it into the crack nearest to my face. Cams are spring-loaded device that climbers use to protect their falls. You pull back on the lever and insert the device into a crack in the wall. When you release the mechanism, it locks in the wall, and in theory should only come out when you pull back on the lever again.

I wiggled and wiggled it until I was at least 50 percent confident that it wouldn't dislodge. To my satisfaction and, equally, my fortune, it would be the first and only piece of gear that I would place, because the remainder of the route was easy rock scrambling. But one impasse lingered before we could stand on the summit.

"SHIT!" I yelled to an empty audience.

I was so caught up in the anticipation of leading my first climb that I forgot that I lacked an essential skill—the omission of which could have spelled doom for any other gumby. At the time, I didn't know how to belay my partners from the top.

Without the requisite knowledge, I was strapped for options. I searched for a boulder large enough to wrap both ropes around and use as a natural anchor—but there would be a lot more rope drag, or resistance, and effort on my part to keep them secure. A few minutes later, I spotted an unusually large boulder next to a snowfield.

I rigged an impromptu belay system on the boulder so if anyone fell, the boulder would catch them as long as I didn't let go of the rope. But it became apparent when I started to belay them that their lives were actually in my hands. You know, like literally *in* my hands.

My body trembled as I held on tight to both ropes with both hands and started pulling the slack in. Because it was near impossible to communicate with the guys, I pulled as hard as I could until they knew it was time to climb. By my estimation, they were up standing next to me within six and a half minutes, without having broken a sweat. On the contrary, I never pulled something harder in my life. The friction was inexplicable—and by the end of it all, I was drained.

"Christ, Justin, do you have any idea how to belay?" Dorian remarked, as he removed a cigarette from his pocket.

"Of course!" I fibbed. They both made it up alive—that's what counts, right?

Thankfully, he forgot all about it soon thereafter.

"Eitheruh you gotta light?"

"I've got some matches in my bag," Curtis said.

"Give it here."

"It's in my bag at base camp," he clarified.

"Well shit. Guess we're runnin' outta daylight anyway. Might be time to git goin'."

Indeed, daylight was fleeting. We would be lucky if we made it off the summit before the sun set. Thankfully, the last portion of the climb was a short traverse over a snowfield and a brief scramble to the summit. It wasn't until I got a moment to breathe at the Grand's pinnacle that I bothered to stop and soak in the scenery around us.

Vibrant hues of orange and purple painted the sky, a canvas that could only be recreated in the backdrop of Big Wyoming. It was a sight for sore eyes, and believe me, our eyes were sore. We had been climbing for fourteen hours and keeping focused became a struggle. But despite our deteriorating physical and mental well-being, something clicked into place in that very moment that allowed our weariness to temporarily escape in favor of a rejuvenated outlook. It was getting really, *really* dark out.

"No time to be standin' around here, gentlemen, let's get our asses movin'!" Dorian was quick to announce, as if we hadn't come to the realization ourselves.

We began to scamper down the precarious ledges that led to the rappel station off the summit. Appropriately, we had no clue how to rappel at the time, so Dorian gave us the brief run-through.

"Now if ya die, I'm not gonna rescue you, ahlright? We'll get them rangers to come up and get your dumb asses on a helicopter."

"I'm pretty sure if we die, we won't care who rescues us, since we're already dead," Curtis snickered. Notwithstanding the fact that our immediate fate was uncertain, a somewhat mild temperament filled the air. What a motley crew we were.

When we reached the rappel station, Dorian had to tie both of our ropes together and run them through the existing anchor. Therein lies an important consideration for all climbers: to trust or not to trust the anchor. Many climbers opt to build their own anchor rather than use old wind-, rain-, and sun-worn webbing. But it appeared as if the existing apparatus was in good enough standing that Dorian placed all his trust in it. He was to oversee us while we prepared to rappel, which proved to be a more daunting task than he envisioned.

I was first to go. I secured my belay device to my harness and began my descent. As I looked down, I saw nothing but air. The drop is only about 120 feet, but it felt more like a football field. I could see endzone to endzone, but the pylons were barely distinguishable from inside my own ten-yard line, down four points. It was touchdown or bust.

On the first play, I picked up huge chunks of yardage. I bounced off the wall in front of me, giving my feet the false sense of security that the ground was closer than I thought. Second down reminded me that this was far from the case. At some point, the wall gave way to more open air, and I almost smashed my noggin against the roof of the overhang. Despite being nearly beheaded, I was able to scramble for a few yards.

Third down proved to be disastrous. As I sat back in the pocket, I saw a defender charging at me like a bullet, and a well-timed expletive followed.

"SHIT!"

Curtis's apprehensive voice sent an icy chill down my spine. I was sure that a part of the anchor had snapped off and I was seconds away from being eaten alive by the ground below me.

An object no larger than my hand whooshed past me and careened its way into oblivion. I lost sight of it as it made its final leap of faith off a thousand-foot cliff.

"WHAT THE HELL WAS THAT?" I shouted up at the belay station.

"My belay device," he responded, barely audible.

While I converted on fourth down and made it to the bottom unscathed, we still had eighty yards to go. And I wasn't too confident with our prospect of prevailing. It wasn't until that moment that I finally realized we were in over our heads. Only an inexperienced climber would have no clue how to rectify such a simple dilemma.

"HEY JUSTIN! TIE YOUR BELAY DEVICE TO THE ROPE AND WE'LL RIG IT UP," Dorian shouted confidently.

"OKAY!" I yelled back, unaware of how much of an idiot I was for not thinking of that myself. Problem solved.

But we had one last hurdle to cross. After completing our rappels, it was essentially pitch black. We would have to retrace our exact steps over unstable terrain to make it back to base camp. We had no water left, nor did we have a reservation to stay another night at camp. Fortune favors the bold though, right?

* * *

Remember when you were a kid and your mom was always on your case about drinking fluids when you were outside all day in the hot sun? Meanwhile, she was already on her sixth cup of coffee for the day and couldn't for the life of her understand why she was "so goddamn tired" or why she got splitting migraines all the time. I don't have to be the person to tell you that water is the foundation of life. Yet countless morons like us go off into the mountains with an inadequate water supply and, in turn, find ourselves in seemingly unconquerable scenarios. I need not elaborate, for there are myriad cautionary tales laid out in outdoors publications across the world that posit questions about why people die in the woods, when the answer is as simple as they ran out of water, collapsed, fell off a cliff, and died. Or something along those morbid lines.

At altitude, dehydration is even more prevalent—heavier breathing, lower humidity, and loss of appetite for food and water all contribute to hastened dehydration at higher elevations. Ultimately, it becomes more difficult to discern just how much water you really are losing because your sweat dries up rapidly in a more arid environment. So what did that mean for the trio of idiots (really, two idiots and our guide) trying to descend Grand Teton, approaching hour nineteen of their perilous journey? Delirium. Not quite on par with what we endured in the Grand Canyon, but our heads certainly weren't in the best of shape.

We made it through the hairiest sections of the descent, where we constantly found ourselves on all fours in an effort to not collapse, fall off a cliff, and die. If downclimbing nearly vertical sections wasn't hard enough, the difficulty was exacerbated by a dearth of moonlight thanks to the approaching clouds. Those wispy buggers wouldn't foil our plans to make it back to camp though, because we were just a wee bit tired of being tired.

Dim headlamps illuminated our path to safety as we scurried down a series of interminable switchbacks, our eyes finally starting to adjust to the darkness. We were sure that the parties below were preparing their tents for the evening, looking up at the forlorn figures above, and laughing to themselves, "look at those idiots," or "I *so* do not feel sorry for those morons." Their judgments, sadly, were not without some verisimilitude.

After an eternity of knee-pounding down the mountain, we spotted a structure in the distance. It had to be the ranger station on The Lower Saddle, the high camp of the Grand—which meant that we still had another fifteen hundred or so vertical feet to go before we reached our own camp. If we were going to have any chance of camping another night without consequence, we would have to pay the good ol' warden a visit.

"I've got this," Dorian said, as he knocked on the door to the building.

I found it kind of unbelievable that the ranger lived in his own little house at the highest camp in the park, but I guess that's what happens when you have dumbasses like us scaling the tallest mountain simply because it's the tallest mountain, all but ignoring the technical knowledge required along the way. It's better to have that insurance than to burden the taxpayers with our rescue.

"I reckon you were sleepin'?" Dorian asked, as a middle-aged ranger in his pajamas appeared in front of us with a quizzical expression on his face. He was short and stocky, his face weathered and tough.

"What is it?" He said somewhat angrily while he rubbed his eyes.

"Well, to make a long story short, sir, we just made it down the mountain and we've found ourselves in a bit of a pickle."

"A dill pickle?" He smiled.

I couldn't help but chuckle in my weakened state.

"We ain't got no water left—"

Curtis interjected mid-sentence.

"And we don't have a reservation to stay here another night. We weren't exactly expecting to finish this late, but we had some route-finding issues."

The ranger gave us a somewhat stern face in response, obviously annoyed that we disturbed his beauty sleep. Nevertheless, we received a favorable answer.

"Alright, no worries, as long as you're all okay? I have some extra water here. There's some more in a stream further down the glacier if you're up for the trip."

"We're up for the trip whether we like it or not," I added, as my voice trembled, an indication that my body was craving dormancy.

"Not a problem gentleman."

The courteous ranger gave us about a quart of water each, and we were on our not-so-merry way back toward camp.

* * *

Back at camp, I had no thoughts on my mind. We slept on a moraine that night, a grim preview of what our planet will one day become when the glaciers are all gone. But I didn't think too much about it at that moment. I was just happy I had a place to put my head down. I fell asleep within minutes of laying my head on a rather uncomfortable backpack. My brain stem dictated the only things I cared about in the moments leading up to my slumber. Sleep, survival, food, and water were my only concerns. I hadn't thought about law school in two and a half months. I had no reason to. Everything I ever wanted, but never expected to get, had transpired in that brief time period. All for the price of a few month's rent, an amount that I had toiled for relentlessly in my last semester, driving a van for minimum wage. And to be honest, the trip could have been done for half that, if we weren't so indulgent.

Our fairytale was coming to an inevitable end, and I was surprisingly enthusiastic about it. I missed home, my family, friends, and everything I had grown to love. I couldn't help but wonder, though, about how I was going to settle back into our deeply misguided society of greed, corruption, and vitriol.

I feared that my legal studies would lead me down a wayward path. Could I resist the ambulance-chasing mentality of some attorneys? Was I destined for a life of great opulence, maximizing billable hours, cutting corners, and taking extravagant journeys to tropical paradises? Or what? What the hell was I going to do with my life?

We had survived another day in the mountains, but at the expense of our pride. Though we didn't want that shock of a close call, it was the tremor that we *needed*. Too many times we were immersed in difficult situations that we just narrowly escaped not because of our ingenuity, but because of our good fortune. We welcomed the luck, but it wasn't realistic. And I think that we mistakenly thought it was. Ever since that fateful day in the Great Sand

Dunes, nothing could go wrong. And aside from a few minor missteps, nothing did go wrong.

But we needed something to go wrong. We needed our mortality to be tested. Not because we craved danger, but we needed a reminder from nature that we are, indeed, transient beings. Otherwise, we would remain complacent and our lives would pass by without incident. We would die as we were born, clueless and fearful. Until a human being is put in a seemingly insurmountable situation, they never think about life's fragility. I never wanted to learn the truths about life; that our deaths are as uncertain as our origins. But I had to. Otherwise I would succumb to first-world ennui, trapped and blind to the world around me. I needed the shock.

For Curtis and me, the experiences of the last few months had coalesced into our own distinct *reality*. For the next twelve months, we would bear the brunt of a merciless version of life, eventually culminating in a profound realization: the itinerant life was the sole means to achieving enlightenment in a world obscured by a diaphanous haze. The truths were self-evident. Routine was destructive; wanderlust was *reality*.

* * *

South Dakota. Minnesota. Wisconsin. Illinois. Indiana. Ohio. Pennsylvania. New York. Each state a little different, each highway sign a reminder that the end was coming near. In South Dakota, we saw Mount Rushmore, Wall Drug, and the Badlands; in Illinois, we ate deep-dish pizza; and in Indiana and New York we visited old friends. But my drive to be on the road had swiftly begun to dissipate. I was craving home in a big way, despite Curtis's insistence that adventure was still to be had elsewhere. Maybe it was the impending grip of law school; maybe homesickness. Perhaps falling asleep in department store parking lots at 5 a.m. was catching up to me. Or peanut butter and Nutella, creamed honey, or jelly sandwiches were becoming inadequate. Realistically, it was a combination of all these things. The perks of the road were endless; the amenities were unaccommodating to say the least.

For better or for worse, I guess, I was prepared to begin my new reality. Both the momentary safety net of college and the unlimited freedom of the road had collapsed into oblivion. In their place, an immense responsibility had materialized. I was going to commence my studies as a prospective lawyer. I had no idea what to expect or what the hell I was getting myself into. All I knew was that I was ready to get back into a new routine distinct from the discomforts of the road. Whether I liked it or not.

PART 2

Chapter 15

This land has been ruined by opulence, destroyed by materialists, and ravaged by harvesters. But the freedom of the high peaks has yet to be compromised. They dwell in the clouds, ice-capped and frozen in place, where man is separated from machine, pillager from conservationist. It is in these mountains that we find solace, purpose, and vitality. So long as we extract ourselves from the death grip of wealth, privilege, and entitlement, we will find ourselves equal in the eyes of our one true provider, the very earth that we wander with courage, with strength, and with grace.

* * *

The first time that I stared at death was from afar. I guess you can't even say I was looking at it. Its features were indistinguishable, inhuman even. It came in the form of an urgent email from an employee at my college during the summer between my sophomore and junior year.

To minimize my course load during my last year, I opted to take a summer class—Mountains, to be precise. The last class of the semester was that coming Saturday, and we had a simple final project: create a presentation about your favorite mountain. At the time, I had yet to discover my unending love for the hills, but one place stood out in my mind: Mount Pisgah.

When I started running track and field in high school, I was introduced to a trail system not five minutes from my childhood home. Among the local youth, it was known as the spot to get stoned. But for those looking for isolation in crowded Central

Massachusetts, it was a place to blow off steam. It wasn't until my senior year when I actually started to train for track and cross country that Pisgah became both my psychological safe-haven and my physiological battleground. Though it's a dinky hill in comparison to the peaks you find up in New Hampshire, runs at Pisgah always proved to be a challenge, with relentless inclines and rocky terrain.

But I had no idea what real mountains were until a few years later when Hans and Francine picked us up after our traumatic outing on the Franconia Ridge. That experience might never have happened if it wasn't for Lionel Sanders, though. Lionel was a photojournalist for our local newspaper for several years, documenting everything from skiing to the War in Afghanistan. He was also a lover of all things nature and, appropriately, taught the Mountains course at my college.

The email came on a Sunday, the day after the last class hike on Mount Monadnock, the second-most hiked mountain in the world, but the story begins a week before that. On our penultimate hike, Lionel brought the class to Mount Watatic in northern Massachusetts. I fondly remember that day not for its visual splendor, but for how obscure and perplexing it was.

Having hiked for five straight Saturdays with Lionel, we were accustomed to the routine of dripping sweat and listening to an informative lecture to commence the weekend. Every half-mile or so, our knowledgeable professor would describe the abundant flora and fauna along the trail. He would stop suddenly when the forest shifted from oak to pine, or maple to birch. Even the discovery of a non-human footprint would elicit a prompt statement. But on our Mount Watatic hike, he brought a mystery woman along.

"Class, this is Stephanie. Stephanie, this is everyone."

An attractive blonde woman in her late thirties or early forties gave our group of eight a wave and smile as Lionel embraced her with a hug from the side. It only made sense that she was his daughter, and Lionel didn't tell us otherwise.

Lionel was a good-looking guy himself. Even though he was in his mid-sixties or so, he was the archetype of a fit grandpa. He had gray hair and facial wrinkles, but he was built like a Colorado hard-meat. Despite his appearance, he spoke softly and intelligibly, and was as compassionate a teacher as I had ever had the privilege to learn from. Regrettably, he, like everyone else, had his vices.

Our fearless leader took the helm as we commenced our hike through a dense New England forest and quickly began to gain some elevation. The terrain spread out the group, and Stephanie stayed ahead of the pack with the more ambitious hikers.

"So, what are you all majoring in?" Stephanie asked.

"History," I said, rather unimpressively.

"Microbiology," one of my classmates said, as he struggled to catch his breath.

"What about you, Stephanie?" I awkwardly mumbled after the air had gone still.

"Well, I'm a photographer. And I love what I do."

Stephanie was pleasant and easy to talk to and clearly enthusiastic about life. She explained that she had fallen in love with hiking and the outdoors at a young age and had recently begun to dabble in nature photography. But *who* she was remained enigmatic.

Lionel and the others were still a ways behind us, so we caught a break at a trail junction where we weren't quite sure where to go next.

"Lionel must be a proud father," my mouth-breathing classmate said, huffing and puffing.

"Oh, he's not my father," Stephanie laughed hysterically.

What was so funny? Unfortunately, our curiosity was only intensified, as Lionel and the crew began to roll in just as Mouth Breather was about to ask an ill-timed follow-up question.

"Hey there, speed demons," Lionel proclaimed. "I was just telling your classmates about the different variations of hardwood trees that we walked by on the way up. I'm going to have to fail you both for missing the day's lesson." He chuckled.

Mouth Breather started to panic.

"He can't do that!" He whispered to me.

"Oh, but he can," I quipped.

His face turned red and he scampered to the back of the group.

"Is everyone ready for the steep ascent?" Lionel inquired.

We all nodded in approval, some more emphatically than others. I could tell that Mouth Breather wasn't the only one having a hard time; most other people were sweating bullets. As we prepared to continue upward, Stephanie took a few steps down the other way. She motioned to Lionel, who made his way over to her. He gave her a kiss on the lips and they smiled at each other before she began to descend the trail.

"Where's she going?" Mouth Breather asked.

Lionel waved at her and waited for her to be out of sight "She's gotta go to her kids' baseball game. Hope you all liked her!"

I looked at one of my classmates, Jen, whom I went to high school with but had only recently befriended. We gave each other quizzical looks and shrugged our shoulders. I didn't really give it any more thought that day, and we were well on our way up the mountain soon thereafter.

* * *

The first person I called after I received the email was Jen. I needed to talk to someone who would empathize. I was having a hard time grasping its contents.

"How could he have done that? I just don't understand." Her voice rattled as it came through the earpiece.

"I don't know. I really don't." I replied, softly.

Just the day before, our class had successfully hiked Mount Monadnock. After a quick debrief in the parking lot and an explanation of our final project, we'd all gone our separate ways. I was the last student who saw Lionel that day. After leaving Monadnock State Park, I waved goodbye to him at a stoplight. I went left. He went straight. It was the last time I would ever see him.

Lionel Sanders took his own life later that night. The details, to this day, remain vague and unclear. But it was the first time that a person close to me had passed away during my adult life. And it hit me hard.

"I haven't seen the email yet, what did it say?" Jen asked.

"Nothing really, just that he passed away. Haven't you seen the news article?"

"No. I'm just hearing about this for the first time. This is just insane." She sounded as if she had just seen a ghost.

On the evening after our hike, Lionel got into a scuffle with Stephanie's husband at their family home. Contrary to our initial belief, Stephanie was not Lionel's daughter, but his lover. The cause of the dispute was never disclosed to the public, but Lionel allegedly attempted to drown her husband in the pool and bashed him on the head with a cinder block. How such a gentle and soft-spoken man could commit such an act is an unanswerable question. There was some suspicion that Stephanie herself conspired with Lionel to murder her husband; the preliminary evidence showed that Stephanie called the police once, hung up and then called again to report an attack on her husband. Who knows what her intent was that night. Nonetheless, the whole situation continues to perplex me as the years continue to pass. We may never truly know what happened.

After the purported attack, the police were en route to the house, and Lionel fled the scene in his car. A high-speed chase ensued, leading to one of the highest bridges in Massachusetts. Despite pleas from the police to stop, Lionel flung himself off the fifty-foot section of the bridge. He presumably perished on impact with the ground. It was a tragic end to an otherwise storied life. Coincidentally, beneath that bridge is one of the most scenic rail trails in New England, which I continue to run on to this day. And never a run goes by without remembering Lionel, and his substantial influence on me.

What died with Lionel that day has evolved into something bigger than he could have ever envisioned. His love for the mountains and zest for life inspired me to seek out the solace of the hills to absolve myself of the great apathy of college living. Mountains became my therapy because Lionel instilled those lessons in me. He gave me a reason to love them too. Just one month after his death, I found myself near hypothermic on Franconia Ridge—and only two years after that, atop Mount Rainier, still as clueless as when I began my obsession. To this day, my love for the high peaks has not faltered, and I doubt it ever will.

But Lionel—what happened to Lionel? Had his love for the mountains lost its meaning because he could not find it elsewhere? Is it love that keeps us going through life, and did he die because he no longer loved or was loved? I will never discover the answers to those questions. Nor will I ever be able to thank him for the seed he planted. But I will continue to harvest its fruits, from now until forever.

Chapter 16

"A human being is a part of the whole called by us universe, a part limited in time and space. He experiences himself, his thoughts and feeling as something separated from the rest, a kind of optical delusion of his consciousness. This delusion is a kind of prison for us, restricting us to our personal desires and to affection for a few persons nearest to us. Our task must be to free ourselves from this prison by widening our circle of compassion to embrace all living creatures and the whole of nature in its beauty."

—Albert Einstein

* * *

Why did we desire to leave? What was so unfulfilling about our lives that it provoked us to stuff Mindy with all our belongings and take off westward? It was as if we wanted to live like we were impoverished, deprived of a roof over our head every night. We seemingly romanticized a life devoid of commodities, pontificating that it would be far better than the depression and anxiety that stemmed from our privileged lives. We were fed, cleaned, clothed, housed, and educated. And yet, we were devoid of struggle, devoid of strife, devoid of desire. We were missing a key element in our lives that could only be satisfied by a monumental alteration to our familiar privilege.

Truly, I worried about finding meaning in my life so much that I drove myself to search for more. I was not simply content with the life of a spectator anymore. The onerous routine of procrastinating, doing the bare minimum, and taking the easy way out was no longer rewarding. I wanted to challenge my instincts and my ambition. What better way to do that than to live in your car for nearly two and a half months? Or something like that.

When I left college, I felt as if I had been trapped in a bubble for four years. The endless weekend nights in my room wondering why I didn't have the courage to socialize. The anxiety about arbitrary letters and numbers on my transcript. The complete disregard for the poverty and gentrification that surrounded my campus, and the naïve belief in its reputation as a "bad neighborhood." All of this and more contributed to my desire to do something unique, to take to the road. Whether what I was doing was the right thing to do is debatable. But we left everything behind and we learned from it. That's all we could have asked for.

September came, and so did my first year as a law student. They call it the 1L year. It's supposed to be a crash course in learning to become a lawyer. Torts, Property, Contracts, Criminal Law, Constitutional Law, and Civil Procedure. Each distinct subject is supposed to prepare you to think like a lawyer, though no one can define "thinking like a lawyer." The truth is, nothing prepares you as well as learning on the job. So just as with college, I became quickly jaded. If all I was doing was getting a piece of paper to say I learned something, what was the point? In that sense, my 1L year was more of the same. The new routine became an old one, attentiveness became a chore, and doing more than the bare minimum was impossible when my already good grades discouraged me from giving it my all. Not to mention, the open-mindedness that we embraced on our trip became a thing of the past.

All things considered, "normal life" was stale. I wanted nothing more than to get my degree and be done with it all. I wanted to start helping people now, not later. And my impatience bred a new kind of desire: to get away from it all. Sound familiar?

When Curtis and I had returned from the road trip, it became clear that it was a trip about "growing up" and "finding ourselves." Friendship was essential to the success of the trip, but our own camaraderie was inadequate. We depended on human interaction with others, and it became imperative to branch out and meet strangers more than we ever had before. So, aptly, we hoped that we could emulate this in our travels back home. My saving grace in that first year of post-road-trip apathy was one of the few loves of my life: the mountains. And the people I shared them with.

* * *

"Are you serious?" I mumbled to myself, a familiar occurrence when it came to Curtis-related matters.

At 1:45 a.m., hours after arriving at the southern terminus of the Presidential Traverse, I heard a faint tap on my window. At sunrise, we would begin our hike over seven or eight of the four-thousand-foot summits in the White Mountains—Madison, Adams, Jefferson, Washington, Monroe, Eisenhower, and Pierce, with Jackson being optional. (This is because Mount Jackson is named after former state geologist Charles Thomas Jackson, and not President Andrew Jackson). New Hampshire's four-thousand-footers list is similar to the Colorado fourteeners. There are forty-eight of them, and peak-bagging them has become an extremely popular and quintessentially New England achievement. Perhaps surprisingly, the Presidential Range is one of the most rugged, wild, and dangerous mountain conglomerates in the world. Formed by vicious freeze-thaw cycles and ferocious winds, the range is also notable for its many ravines—Tuckerman, Huntington, Ammonoosuc, and King, to name a few—carved by long-extinct glaciers.

The Presidential Traverse spans a minimum of around twenty miles with approximately 8,500 feet of elevation gain, and we planned to do it in a day. It would be our first big hike since the road trip and last big hike before I would start law school. But it didn't seem as if we would be getting much rest the night before. We still had to shuttle one car to the northern terminus before hitting the hay that night. By the time Mindy rolled into the parking lot for the northern terminus, it was 2:30 a.m.

"I still can't believe you didn't see my car when you pulled in," I said to Curtis, in my typical "I'm mad at you" road-trip tone. We were supposed to meet up before midnight, but of course, it didn't work out that way.

"It's dark out and I had no service!" He fired back, combatively.

Rather than needlessly escalate the situation, it was mutually agreed that we sleep. Clearly, our original 4 a.m. wake-up was out of the question. But by 6 a.m., our excitement to get on the trail could no longer be contained. Rest and being mad at each other would both have to wait.

* * *

Before embarking upon our road trip, we would occasionally say hello to people in passing on the trails but would never engage in chats for more than a few seconds. On this hike, we sought to make conversation as if we were still on the road. We decided to assume the approach that we oft took while traveling—stopping to think, to talk, to socialize, to appreciate. It seemed as if we were always in a rush before we left for our journey, but a lot had changed since then.

We began our hike in a near-sprint up three thousand vertical feet to the summit of Mount Madison. It felt good to get our legs moving like we were used to on the road. Atop the summit, I ran into a guy I went to college with. At first, neither of us recognized each other. As he put it, we stared inappropriately at one another for a good minute before I finally approached him. Like us, he was working on his forty-eight.

It wasn't quite Colorado, but the alpine zone of the Presidential Range was something else. Sweeping views of Mount Washington and the surrounding peaks came at us as fast as the heavy winds the range is known for. This time there really, *really* was wind though. A lot of it. But it felt pretty darn good on our tired bodies. Especially with at least fifteen miles to go. We could see most of the remainder of our route right in front of us.

Peak number two for the day was Adams. Typically hiked together with Madison, its summit views are some of the best in the range due to its position between Madison, Jefferson, and Washington. As we reached the top, another guy came up and tagged the peak at the same time. It turned out that summit was his forty-eighth and final four-thousand-footer. We felt lucky to share that moment with him.

As we continued along and summitted Jefferson, Clay (an optional sub-peak), and Washington, we crossed paths with a girl carrying eighty pounds of food on her back. She was a "croo" member, one of the select few who live in the mountains all summer to cook and clean for guests at the Appalachian Mountain Club's (AMC) huts. I suppose carrying eighty pounds of supplies up from the trailhead to the huts isn't so good for your posture, but it beats working in an office cubicle. Somehow during our chat with the croo member, we found out that we were born in the same hospital. How one gets into that discussion on a mountain is beyond me, but these are the small-world revelations that unveil themselves when you stop to listen every once in a while.

Monroe was next, and with it, another conversation-provoked coincidence. I got a little ahead of Curtis on the trail and happened upon a man wearing a Grand Teton hat. I chatted with him about our epic ascent just a month earlier, whereupon he told me that he had stayed at the Climber's Ranch where we had also stayed and met Dorian for the first time.

Along our route from Monroe to Eisenhower, we also ran into about a dozen Appalachian Trail (AT) thru-hikers who were on their way to Mount Katahdin from Georgia. We stopped to talk to a few groups, and before long, we discovered that one of them lived in the town next to our hometown.

By the time we reached Mount Pierce, we had encountered the same family of four on three separate occasions. To tag each peak, we had to take a spur trail off the Crawford Path, and then meet back up with it. We first saw this family at Lakes of the Clouds, which is the high-alpine AMC hut between Washington and Monroe. We took the spur path to Monroe, descended back down to the Crawford Path, and bumped into the family again. The same situation occurred after we descended from Eisenhower. On the third occasion, I emphatically said to them, "we've gotta stop meeting like this."

Just before hitting the summit of Pierce, we contemplated whether we were going to tag Jackson afterward, which would add a few more miles and extra elevation gain. But then we met three more AT hikers—Rubber Ducky, Boulder, and Remedy—and clearly Jackson was off the table. Not to mention our feet were killing us. We spoke with the thru-hikers for about an hour, discussing the parallels between life on the road and life on the trail and exchanging stories about our travels.

"So, do you guys find yourself sticking together with a particular group?" Curtis asked.

"We run into some of the same people every few days. It's just the nature of the trail," Boulder said. He looked exactly like you'd expect: gruff and buff. He had a calm demeanor despite his rugged appearance.

"Sometimes we even lose sight of each other a few days, but these two guys are the best friends I have on the trail," Rubber Ducky chimed in. She was the sole lady in the group, but she was tough as nails. Anyone who can walk with the blisters she had and not complain was a total badass in my mind. Her trail name was a little misleading, if you ask me (no offense to rubber duckies).

"Hey, you're the one who runs ahead," Remedy chided. Unlike Boulder, he was beardless, and frankly looked a little out of place on the trail. Who shaves on the AT?

The small talk quickly transitioned into meaningful conversation about why they decided to thru-hike, and it seemed that boredom with their lives was the primary reason for starting on the trail. Curtis and I were empathetic to their cause, given our desire to take to the road, especially now that we were back home and familiarizing ourselves with old routines. It was at that moment that a monarch butterfly flapped by us and rose gently through the sky.

"Pretty butterfly," Rubber Ducky said, as she folded herself into a yoga pose.

"Funny you say that," I remarked, "you actually remind me a lot of our friend we met on the road. Her name was Butterfly."

"Funny *you* say that, actually," she echoed. "We know a Butterfly as well. Do you know Cowabunga and Indian?"

Curtis and I looked at each other and shook our heads.

"They were on the trail with us a few months ago but ducked out and decided to go to Wyoming. Last we heard, they were driving a girl named Butterfly up to the Tetons."

Curtis and I smiled and gave each other that look when both of you want to talk but it's a race to get the first words out. Curtis won.

"That's insane!" he exclaimed. "When we left her, she was hitchhiking with two AT hikers to the Tetons. What a small world!"

A small world, indeed. From Arizona to New Hampshire, a brief conversation prompted by a tiny butterfly and a chance encounter with a trio of thru-hikers led to the biggest wow moment of a day already filled with them. These trails we tread, from the White Mountains to the Grand Canyon and beyond, are tightly knit. No matter where you choose your adventure, you'll find enjoyment and serendipity. That day reinforced to me that our open and outgoing road-trip personae were the only way to make those wholesome connections, lest we walk our walks without ever stopping to say hello.

* * *

It was Cole, with his carefully crafted metaphor, who told us to live outside the box so we could read the instructions ourselves. Not long after meeting our thru-hiker friends and just after I started law school, he made a surprise trip up north, now sixteen months into his road trip. He wanted to see the New England fall. Appropriately, we decided to give him a hell of an experience high up on Mount Jackson, which we had bailed on just a month prior.

When you settle back at home after a long trip, old habits tend to reemerge. Like when you're trying to make evening plans: *Should I go out with friends or stay in tonight? Ehh, I can see Jimmy and Al another time. Besides, the new season Game of Thrones' starts tonight. Plus, I can't stand Jimmy and Al.*

Or when you brush into someone in the hallway: *Hey look, it's Jonny! Should I say hi to him? Maybe a head nod? Nah, I'll just walk right by him without even acknowledging his existence so that every time I see him going forward, it'll only get more awkward.*

And especially when you want to make weekend plans: *Hey Sally, sorry I have to bail last second, but my cat has the flu and I need to watch her just in case the little furball needs some hot soup.*

But Cole reminded us that although we would inevitably sink into these awful idiosyncrasies, we needed to remember to appreciate what we had in our backyard. We met him at the trailhead for Jackson on a crisp late September day.

"Gentlemen! It's so good to see you." Cole beamed a pearly smile and we mirrored his with our own.

"It's like we're still on the road," I joked.

"What's the plan for the day boys?"

"We're thinking we do Webster and Jackson, since the weather is perfect," Curtis answered. It was almost 11:30 a.m. with baby blue skies, and we were confident in our ability to hike roughly six miles before dark.

As we took to the trail, we began to tell Cole about the profound coincidences we'd experienced in this very mountain range just a month before. Not even a few minutes after that conversation, we encountered another group of hikers. One of them asked me about my shirt, which was from my high school track and field team.

"I graduated about five years ago from there. You've heard of it?"

The man gave me a smile and replied gleefully.

"I graduated from there a few dozen years ago and just started working there!"

There's just something about these mountains, I tell you.

The remaining miles to the summit of Webster were quiet, with Curtis and I getting a little ahead of Cole. We were already returning to old habits that we had tried to unlearn on the road. But Cole wasn't far behind and met up with us at the open summit of Webster just a few minutes after we arrived.

Directly below us was a whirlwind of colors. The trees were bursting forth in an aurora of dazzling yellows, crimson reds, emerald greens, and juicy oranges. There are only a few good weeks a year when the fall foliage is out, but those weeks alone make the other fifty weeks tolerable.

Looking toward the remainder of the Presidential Range, however, we already could see signs of winter. Cole explained to us that the New Hampshire natives he had spoken to earlier in the week call the period between foliage season and snow *nuclear winter* because there is nothing redeeming about trees with no leaves. To me though, leafless trees mean less crowds, and I'm all about less crowds.

"At least the leafers will be gone soon," Cole chuckled.

"Enjoy it while it lasts!" I countered.

"There really is nothing like a New England fall," he replied.

"It's one of the few times all year the air feels crisp. It's humid as hell most of the time." Curtis said.

"Crisp like an apple," I said, as I munched on a McIntosh.

While I took a bite, a flock of gray birds perched themselves on the short pine trees near the summit.

"Do you boys know about camp robbers?" Cole extended his hand with a piece of bread.

We looked at each other and shook our heads.

One of the gray birds flung itself onto Cole's outstretched hand.

"See, camp robber!"

The gray jays followed us all the way over to Mount Jackson, and we couldn't help but think we should have abstained from feeding them. On the summit of Jackson, one even tried to swoop down and steal my sandwich right out of my hand.

I remembered back to our days on the road, and all I could think about were the signs that said, "Don't feed the wildlife." But I was so awestruck by the bird crawling on my hand that I just couldn't resist. Sorry Ranger Rick! If it's any consolation, I haven't fed the wildlife since that day.

As we completed our short loop, Cole thanked us for showing him around our neighborhood.

"It was wonderful to see you both again. And I know it won't be the last time."

As he got into his bulky Expedition, he left us with some parting words.

"Do what makes you happy. But remember Justin, don't become an ambulance chaser!"

Words to live by.

Cole's presence reminded me just how far I had to go on my quest. I remembered his Black Canyon advice to do something significant, which he reiterated at the base of Mount Jackson. But if my first year of law school was any indication, I had a long way to go. The only thing that got me through it without pulling my hair out was the excitement for a new journey. One that would change everything. And one that would remind me that the grand delusion that our lives would transpire without incident was far removed from reality.

As time elapsed, it became evident that everything was creeping back toward business as usual. On the road, I was so familiar with waving to people, introducing myself to random strangers, and stopping to listen, but it was hard to even get a returned smile in the hallways at school. I felt as if I was slowly sinking back into the sadness that brought me to the road in the first place.

For much of the year, I struggled with anxiety about the future. I was bogged down in school work which became more pointless to me with every passing day. As the busy first semester ended and the next one started, I wondered what the hell I was doing. I thought of nothing but the mountains. Whereas most of my classmates were studying all weekend, I was playing. It was a necessary distraction to keep me sane. Whereas most of my classmates were binging on caffeine, alcohol, and anxiety meds, I was hooked on nature. It was the only remedy I had for my problems.

February rolled around, and I fondly remember sitting in Constitutional Law thinking to myself, "Can I do this? Am I actually going to be able to finish law school?" I had lost all drive and desire to do anything productive in class. Instead of taking notes, I was surfing the web, doing whatever I could to occupy my time. I became a pessimist and a cynic. And I thought about how crazy my prospective profession was. Why do we need laws? If people were honest and good, philanthropic and open-minded, kind-hearted and receptive; would we even need to make rules? My future job relied upon conflict, disagreement, and committing morally objectionable acts. If people got along and behaved, I would be doing something entirely different.

My drive had all but dissipated as I sat in a classroom day in and day out. I had been so passionate about what I was doing when I started. I had genuinely enjoyed the long afternoons of reading, of taking notes, and of learning. But the honeymoon period had passed. And I was left with nothing but a spinning mind. In class, I stared emptily off into space. I was anesthetized to everything and the rut was inescapable. That is, until my grandfather died.

* * *

Milton "Milty" Raphaelson was born to Russian immigrants who had fled their home country between 1905 and 1917 to escape the revolution. Had they not done so, they very well may have perished.

When Milty finished high school, he enlisted in the military and married my grandmother around the same time. After finishing his stint in the military, Milty began working in his father's grocery store. He was a meat cutter by trade, and the store became the go-to place for families who lived nearby.

He began his studies at my alma mater, Clark University, using his GI bill benefits. Without them, who knows if he would have ever gone to college. But he went to school by day and worked at the store by night, and when he graduated, he decided to use his remaining GI benefits to enroll in law school at Boston College.

The commute to Boston was a little more daunting than going to school down the street. But he worked and went to school full time. For him, getting an education was imperative. He wanted to help the most vulnerable people in his community—the unrepresented and the voiceless.

After he graduated from law school, he took as many court-appointed cases as he could. His first office was on the second floor of the grocery store, and many of his initial clients were the people he continued to serve in the grocery store. He caught the eyes and ears of one of the more prominent judges in Worcester County, who began to appoint him to even more significant cases.

He argued a case in the Supreme Judicial Court of Massachusetts that changed the way we allocate funds in the court system. There was an issue getting a tape recorder for one of the courtrooms due to financial restrictions, and he successfully argued that such supplies should be state funded. In 1980, he represented a defendant in a case that eventually ruled the death penalty unconstitutional in Massachusetts. The case continues to be guiding precedent after.

After, Milty was appointed a district court judge, and attention as a radical and intriguing figure in the pioneered the idea that drugs and alcohol are the ely 80 percent of crime. Although there are to crime, he wasn't far off the mark. He the course of his judgeship, and, something needed to be done

to
what

nted to
admired
at of hun-
But this, I
I wanted to

about the system. He felt the courts were locking up too many people for substance abuse problems and overflowing the jails.

He started what he dubbed the Honor Court. It was an after-hours program in lieu of jail that gave drug and alcohol offenders the opportunity to participate in sobriety programs. While many people benefited from the program, some of my grandfather's critics weren't too keen on the idea of allocating court resources to such a program, and it abruptly ended.

A rift in my grandfather's local court caused him to take a leave of absence. In his journals, he wrote of deep depression stemming from his ouster. But he returned to the Worcester Court a stronger person and a better judge. When he retired in 2000, an enormous reception was held for him at a large, historic venue in Worcester. I was only nine years old at the time and didn't understand the gravity of what I was witnessing, but it was clear that he made a difference in many people's lives.

* * *

I visited Milty the day before he died. He had indefinitely fallen into an endless sleep, and not even a nudge or a hand on his could wake him up. But he knew I was there. His body moved ever slightly as I patted him gently. As I sat by his death bed, I began write notes about how he had affected me. I wasn't quite sure I would do with them, but I wanted to record my memories.

The next day, he passed. I immediately told my dad I wa give his eulogy. It was important for me to recall the man I and looked up to. I was told that I would be speaking in fro dreds of people, and this initially made me nervous. thought, was why I went to law school in the first place make a difference, no matter how large the audience and how nervous I would be. Someone was bound to take something out of my words. And that was special to me.

I wanted to embrace those qualities. Though I knew I could never truly emulate them, I would at least try. At the funeral, I tearfully told a large assembly about my grandfather and his impact on me. It was Milty who created my desire to share my gifts—to try to capture his wit, charm, and intellect—and to help those in need. Much like those who helped me growing up and while on the road. But first I needed to finish school, which would likely sap all motivation from me by the time it was over. Because even with a renewed and rejuvenated outlook, it would still be a difficult endeavor. So, to make it more tolerable, I would continue to supplement my apathy with alternative inspiration: the mountains, and the road.

Chapter 17

At home, in our purported element, our voices are
stifled. But the mountains are different.
When we speak, they listen.

* * *

It had been nearly a year since we returned from the journey that we jokingly deemed "celestial." But the stars were certainly aligned when we took off on that road trip, a culmination of four years of indomitable yearning. If you had asked me after the trip if I would do it again, I would've impulsively nodded in the affirmative. If you'd asked me when, I would've shrugged my shoulders and winced uncertainly.

In the wake of that uncertainty, the drive to transcend reemerged. I was so jaded from another year in school, so frustrated from the familiar regiment; I wanted nothing to do with anything run-of-the-mill before going back for my second year. The extraordinary, it seemed, was the only way to satisfy my altered desires. Sitting in my room playing video games was no longer a permanent resolution to escape from monotony. The freedom of the road had taken hold, and I needed to go. To feel the liberty of its openness; to smell the cows in Ohio and the exhaust in Chicago; to see the mountains in Colorado and the deserts in Utah. Again.

The stoke was high. So much had taken place in the last year for both of us. Curtis had started a master's program in entrepreneurship, and I was knee deep into law school, but we had both continued our outdoor pursuits to maintain our sanity. By spring's end, we found ourselves part of a like-minded group of individuals whom we had met at the climbing gym. Consequently, that summer, we spent more time suspended from cliffs than we ever would have imagined, all in the company of good friends.

With our new repertoire of climbing skills and an increased drive to spend all our free time in precarious situations, we had caught the eyes and the ears of College Outside, a local company that connects college students with outdoor brands and discounted gear. We met the founders of the company multiple times at outdoor events over the year and became friendly with them, and they offered to sponsor us for another road trip that August.

During the planning stages of our trip, we decided to see if they would reach out to some of their partners to see if anyone would be interested in supporting our trip. They penned our idea to Adidas Outdoor, who agreed to fully outfit our trip—all we had to do was post on social media and write gear reviews and trip reports. I remember standing in a bathroom when I got the call from College Outside's cofounder. He informed me of our eight-thousand-dollar budget to buy whatever gear we needed. *Holy crap*, I thought to myself. *I've never won anything before in my life.* Mostly though, I thought, *Wow, we're sellouts.* In all honesty, it was the first time that anyone had given me any sort of compensation to write, and I was ecstatic. I would have done it for free, but the incentive was impossible to turn down, and damn did I need a new pair of boots.

Aside from our generous sponsorship, why did I want to hit the road again in the first place? Well, meeting new people, challenging ourselves physically, and getting away from the fast-paced East Coast culture were as alluring as ever. I had gotten far too complacent and comfortable. When that happens, my productivity level plummets and my anxiety and depression flourish. Not only that, I was living by the adage of "do it while you're young." (Except I knew I wanted to do it even when I'm old).

But truly, the only reason that we had the option to even travel in the first place was because of our privilege. We worked two-thirds of the summer but had a month off. We were pampered and spoiled. And we were bored. Because we were given everything, we desired nothing. The idea that our generation values experiences over material goods is all too accurate a statement. Having things only makes our lives more cluttered and messier. We just need the basics to satisfy our Hierarchy of Needs: to feed ourselves, to feel safe, to be loved, and to feel good about ourselves. With all that in place, we strive toward the elusive self-actualization. Sitting at a desk was simply not going to get us there. We wanted the simple life—to wake up to a mountain sunset, to work up a sweat, to share priceless evenings with old and new friends, and to sleep among the stars outside of the realm of light pollution.

We knew that this trip was going to be substantially different from our first. For starters, we would be much less spontaneous. We had two destinations: Colorado and California. We already had our mountains mostly planned and had a good idea about where we would sleep each night. We also knew whom we would spend time with. Meeting people the previous year had opened up opportunities, couches, and guest bedrooms. To that effect, we didn't have to rely as much on making new friends.

The anxiety we first experienced in the Great Sand Dunes was a thing of the past. The necessity to be open was no longer a prerequisite. It seemed as if our fairy-tale coming-of-age adventure had already come and gone. The serendipity and excitement weren't as vivid as the journey we had ahead of us. Nothing could recapture the mysteriousness of the places we had once only dreamed of.

Nonetheless, even though we had "been there, done that," we still needed the road. Its fruits were far more desirable than those borne by our own mundane lives. And we were much more experienced climbers this time around, which opened far more doors to us. But the open road that we thought we knew became little more than an adolescent dream when the reality of life finally bit us in the ass.

* * *

Talia woke us up after 9 a.m., over an hour after our proposed departure time. Curtis and I appreciated this gesture, as we were both reeling from head and chest colds. Though somewhat nervous, we were confident of success on Capitol Peak the following day.

We had only been back on the road a few days, and it felt familiar, but we were in a fundamentally different place than we were on our last journey to Colorado. We knew where we were going to sleep at night. That certainly took away a bit of the surprise.

From our homes just a few days prior, we'd driven over fourteen hours in a day to Chicago where we unsuccessfully tried to convince our friend Daphne to come along with us to the Rockies. She had just graduated from college and was still looking for a job, three months after leaving school. To our dismay, we could not lure her away from her familiar home. Thus, our trek through the Midwest out to Colorado was about as eventful as you'd expect it to be.

We had been chatting with Talia all summer about our plans for August, and she convinced us to tag along with her on a long weekend trip to the Elk Range. The range is accessible, yet hazardous, and is home to some of the hardest standard-route climbs of any four-teeners in Colorado. Each of the peaks is a challenge to climb, and Capitol and the Maroon Bells, our two biggest objectives on this trip, are some of the most dangerous and exposed of all. Fatalities are common. We planned to do all of them in one fell swoop. Talia was only a few peaks away from completing all her fourteeners, and we felt privileged to be able to join her for two of the hardest climbs she would have to complete on her quest. But we weren't the only company she would have along for the ride.

"Moooooooooooooooo," was the first noise we heard upon va-cating Mindy.

At the trailhead, we were greeted by a large ensemble of filthy, smelly creatures. We were perplexed by their enormity and charis-matic nature. They seemed out of place, less suited for the moun-tains and more suited for an enclosed area. Good for them, we thought, breaking free of the traditional cattle mold.

At a loss for words other than "moo," we continued into the depths of the forest, only to be greeted by probably a hundred more of them along the way. They were omnipresent, omniscient, even. We felt as if we were being watched at every corner. Our belief was confirmed as we stared up into the adjacent hills and saw a half-dozen of them giving us the stare from two hundred feet above. We decided to call them mountain cows.

One such mountain cow was brave enough to lead the way on the trail toward Capitol Peak. We named her Columbia, a tribute to the immense capitol that now loomed above us.

"Quite the service here, huh?" Talia joked. We stopped to ad-mire the scenery as the first views of the peak came into sight above a bucolic meadow. The peak was sharp and still snow-covered along parts of its slopes, and the clouds had begun to dissipate around the stunning monolith.

"Maybe she'll carry our backpacks." Curtis replied.

"Why don't you go ask her?" I gasped. We were barely at ten thousand feet, and I could barely breathe. When we started up again after our brief break, Columbia took the lead once again, allowing us to follow her along the well-established trail. It was a benevolent gesture for a cow. If only she knew how badly we humans treat her kind.

* * *

We settled into our basecamp for the evening at 11,600 feet. In front of our tents, the towering west face of Capitol Peak wound itself along the base of its eponymous lake. To either side of us was pristine wilderness. Nearly eight miles from the trailhead and even more to the nearest main road, this was truly unscathed territory.

We were one of three parties who settled down at the established campsite that evening, but we exchanged only pleasantries with the others. We were too worried about what was going to happen in the morning. My sickness had traveled from my head and into my chest just since the time we had begun hiking earlier in the day, and I felt like shit.

"You going to be okay buddy?" Talia remarked, as she set up her one-person tent.

"I hope so," I responded, apprehensively, as I watched Curtis fire up our backpacking stove. Freeze-dried spaghetti was on the menu. When wasn't it? Our bowels hadn't forgotten the last time, that's for sure.

I started feeling feverish and my appetite swiftly waned. I wanted nothing to do with diarrhea and indigestion from the spaghetti, so I stuck to electrolytes and insoluble fiber. If I was going to go down in flames the next morning, it wasn't going to be from corrosive carbohydrates. In hindsight, shitting water sounded a lot more appealing than what ensued.

At 2 a.m., the fever broke. I was drenched in sweat, and our alarm was a mere two hours away. Alpine starts are already brutal enough, but this one would likely take the cake for the worst to date. I didn't sleep a wink before the familiar sound of torment rang through the still night sky. Rather than rise, I turned it off immediately and put my head down, hoping neither Talia or Curtis heard it. Not five minutes later, I found myself outside of the warmth of our tent munching on Pop-Tarts and in high spirits, despite still feeling feverishness. And so, we began our assault on the Capitol, fragmented, but functional.

* * *

"Are you okay?" Curtis yelled back to me from his perch at the saddle between Capitol Peak and K2, its sub-peak. To get there, we had traipsed up a series of switchbacks, down across a snowy valley, and up a steep scree field on the way up to our next big task.

The notorious Knife's Edge began just a few feet from where I stood, but I had neither the mental nor physical ability to move any further. Before this, I had never experienced any severe altitude related ailments sans a little light-headedness and a decrease of appetite. But I was *hurting*.

"FUCK OFF!" I screamed back at Curtis, delirious and borderline hallucinating—two of the early signs of HACE and HAPE.

High-altitude cerebral edema and high-altitude pulmonary edema are two of the leading causes of death among those afflicted with severe altitude sickness. HACE relates to fluid in the brain, HAPE to fluid in the lungs. Both can be catastrophic if not treated promptly.

I was furious because I knew I wasn't going to make it to the top. But if I had stayed just a few more minutes, there's no telling whether I would still be here today. Ahead of us, the crux of the climb begged me to forget about my crippled state. Ever since the first time I hiked Katahdin back home in New England, I dreamed of Capitol Peak's exposure. It was cloudy, so it was impossible to know what lay ahead. As I later found out, with considerable drops of well over a thousand feet on either side and not more than a few feet to maneuver across, there would be no room for error. Much of the Knife's Edge must either be straddled or traversed along its side. Dropping too far from the ridge proper is a death sentence of loose rock and phantom paths carved out by years of oblivious climbers. All but certainly, I would have found myself a casualty that day if I had continued with my plan to summit.

"What are we going to do?" Curtis said to Talia. They were just a few exposed moves away from me, but there was no way I was going to reach them. I had started to shiver uncontrollably, and my head felt like it was going to explode. *I should be on top of this god-damn mountain*, I thought to myself, as I started to punch rocks for no reason other than my deliriousness.

As if his prayers were answered, a couple poked out from behind some rocks coming from the direction of the summit. They yelled to us that it was too wet and dangerous to continue. Just behind us, another solo climber made his way up to our general area.

I looked below my feet at an endless cliff and finally realized that I didn't want to die here, not like this. I knew that if I was healthy enough, I would have followed my two comrades into battle to seize the Capitol. But instead, Capitol punishment would have to suffice.

I was accompanied down back to base camp by a man named Ryan. Talia and Curtis had decided that they were going to give it a shot and keep going despite the warning to turn back. They were the only two people to go for the summit despite the worrisome weather that day.

"Have you eaten anything?" Ryan said, as he rummaged through his backpack on one of our many stops on the way down.

"Not since breakfast," I answered, as I grabbed my head and avoided looking into the bright sky. The clouds had begun to taper off, ever so slightly, but we could hear thunderstorms starting to roll in.

I coughed uncontrollably as Ryan handed me a chocolate GU. Though a generally mediocre flavor, I quickly devoured the caffeinated delicacy. We got into a great conversation on the way down about his work in the CIA. He couldn't tell me a lot, as much of what he does is confidential, but he did explain to me that he had been relocated from Denver to Maryland and missed every minute of being in the mountains.

"There's nowhere quite like Colorado," he explained. "The closest mountains to me aren't very close at all. But at least the Rockies will always be here."

"I guess so," I responded, feeling defeated.

"Justin, you've gotta understand. Bailing happens. I've been doing this stuff for years, and what I've realized is that you're not a true mountaineer until you've bailed."

As a born and raised New Englander with an ego the size of Maine, "bailing," as Ryan described it, doesn't happen very often. Altitude sickness is not a concern back home. Weather seldom factors into a safe mountain ascent unless you're in the dead of winter or on one of the Northeast's few exposed ridgelines. The first and only time I had bailed up to that point was in a very similar scenario on the Presidential Range. The only lesson that I took out of that experience was that I never wanted to do a three-day backpack in the dead of winter on or around Mount Washington ever again. But this time on Capitol Peak, I was humbled.

Ryan left me back at our campsite and took off. I was left to my own devices for the next several hours while I pondered probable scenarios for Curtis and Talia's demise. Between the risks of wet rock, lightning, and poor visibility, they hadn't put themselves in the best of situations. At least they didn't have me as baggage for their daring summit bid. My head was on fire and I felt like I had to throw up but there was no food in my stomach to expel. Instead, I laid down for a while until I realized I hadn't had water all day. I often wonder how many years I shredded off my life that day.

Some four hours or so after I left them, Curtis and Talia's frames emerged high up in the switchbacks. I breathed a sigh of relief and began to walk toward them, immediately wishing I had just stayed where I was. Each step caused my violent headache to intensify, and I knew that we had to go as soon as they got back.

Not five minutes after they arrived in camp, we heard a sound that seemingly didn't belong coming from down trail. It was the unmistakable gallop of a horse, and it quickly interrupted us from disassembling our camp. Talia was the first to arise from her packing duties. She was quick, and to the point.

"Hi there, are you heading back down perchance?"

Two teenage boys dismounted from their horses and began to untie the gear that they hauled up for a lazy party who apparently couldn't do it themselves. Not going to lie, if you can't haul your own backpack up and down a mountain like Capitol Peak, you probably shouldn't be up there in the first place. Nonetheless, the boys were quick to give us sass.

"Duh, we're not taking the horses up the Knife's Edge," one of the two boys said. He was wearing a cowboy hat and a yellow rain jacket to go along with jeans and cowboy boots. Not the most mountain-appropriate outfit I've seen, but not the worst either.

"Well, I know that, silly," Talia remarked.

The other boy, who had a similar outfit as his partner, seemed to be tipped off by Talia's tone. He quickly stepped into action.

"Y'all want help bringing your stuff down?" His voice cracked. He couldn't have been older than thirteen.

Talia insisted that we would be fine, but as if Curtis knew to play along, he told them that I had a horrible bout of altitude sickness.

"Okay, we'll help you folks out, it's the least we can do," the second kid said.

Curtis smirked at Talia who gave him a similar look in response. Meanwhile, I was pissed. After we retreated to our belongings to finish packing, I made it known to them.

"Seriously guys? I couldn't even finish the climb and now you want them to take my stuff? I can manage, I'm fine."

Irrationality, it seems, has a way of following me around when I'm in a lousy mood or I'm feeling like crap. Granted, I was still pissed that I didn't summit. Even though my friends had good intentions, it didn't come off that way to me.

"You can take your own bag if it's that important to you but we're just trying to help you out," Curtis said, genuinely.

So I did just that. After loading up Curtis and Talia's bags, the first kid who initially gave us sass retreated to his initial unfriendliness.

"So, about payment. That will be one hundred dollars. You can pay down at the car if you don't have anything on you."

We looked at each other in bewilderment. He wasn't kidding either.

"You can take off our bags now then, we can just carry them," Talia responded, angrily.

It had taken about ten minutes to load everything up. Curtis and Talia's bags, our tent, and a trash bag full of odds and ends were strapped to the horses. It would probably take another ten minutes to take everything off. I was quickly losing patience and brain cells, as my headache was not going away anytime soon.

The second boy pulled his comrade aside and they whispered among themselves. He then turned around and quickly retracted the previous statement.

"It's okay guys, we'll do it for free for ya." We all breathed a sigh of relief.

On the way down, I was so ready to be off the mountain and away from the altitude that I practically sprinted the last five miles after we got through the most rugged part of the descent. I must have seen a hundred cows, and no matter how many I ran into, I gasped at the not-so-surprise encounters each time they popped out around corners.

At the end of the day, we did feel bad that we caught those kids in an awkward situation. After all, they need to make a living too, no matter how silly we thought it was that they were hauling people's gear up to camp. Especially since we took advantage of their services. Before I ran ahead of the others, we mutually decided that we would tip them as soon as we got back to the car. Unfortunately, they had left our items by Mindy and just taken off. Oh well.

I still look back on that day on Capitol Peak. I long for another chance to tackle its steep slopes and jagged ridge. Even if I had made it to the top that day, the clouds would have obscured the dramatic views that one normally has in more favorable conditions. Someday, I will be back. And on that day, I'll bring a cowbell. You know, just in case the cows try to attack me next time.

Chapter 18

"The beautiful Maroon Bells, and their neighbor Pyra-
mid Peak, have claimed many lives in the past few
years. . . . They are unbelievably deceptive. The rock is
downsloping, rotten, loose, and unstable. It kills quickly
and without warning. . . . Expert climbers who did not
know the proper routes have died on these peaks. Don't
repeat their mistakes, for only rarely have these moun-
tains given a second chance.

—The Deadly Bells

* * *

"Guys, get up, breakfast closes in five minutes! They have eggs!"
Talia proclaimed.

Complimentary hotel breakfast? With eggs? No self-respecting
non-vegan outdoorsman would turn down such a grand opportunity after a day of extreme calorie deficiency.

Even with ten hours of sleep, our minds were tired. I was still
reeling from my altitude sickness and chest cold. It seemed to be
getting better, but that could have just been relative to how brutally
awful I felt the day before. It's ironic, really, that I'm the guy that
prides myself on being in the best shape of everyone, yet I was the
only one to not summit the mountain. That's altitude sickness for
you. Relentless, and unassuming.

We spent the bulk of the morning cleaning Mindy, which aptly
reeked of cow and horse shit. Our initial plan for the day was to head
on over to the trailhead for South and North Maroon Peak, but given
the way that Capitol Peak had unfolded, we decided that we needed

another day of rest. What better place to recover than the local hot springs?

* * *

The hot springs were full of intriguing individuals, and we enjoyed hearing strangers' stories as we so often had during our first road trip. Jack and Danielle were two adventurous Floridians with whom we struck up a thirty-minute conversation with about the great outdoors. They were on a multi-week vacation in the Rockies, with aspirations to climb North Maroon Peak just like us—and on the same day as us, no less. You'd be hard-pressed to find a more badass couple from the Gulf State. At home, Dave runs a company called Outdoors Life, where he gives paddle tours of all the islands in the surrounding area. He offered to take us on a thrill ride if we ever find ourselves in the Florida Keys.

Allie and Jorge were two twenty-somethings with a cheap taste in beer and a wild sense of spirit. It seemed as if they make the trip out to the hot springs whenever they get a free afternoon. How could you blame them? Allie played with her daughter, Malia, as her father, Joe, told us stories about his many years as a firefighter. He began his career as a local firefighter, but now worked for the federal government. Burning down houses that fail to mitigate for fire-resistance purposes is commonplace, he told us. If incinerating one promises to save dozens of other houses and lives, then he would have no problem letting someone's roots burn out from under them. It is harrowing, but necessary.

Josh and Rachael were nervous at first, but eventually they got to talking when everyone else left. They heard us chatting about climbing, and suddenly their eyes lit up like kids in a candy store.

Josh told us about all the local crags, and I think he assumed that we were better climbers than we were. He started to name off some of the harder routes nearby that he thought would strike our fancy—5.12s and 5.13s. We played along with him for fear of coming off as fanboys, but we totally were.

Brent and Elyse were two of the receptive Colorado types that we have gotten used to meeting over the years. They were bubbly, sarcastic, and kind-hearted people who were some of Talia's most trusted climbing partners. They were gearing up to hike Snowmass, one of the longest, but not necessarily most difficult fourteeners.

After sufficiently replenishing our worn bodies in the hot springs, we met Brent, Elyse, and my high school friend Nel at a local brew pub. Somehow, we convinced Nel, a recent migrant to Colorado, to partake in his first fourteener—South Maroon Peak.

Nel is a super-athlete. Not in the sense that he's the most athletic person in the world, but he is legitimately the most active person I know. Often he will bike a hundred miles and then go for a run in the same day. While he has since hiked and climbed his fair share of difficult fourteeners, this would be his first. Nel only had one problem—he didn't have a helmet. While it isn't necessarily a requirement, the rockfall is so dangerous on South and North Maroon Peak that not having one is borderline reckless.

"What are we going to do now?" Talia said, frustrated. She knew Nel was new at this, but this wasn't what she signed up for when we told her we had a friend coming along.

"It's okay Tal, he can use mine," Brent said, as he took a munch out of his burger.

"Oh no he can't!" Elyse exclaimed. "We're going to need those this weekend!"

"It'll be fine, it's less weight anyway."

"There's got to be a better option," Curtis, ever the problem-solver, opined.

"Guys, I've got it!" A gleeful Nel interjected from out of nowhere. He quickly got up from the table and headed out of the pub. We all looked at each other in bewilderment.

"I don't reaaally need my helmet," Brent reiterated, french fry hanging from his mouth. Elyse and Talia glared at him without a word. He got the message.

Nel returned after five minutes outside. As he walked over, we saw he was clutching something in his hand. It appeared to be made of fabric or nylon. When he moseyed back over to the table, he set the mysterious item on the table in emphatic fashion. It was at that moment that we realized it was a fanny pack.

"OK, so I've figured it out." He unzipped the fanny pack and emptied out its contents. "I have a bunch of extra layers in my car that I wasn't planning on using. If I take all of them and stuff them into the pack and fill it to capacity, I can give it some solid padding."

We all gave each other looks of mutual confusion.

"Yeah, I know it sounds silly. But here, give me all of your extra layers." We all silently obliged, wondering what the hell was going on.

He stuffed four light jackets into his fanny pack, which to be honest, was quite spacious. They get such bad reputations, but gosh darn are they handy!

With the bulky fanny pack sufficiently filled, Nel secured the pack on top of his head and buckled the strap under his chin like a helmet.

The rest of us gave each other a look and burst out laughing.

"Is this—your idea—of a helmet?" Talia said, as she tried to contain her uncontrollable laughter.

"No really guys, this is going to work! All I need to do is find some sturdier layers and the loose rocks will wish they never fell on my head!"

When the laughter subsided, and everyone realized that Nel was serious, we got our heads together to brainstorm.

"Well, we could ask someone around the restaurant if anyone has one that they would be willing to loan," Curtis suggested. He sipped his local IPA and pulled at his beard hairs, which had become a distinct habit ever since he started to grow it out on our first trip. Both the IPA drinking *and* the beard pulling.

Springing into action, Nel again rose from his perch and asked the first group of people he saw at the table adjacent to ours. Embarrassed to be a part of this silly situation, I put my head down, so I couldn't see or hear what was going on, and pretended I wasn't there.

By some miracle, Ned returned to the table not five minutes later with a bike helmet in hand.

"That works," Talia said with a genuine smirk on her face.

"Yeah guys, it worked out great. These guys actually live a few streets over from me in Boulder. I had to put down thirty dollars for collateral, but such is life, right?"

Oh, brother.

* * *

What's in a name? The Maroon Bells earned the nickname *the Deadly Bells* in the mid-1960s when they claimed the lives of eight unassuming climbers. In the years since, many have perished along their auburn-hued escarpments. Home to some of the crumbliest rock in Colorado's many mountains, the Deadly Bells are composed of metamorphic sedimentary mudstone that has been sculpted into rock over millions of years.

Even a day after our hot springs R&R, my body and mind were still destroyed. The night before our bid for the Bells, we base-camped in the trailhead parking lot, per usual. Initially, Nel, Talia, Curtis, and I were supposed to go up together. Per usual, it didn't work out that way.

I woke up at 4:30 a.m. alongside Curtis in the front seats. Talia, who slept on our stuff in the back, was already up and packing her gear for the summit bid.

"No way," I mumbled to Curtis from my cozy sleeping bag, as Talia and Nel conversed about the day's plan. They intended to set up a base camp at Crater Lake, just under two miles from the trailhead, and then summit South Maroon Peak that day. In contrast, Curtis and I originally anticipated that we would summit South first, and then traverse over to the North Peak. There was no way in hell that was going to happen.

"Go without me," I said, disappointedly, "I'll meet you guys up at the camp later in the day."

"Are you sure?" Curtis asked, not wanting Talia and Nel to hear us.

"Yes." Sleeping at 9,500 feet did not agree with me. And more sleep was the only remedy.

After hearing of my plan from Curtis, Talia tapped on my door. I rolled down the window to an unsurprisingly perplexed Talia.

"What's going on?" She asked. I could tell she was a little annoyed, but deservedly so.

"I'm still feeling pretty sick. You guys can go ahead. I'll meet you at camp. Hopefully I'll feel better tomorrow and maybe try then."

Curtis decided that he would head up to base camp with Talia and Nel but would wait a day so that he could summit with me. Talia was torn about what she wanted to do. She had never intended to take Nel alone. She desired partners who were more experienced in route-finding and dependable at altitude. Maybe the helmet situation had something to do with it too—which could have been avoided altogether now that I wasn't going to go.

Although my door was closed, and I was about to doze off again, I could still hear their conversation outside.

"Nel, if I'm going to take you alone, I'm going to be responsible for you. This is not going to be easy. Do you understand?"

I couldn't hear the response, but judging from Talia's stern tone, I knew he had been put into his place. Surely, this wasn't an ideal situation for anyone, but I wasn't going up there to have another Capitol Peak episode. I bid my peers goodbye and drifted back to sleep for another five or so hours.

* * *

3:20 a.m. the next morning. The phone alarm was offensive, menacing even. Our bags were packed at least, and, barring an untimely event, we would likely be on the summit of South Maroon Peak, followed by North Maroon Peak, within the next several hours. Nel and Talia had successfully tagged the South summit the day before, so now it was our turn.

It was awfully dark out when we began our slog to the top. Our headlamps illuminated the easily navigable trail until we reached a confusing boulder field about fifteen minutes later. We spent the next ten trying to figure out where the hell we were. Fortunately, a pair of climbers passed us and affirmed that they had the GPS coordinates of the trail. We trusted their judgment over that of the group of gumbies in front of us who continued to follow a path to who knows where.

The sunrise was breathtaking, almost Rainier-worthy, as we pushed harder and harder to the summit. Perhaps it wasn't the sun taking our breath away, but the increasing altitude. The sky was still kinda cool though, if you like sappy mountain sunrises and all. We reached the saddle roughly a half-hour after the sun put on its vivid display. Somehow, I was feeling great, notwithstanding my ongoing cough. That was probably due to the afternoon run I went on the day before when I'd gotten stir-crazy.

"So far . . . *cough* *cough* so . . . *cough* good." I erupted into a relentless bout of hacking.

"You sure?" Curtis said, breathing heavily.

The summit was calling our names. I wasn't about to let this measly sickness, which had already incapacitated me twice, consume me.

* * *

Two guys whom we met on the trail shortly after, Dirk and Dan, led the way as we traversed a sketchy scree field toward the summit of the South Peak. They were proficient route-finders, and we were content with their judgment, even though we met them five minutes prior. We tagged the top together, as a team, a notion that we are all too familiar with. Despite the numerous, transient encounters we have had on the trail over the years, they never become any less special.

Our celebration was short-lived, however, as we would have to part ways with our new peers, who planned to head down the way we came. We were going to press forward, however, to North Maroon. In between us and it lay a highly dangerous and highly exposed vertical scramble. Per the advice of the guidebook, we left the rope at home even though we would have to do a decent amount of vertical climbing and downclimbing.

"How are *you* feeling?" I sarcastically asked Curtis, as he posed for a grandiose picture with the majestic North Maroon in the background.

"Better than you!"

Gingerly, he took a step down from his perch and toward the ridge. Without even looking back, he began the traverse, fearlessly.

"Hey, wait up!"

I guess he didn't hear me. Typically, it was windy up there.

* * *

The granite was rough and sticky, just how we liked it. Nonetheless, we were careful in each of our steps, because, death. Thousand-foot drops were just a few feet away.

At the lowest point of the traverse, the so-called Bell Cord, the real challenge commenced. A series of forty-foot cliff bands rose straight up from where we cowered with little to no horizontal relief. A fall here would likely be fatal.

Without thinking and without consulting our handy-dandy pocket mountain guide, we took off swinging. Soon, we went from swinging, to flailing, to shaking uncontrollably. Not surprisingly, Curtis and I ended up off-route. While such a mistake likely would have ground us into minced meat the year before, we kept calm and collected while we carefully evaluated our route. We realized that we had strayed too far left and were now in no man's land. Only the mountain goats and bighorn sheep probably treaded out to these parts. Maybe the occasional marmot or gumby.

At this point, we were practically hanging by a thread. Well, a rock, to be precise. Curtis and I both thought that we had found the correct route, but the rock got steeper—more like 5.5 than 5.2. As I placed my sweaty hand in a blind spot just above my helmet, a handhold abruptly snapped off the mountain.

"Holy sh-sh-it," I nervously shouted, as I somehow maintained my balance. My body quivered at the thought of what could have happened if my other hand had lost its grip.

"WHAT HAPPENED?" Curtis yelled down to me from about fifty feet up. His voice echoed over the crumbly, sheer face. I was convinced his voice would cause a rockfall, as I dangled with my one good handhold.

"I'M OKAY," I yelled back while I scrambled to find a better spot for my free hand. Thankfully my feet were in a somewhat decent position. But there was no telling when those holds would blow. I stared down at my boots just to make sure I was still standing on solid ground before I made the next lunge up to a bomber horizontal crack where I wedged my free hand into it and pulled my ass up to a secure ledge.

Not long after that episode, Curtis yelled down that he had found the next trail marker. After regaining the correct trail, we swiftly gained the summit of North Maroon Peak, where we encountered a herd of mountain goats. It was the first time that we had ever seen them in the flesh, and by golly were they beautiful creatures. Their fur was as white as snow, and their horns as sharp as a bull's. Though nearly as big as a horse, they moved effortlessly through the crumbly boulder fields on the sustained flanks of the peak.

"Wouldn't it be nice to have hooves like that?" I joked to Curtis, as I continued to cough uncontrollably. Somehow, I wasn't feeling the effects of the altitude despite my cough; I suppose proper acclimatization, no matter how sick I was, was the gamechanger.

"I'd rather have climbing shoes," he responded, poking fun at the fact that we had climbed some gnarly rock in our hiking boots.

Before our descent, I stared out at the neighboring peaks and wondered. Of course, I wondered. What the hell else do you do when you're on top of a mountain? Specifically, I thought about how silly we were, up here in the hills, risking life and limb and braving nasty chest colds just to stand on top of some rocky structure. After all, I had an important career ahead of me. What would my friends and family do if I threw everything away just to feel a sense of accomplishment and exhilaration? At twenty-three years old, I still had a lot to learn about risk and reward. Everything had gone so right for so long. But if the past few days had taught me anything, it was to be humble. The mountains will always be there. We won't.

Curtis, on the other hand, had yet to have his day of reckoning. He felt invincible, and rightly so. Though he wasn't nearly as fit as me, he had an iron physique built for the mountains. His stamina was barely affected at altitude, and he could run laps around me while my inflamed sinuses cursed me to near death. Not to mention he had spent the entire year obsessed with climbing. And here he was. At the apex of his latest daring quest. Accomplished, but familiarly so. He may never admit it, but from the outside looking in, I think he was getting in over his head.

* * *

We spent the next few days back in Denver before taking to the road once again. Talia graciously let us crash at her place, and we needed the relaxation. Though much of the intention of this second trip was to rock climb, we hadn't done so yet. You would think that climbing two of Colorado's hardest fourteeners would qualify as rock climbs, but for us it wasn't a true rock climb until we got the rope out. Curtis suggested that we climb Mount Thorodin, located in Golden Canyon State Park. Though only a 5.5, it would get us re-accustomed to climbing out west, so as to avoid a repeat of the previous year on the Grand Teton.

We pulled up to the trailhead located at Panorama Point. The route description online wasn't very helpful: "Hike to the buttress on the right side. It may take a while." Between the parking lot and the base of the climb, we wove through thick juniper and pine, often finding ourselves astray. There wasn't a defined trail, so we had to resort to intuition.

"SON OF A . . . ERGHHH!" I shouted.

Curtis spun around. "What's wrong?"

"I hit my damn funny bone!"

So much for intuition.

About forty-five minutes into our approach, we reached the base of the climb. Curtis prepped his gear and I put him on belay.

"You good to go?" I asked.

"Climbing!" He replied.

"Climb on."

I watched as my best friend fearlessly scampered up a short ramp, to the left of a tree, and then into a system of discontinuous cracks. He must have used half of the rope without placing even one piece of gear.

"HEY CURTIS!" I screamed.

"YEAH?"

"PLACE SOME PRO!"

"IT'S SUPER EASY."

"STILL."

He climbed up another ten or so meters, about two-thirds of the entire rope length before he placed his first piece of protection. I couldn't understand for the life of me why he hadn't done so a lot earlier. After all, he was no Alex Honnold.

After placing a few cams, Curtis continued to climb without looking back. I lost sight of him as he scaled the face.

Minutes went by, and so did meters of the rope. I thought to myself, *what the hell is he doing*? I glanced down at the rope under my feet and panicked.

"CURTIS!!!!!"

"WHAT?"

"YOU'RE OUT OF ROPE!"

He had maybe five meters left of our sixty-meter rope, and it seemed like he would have kept climbing until it was all gone. With two meters to spare, he yelled down to me that he was off-belay. Within a few minutes, I was on my way up.

I could understand why Curtis hadn't placed any gear. The climbing was easy, and I cruised all the way up to his perch on a windy ledge. Clouds were starting to roll in from the west, and we didn't intend on getting caught in an afternoon Colorado thunderstorm. We took a moment to soak in the scenery. It wasn't quite the Elk Range, the San Juans, or the Sangre de Cristos. But even the humblest of vistas can make you smile when you realize you're the only ones on the mountain.

"Gotta be quick," Curtis remarked. "I'll take the next pitch."

The route we were climbing is typically done in three pitches. Curtis had planned to let me do one of the three. But as he took off and started weaving his way up toward the summit, I could tell he was going to finish this one on his own.

"HEY, ARE YOU GOING TO PLACE ANY GEAR?" I yelled up toward him. Indifferent to my yells, he kept on chugging along toward the top.

"OFF BELAY!" He shouted down to me.

I took my belay device and carabiner off the rope and waited for him to pull me up. What did he have to prove? It was one thing if we were more experienced and confident in our abilities, but it seemed as if Curtis was pushing the boundaries of what was safe.

"YOU'RE ON BELAY!"

I began my wayward climb to the summit of Mount Thorodin as my partner in crime belayed me. After a series of easy cracks, I pulled through the crux dihedral, which is essentially a wall angled to look like an open book. I wondered why Curtis hadn't plugged a cam into an obvious crack right before the crux that would have probably saved his life if he had accidentally fallen. No matter. It was his climb to climb, not mine.

As I pulled up to him, I couldn't keep my thoughts to myself.

"Why didn't you place any gear?"

"It was easy." He said, as he pulled his beard hairs.

"Doesn't mean you shouldn't protect yourself. What if you fell?" I jabbed back.

He looked across the horizon down toward nearby civilization.

"I felt comfortable on the route."

I unclipped from the rope and began to coil it up for the descent.

"Watch your foot," I mumbled.

Curtis moved his foot from where he was stepping on the rope and tripped forward, nearly knocking me over the edge of the cliff we were perched on.

"REALLY?" I looked over the edge and pointed down. "And that's why we buy all this gear in the first place."

"Yeah."

I didn't want to press further. It wasn't worth the argument. I had learned that lesson already from the year before. We scampered down some easy class 4 terrain where we often found ourselves sliding on our butts to avoid slipping. Eventually, the steepness tapered off and we were back into the pine and juniper forest on our way back to the car.

As we popped back into the parking lot and customarily threw our shit all over the car, I wondered whether this was the new norm. It didn't feel like the first road trip. Far from it. I had been destroyed by my sickness and the altitude, and at the end of the day getting home in one piece was the priority. I felt as if I had a lot more to lose than the previous year. Either that, or I was becoming more cognizant of risk versus reward. Falling off a cliff didn't sound like the fairy-tale ending that either of us deserved. Whatever the rationale behind my apprehension, it was apparent that Curtis was on a totally different page.

Chapter 19

"Yes, man is mortal, but that would be only half the trouble. The worst of it is that he's sometimes unexpectedly mortal—there's the trick!"

—Mikhail Bulgakov, *The Master and Margarita*

* * *

We so often shield ourselves from thoughts about mortality because nothing is more depressing to think about than one's own demise. But life and death are inseparable. We only mentally detach them from each other because to not do so would lead our minds down a painful void of despair. If we woke up every morning to thoughts about death we would simply be unable to function and live productive existences.

For climbers, death is always one errant mistake away. Cognizance of your own mortality is important when you're dangling from your fingertips three hundred feet off the deck. Whether or not that awareness influences your choices on the wall depends on what kind of person you are. Surely though, a singular moment can define the rest of your life—be it on the walls or elsewhere. One wrong move is all it takes to change everything.

* * *

After Curtis's near free solo of Mount Thorodin, we spent the evening at Nel's house. He kept us occupied with a purportedly rare board game about the American presidential election system. It was about as fun and predictable as you would expect. We got our asses kicked by Nel, the board game aficionado.

The next day, we climbed Grays and Torreys Peak along the Kelso Ridge, a wild and exposed class 3 scramble that dodged all the usual crowds on the standard route.

After our summit bid, we said goodbye to Denver, with eyes set on Park City, Utah, where we planned to meet our friends Jalen and Sandra from College Outside. They were on a business trip of sorts to Outdoor Retailer, the largest outdoor trade show in the country. We found them at Psicobloc, an annual climbing competition where some of the best climbers in the world come together to free solo over a massive swimming pool. It was the perfect place to go to feed into our reckless desires.

Psicobloc, which in the Catalan language means "psycho bouldering," is climbing over a large body of water without a rope, and if you fall, the water "protects" that fall. That is, if you fall properly. It has become a popular climbing competition in recent years likely due to its wow factor. Watching someone climb can be boring, but watching them climb knowing that if they fall, they'll plummet forty feet into a pool is exhilarating for the average spectator. People yipped, jeered, and cringed when the competitors fell.

That evening, we slept in Sandra's camper outside of her friend's house. The Tempurpedic mattress was certainly a step up from the confines of Mindy. The suburban Utah neighborhood we found ourselves in looked a lot like the rest of the so-called American dream—concrete, shaded, and lined with cookie-cutter middle-class homes. That is, until two gnarly dirtbags rolled out of a camper the next morning, disrupting the banal character of the neighborhood.

Our plan that day was to drive to Las Vegas, where we would pick up our friend Randy at the airport. He would join us on our climbing adventures in Yosemite later in the week. Randy was one of our more recent friends whom we had met in the previous year. He had a good engineering job in Providence and didn't get outside too much at the time. This was his first serious climbing trip, and we were excited to have him along.

Prior to leaving Sandra's friend's house though, we got some advice about where to climb and sleep in and around the park. Sandra suggested we climb a few domes in the Tuolumne Meadows area, which is separate from Yosemite Valley, where Half Dome and El Capitan reside. In August, it's typically much hotter in the Valley at four thousand feet whereas the temperatures are nice and cool up at ten thousand feet in the Meadows. Also on Sandra's list were Cathedral Peak and Matthes Crest, two world-famous moderate multi-pitch routes. The options were limitless, so we had to narrow it down to a select few: Stately Dome, Pleasure Dome, Lembert Dome, and Cathedral Peak would be a good start; the rest, we would improvise as the week went on.

The second most important suggestion was where to sleep. We learned from our last experience in Yosemite that stealth camping in the park was out of the question. But we were also very frugal. Thus, Sandra recommended that we go to "the road cut at nine thousand feet." Her advice: "You'll know it when you see it!" We thanked our humble hosts and sponsors and headed for McCarran International Airport in Las Vegas to pick up Randy.

* * *

"What's up guys?" Randy fist-bumped Curtis and I as he threw himself and his stuff into Mindy's back seat. As you would expect, there wasn't much room to maneuver with our shit all over the place.

"Eight-ninety-nine Asian Buffet down the street," I gleefully replied.

"Oh, hell yeah!"

Vegas is known for its buffets, though we opted for one just outside the Strip. It wasn't world-class by any means, but the all-you-can-eat sushi was a plus.

As we scarfed down an endless supply of grease and starch, Randy interrupted our chomping.

"Did I ever tell you guys about the time I got kicked out of an Asian Buffet?"

I slurped my lo mein until the grease from the noodles shot up into my eyes.

"Nope," Curtis replied, as I dabbed my poor eyeballs with a napkin.

Randy was an average-sized guy, and like me, he had the appetite of a horse. At this point in our meal he was on his fourth full plate.

"This one time back home we went to a buffet and I just couldn't stop eating. It was one of those places where the waitresses give you a new plate instead of you going up to get one. So they had to keep coming every few minutes."

"How many plates did you have?" Curtis interjected. I was just about to head to the restroom to clean my irritated iris until Randy replied.

"Oh, I was onto my eleventh full plate."

"ELEVEN?" I burst out while soy sauce burned my eyes.

"So when did you get kicked out?" Curtis remarked, his sodium-free eyes aglow.

"Shortly after. I told them I was parched and needed some water to wash it all down. Then they told me to just leave."

"Without paying?" Curtis popped a chicken finger into his mouth.

"Yeah, they told me to get out, and wouldn't even let me pay."

I gave Curtis a nudge to move from the booth as he listened to Randy's surreal story.

"I'm gonna leave without paying if I don't get this shit out of my eye."

* * *

The drive through Tioga Pass toward Yosemite was an asphalt rollercoaster—it's a damn good thing we don't get car sick. We carefully watched our phone altimeters as we got higher and higher up the pass. When it hit nine thousand feet, we kept an eye out for obvious road pull-outs. We remembered Sandra's advice: "You'll know it when you see it."

We soon found out that it wasn't a pull-out, but a large, established parking lot on the left side of the road directly above a steep cliff. When we arrived, several cars were already in the lot, but only one person was there. We struck up a chat with him, because he sure seemed a hell of a lot more knowledgeable about the park than we were.

"Hey, how's it going!" Randy gleefully called out. Curtis and I weren't far behind him as we walked over to greet the man.

"Hallo there!" The man had a thick accent, which we later learned was Italian. He wore jeans and a plaid shirt with sandals, and carried a pot filled with rice and beans. Something told us we would like this guy.

"Are you a climber?" Randy followed up, cutting straight to the chase.

"Yis I ahm, as a mattera fact. Where-a are ya goin' tahmarrow?"

"We're going to try and do some of the domes in Tuolumne. Lembert Dome, probably, I think we're going to, uh, start there to-morrow," Curtis said, as he pointed to a picture of the dome in our guidebook.

"Oh, I've-a been there before. Vehry nice. A good warm-up." He took a huge bite of his rice and beans with a wooden ladle.

"Do the rangers let us, uh, pitch our tents here?" Curtis asked.

"Well-a, no. But we keep-a comin' back. What can they do about it?" He burst out laughing.

"Well that's reassuring," I mumbled to Randy and Curtis.

"The onlay things ya gotta worry about are the boldickeys!"

"The whaaaa?" Randy asked aloud, though the man likely didn't hear him, because for the next ten minutes he talked about these boldickey creatures like we knew what the hell he was talking about.

"The boldickeys ahra very bad out here. They eat yer food and tap on your windows, so just be-a careful." He started to laugh again, so we all decided to laugh with him. Perhaps a boldickey was some sort of gnome-like creature from the forests of Italy? Or maybe it was a reference to thieves trying to break into your cars? It's not uncommon to hear stories of people having their cars broken into at trailheads.

For the next several hours, we chatted with the man. We never really understood what his name was because of his thick accent, so we decided to call him Boldickey. He hailed from the Italian Alps where he learned to climb as a young boy. We figured that he was probably in his late thirties or early forties but could easily have been older. His grit and extensive knowledge certainly made it seem that way.

Before Boldickey started to tell us about his mountain endeavors, we told him about our background, which, comparatively, was severely deficient. He had attempted to climb Everest twice without oxygen but was unsuccessful on both occasions. His failures came at a great cost. On his second attempt, he and his climbing partner of many years got caught in a brutal snowstorm. Boldickey told his partner that it wasn't wise to continue toward the summit due to the hazardous weather. However, his partner did not yield his advice, and instead continued to trudge through the blizzard. He never heard from him again. No one did.

Stories from his eighteen Denali summits were no more cheery. On one of his many attempts, Boldickey met a Canadian climber who planned to summit on a day that did not promise good weather. Shortly after the climber began his descent, he slipped and fell into a crevasse. Two rangers were dispatched to stage a rescue, Unfortunately, the climber had already perished. The rangers did not realize this at the time, so they pushed forward with the rescue. As one of them was lowered into the crevasse, he fell to his death. The other ranger hung onto an ice axe for dear life. Boldickey was sent out to rescue the last remaining ranger, and he did so successfully.

We realized that his stories could have been entirely made up, and we still have not verified their authenticity. But I'm not sure someone would fabricate stories as detailed as his were.

"How do you still do it?" Randy asked.

"Whatta do you mean?" Boldickey answered.

"How do you keep climbing even though you've seen so much?"

He took a drag of a cigarette and blew a gray plume of smoke into the darkening skies.

"It's-a parta the risks we take."

"When are the risks not worth it?" I asked.

"You will know when. You can't-a make the same mistake once. The mountain will-a bite you in the ass." We all gave each other quizzical looks.

"You know-a the saying? There are the old alpineests and the bold alpineests. But there are no old, bold alpineests. Just know-a when to quit."

It was about that time that we all decided to call it quits for the night. The morbid stories were getting to us and I think we all felt the same way. Curtis and Randy pitched a tent adjacent to Mindy and I decided that I wanted to stay in the car in case the boldickeys came out. Just before going to bed, we found out from Boldickey himself that he was referring to bears. We never did find out where he got the creative nickname from.

To cope with the anxiety that had overtaken me from the horrible stories, I turned on some Sinatra to lull me to sleep. What were we getting ourselves into? I still considered myself new to this whole climbing thing despite our epic adventures the year before and a full year of training on plastic holds in the gym. There were just so many additional variables to consider that I had yet to encounter outside.

Boldickey's advice reminded me of my mortality and of the need to exercise extreme caution. We had taken so many risks in our travels without incident. Sure, we'd had a few run-ins here and there, but never were we seriously hurt in the process. I had all but forgotten that one wrong move could turn into disaster.

Chapter 20

"There's a constant tension in climbing, and really all ex-ploration, between pushing yourself into the unknown but trying not to push too far. The best any of us can do is to tread that line carefully."

—Alex Honnold

* * *

In climbing, every inch matters. The distance between holding onto a bomber jug and a crumbly piece of choss could be the width of a fingernail. And grabbing onto choss that'll just fall apart in your hand obviously poses some grim consequences. On the flip-side, grabbing a bomber, thank-god hold opens a world of opportunities. You can place protection in a nearby crack or use it to rest while you contemplate your next move. You can hoist your body up with one arm and two feet while shaking out the other arm to ensure it does not tire. The peace of mind is unrivaled.

Every so often though, you find yourself in an apparently insur-mountable position. You get to a point where your arms are so pumped that you can't climb any higher. You're on a lousy hold and the nearest spot to place protection is a full body length away from you. In these situations, you have two options. First, you can down-climb and hope to God that you find a better hold to rest on so that you can jam a piece of gear into a shitty crack. If that doesn't work, well, you fall, and hope to God that your last piece holds you.

* * *

Lembert Dome is a shapely granite dome that rises high above Tuolumne Meadows. On the side closest to the road, it rises eight hundred vertical feet to its summit. On the other side, hikers can scale a more gradual face that also leads to the top. Our plan was not to climb straight up, but to ascend between the two sides of the dome up a classic 5.6 climb called the Northwest Books. Since Randy was with us, we opted to take two ropes so that each of us could simultaneously follow Curtis while he belayed us from the top, much like we did on the Grand Teton the summer before.

I took the first pitch. It wasn't anything special. Not even a hundred feet of class 3 climbing brought me to a ledge with a small tree to which I secured an anchor and belayed Randy and Curtis up. We all likely could have made it up there unscathed without the use of the rope.

"Why'd you climb up here?" Curtis asked me.

"Why the hell do you think I climbed over here? It's a pretty obvious line up to this tree."

"Well it looks like we just have to go around that corner to the left and then go back right."

I looked up and scanned the route before responding. It most certainly looked like I had gone a bit too far right. To regain the proper route, Curtis would have to traverse left, climb up a bit, and then go back right.

"Whatever you say. Just rope up and let's do it."

Randy was quick to notice our fragile chemistry.

"Do you guys always fight?"

"No, just on road trips," I quickly responded as I exasperatedly prepared my belay device for Curtis's lead. I hastily turned the carabiner's locking mechanism without checking to see if it was secure.

While we readied ourselves for our respective obligations, we conversed about what Curtis was going to do next, since communication could be difficult.

"Are you actually going to climb to the top from here? It looks like setting up an anchor around the corner so we can see you would be a good idea." Randy logically opined.

"Well, uh . . . it's just 5.6. I probably won't place a ton of gear anyway because there'll be a ton of rope drag."

As a beginner, I didn't question Curtis's intentions. He was much more knowledgeable about climbing than I at the time, and it seemed like he could handle a measly 5.6. The plan was to climb to the left up a slab for about thirty feet to avoid the faceless wall in front of us. He would then forego placing any gear in the cracks, and cut back to the right, going around another wall and into what looked like a cave. From there, he would climb straight up and top out near the summit of the dome.

"You're on belay Curtis," I said as I secured the lock on my carabiner and clicked it just to make sure.

"Climbing!"

* * *

At what point do we tell ourselves that the risk is too much and the reward too little? At what point do we give up and go down? At what point is life more valuable than scaling a rock? The answer is deeply personal. Rock climbing is a spiritual journey for some, a lifestyle for others, and for a few—life itself. Whatever category you find yourself in, each person has a distinct reason for chalking up and getting ready for a climb.

Take people like Alex Honnold. He is the media-proclaimed daredevil of climbing—the only person to free solo El Capitan. He takes unimaginable risks that appear to the layperson as invitations to death. But what people don't understand about elite free soloists is just how calculated and prepared they are before taking on a climb without a rope. They practice, and practice, and practice some more, until they effectively master each sequence of moves that a climb has to offer. This helps ensure that their climb is impeccable from the start. A mistake leads to a fatality. It's as simple as that.

Okay, so we weren't on the same level as Alex Honnold. And we surely had no intention of free soloing. But what all trad climbers should have before they step foot on a climb is a heightened sense of awareness. It doesn't have to be on nearly the same level as a free soloist. But typically, preparation for a climb consists of reading a guidebook, studying the route, and visualizing. When you ascend a sheer vertical cliff, error is not an option. You must be a perfectionist. And if you're not, well, you could find yourself six feet under.

Nearly thirty minutes had passed since Curtis began climbing. Randy and I were getting impatient.

"What the hell is he doing?" I asked.

"Maybe he got lost?" Randy started to walk to the left to see if he could see anything around the corner.

I stood up so that I would take some of the weight off my harness. My feet were getting numb from sitting back for so long. Since I was directly on the anchor belaying, I had a lot less room to maneuver than Randy did.

"Dude, it's a 5.6, where would he get lost?"

He walked back over once he reached the end of the rope, about five feet away from the belay station. "Just a thought."

Ten minutes passed, and our wonder began to turn to worry. We should have never let him go around that corner out of our sight. It is so important to keep your climber in sight. Sometimes it's impossible; but we collectively made the choice to let Curtis climb his climb. Problem is, we couldn't hear each other—which is even worse than not being able to see him.

"CURTIS!" We both alternated yelling his name intermittently for a few minutes. But there was no response.

It wasn't a particularly windy day, but the corner that Curtis had gone around was a massive wind tunnel. Nothing went in, and nothing went out. Except wind, and Curtis—we hoped.

"How are we going to know when to climb?" I said in disgust. "Why didn't he just set up an anchor?"

Not a few seconds later, we heard a thumping sound coming from above us. Sure enough, a yellow cam careened past to the left of us and kept going until it hit a tree at the bottom.

"Wow, Curtis," Randy said. He began to laugh hysterically.

"Well, getting that is going to be a pain in the ass," I replied indignantly.

Suddenly, I felt a strong tug on the rope. I reacted about as fast as I could, given the fact that I was whining just a few moments before. It was enough force to get my attention, but not enough to cause concern.

"My god, what is he doing up there?" I complained to Randy.

We heard a shout from the bottom of the slab to our left. Quickly, we turned around and saw an older couple hiking on the trail below.

"YOUR FRIEND DOESN'T LOOK GOOD!" The woman yelled.

Randy and I looked at each other fearfully.

"IS HE MOVING?" Randy yelled back.

"I DON'T KNOW," she replied.

Shit. Curtis was hurt and there was nothing we could do about it. We didn't even know if he was alive. My head began to spin. We were in a helpless spot. I could climb up myself, but Randy would have to belay me. That would mean that I would have to take Curtis off belay. I had no idea if he was hanging from a ledge, or on the ground.

We heard a faint yell coming from the wind tunnel: "I'M OKAY."

My heart rebounded slightly. In the brief minute between the rope tug and our conversation with the hikers, I had gone from pissed off to thinking that Curtis was dead. But I didn't have long to contemplate what could have been. I still had no idea what *was* and we had no plan whatsoever to assess the gravity of the situation.

"What are we going to do?" I said to Randy. My tone had quickly shifted from abrasive to apprehensive.

"Look, Curtis forgot to tie the other end of the rope to his harness! Well shit. I guess we lucked out."

Had Curtis remembered to tie the second rope to his harness, getting one of us to where he was would have been a little more difficult. A lead climber who has two people following him typically brings up two ropes so each climber can tie onto a separate rope. Otherwise, two climbers would have to be attached to one rope, and if one of them fell, so too would the other. By having two ropes, you make your three-party ascent safer. Fortunately for us, Curtis forgot to tie the second rope to his harness, so I could have Randy belay me up to Curtis's position.

"We could do that. But we may have to call for help."

Based on the expressions and tone that the hikers projected, we could tell that this was going to be a serious endeavor. Neither of us had any qualifications to get Curtis down. And of course, we had no cell service to boot.

While Randy and I were switching Curtis's belay to his harness, a man in his thirties came out of nowhere and perched himself just to the right of us. He was climbing rope-less and only had a pair of shoes and a chalk bag strapped to his back. His hair was dark reddish brown, and he had a five o'clock shadow. There wasn't a bead of sweat on his body. Clearly, this wasn't his first rodeo.

"Hey guys, what's going on?" He continued to climb upward to our surprise, considering we had specifically gone out of our way to go left first.

"Our friend is up there and we think he's hurt. He fell about five minutes ago." Randy said, as I tightened my figure-eight knot and prepared to climb.

"Oh shit, is he okay?" He placed his right hand into his chalk bag and pressed it together with his left until his hands were white as snow.

"From what those hikers down there told us, he's not," I stated.

"Let me go look. I work for YOSAR." Without hesitation, the man effortlessly scurried up the seemingly blank face and was out of sight a mere thirty seconds later.

"What's YOSAR?" I whispered to Randy.

"I think it's search and rescue," he replied. "You're on belay, by the way."

I chalked up my hands and looked straight up where the YOSAR guy climbed up before me and thought *hell no*. "Climbing!"

I took the same path as Curtis and climbed as fast as I could, realizing that I would fall quite far if I messed up. Like Curtis before me, there was no way I was going to place gear on the far left side and cause a ton of rope drag if I had to belay Randy up. As I went further left, I realized that it was highly unlikely that we were on the right route. But I couldn't turn back now.

As soon as I reached the high point on the left side, the opening of the wind cave presented itself to me. The route skirted all the way back right, almost parallel to where Randy was belaying me but about fifty feet higher. None of the climbing was particularly difficult, but without any gear in, this was a no-fall zone.

Even more troublesome than my route though was the sight of my best friend. Curtis was on his back, clearly in pain, being attended to by the YOSAR guy. I practically ran across the hairy class 3 ramp and took refuge next to them.

"Hey man, get on this anchor." The YOSAR guy pointed me to a cord hanging from the wall and I quickly complied. I then screamed as loud as I could down to Randy.

"OFF BELAY."

Once I found a good safe spot to stand, I greeted Curtis, heart pounding.

"You . . . alright?"

"Yeah. It hurts." He was breathing heavily and explained to me that Will, the YOSAR guy, had advised him to not move a muscle in case he had a spinal injury.

"Where's the pain?" I asked.

"Mostly in my lower back. My head kind of hurts too."

I felt my stomach drop.

"Hey buddy, can I see your phone?" Will asked me.

I pulled out my phone and handed it to him. As soon as I did so, another free soloist popped up from below us.

"Jeez, Danny, what timing."

Danny was a tall lanky guy with long brown hair. It looked like he had a body fat percentage of zero. He was solid, skinny muscle.

"What's going on Will?" He asked.

"This is Curtis. He took a nasty fall off the 5.9 section. Looks like the rope barely caught him before he decked."

"5.9 section? Seriously Curtis?" My worry turned to anger with just two numbers.

"Yeah, I realized as soon as I got on it that it was the, uh, the wrong route." He coughed a weak cough and sprawled his body out.

"Curtis, you gotta stay still," Will instructed. "Danny, I'm going to do the assessment on him and give you the phone. Can you bring it down to the station?"

"Not a problem."

Danny found a comfortable ledge directly above us and sat down.

"Okay, Curtis, I'm going to ask you a few questions and record my observations in your phone, is that okay? Make sure not to move. We have to make sure your neck is in a comfortable spot. You good?"

"Yeah."

Will asked Curtis what must have been two dozen questions about his pain, pre-existing conditions, and the like. I felt like I was in a doctor's office. After the medical interrogation was over, Danny took the phone with Will's notes and disappeared above us in a flash.

"Do you need any help?" I asked, feeling like I was doing nothing in a time I should have been doing everything.

"No, thank you, though. In fact, why don't you take Curtis's rope and rappel down to your buddy."

Without questioning him, I helped untie Curtis's knot and pulled the rope down after he had been secured to an anchor. From there, I moved back out left just a bit until I could see Randy and set up an anchor to rappel off.

"How are we going to get our gear back?" I asked, as if I had forgotten that my friend was potentially severely injured.

"Don't worry about it. We'll get it for you."

I began the rappel down to Randy on the first ledge with the tree. As soon as I was within a few feet of him, his curiosity surfaced.

"Is he okay? What happened? What took you guys so long?"

I waited until I was back on solid ground and secured myself to Randy's anchor.

"I don't know if he's okay. He says he is, but you know Curtis."

"What are they going to do?"

"I don't know, Randy. I really don't."

We were silent for a few minutes. It was the kind of somber silence you experience when you're feeling helpless, like nothing can clear the air. Except stupid questions.

"Is he going to be alright?"

"Dammit Randy, I told you I don't know. He hurt his back, they're stabilizing his spine, that's all I know!" My blood was boiling. Why would he do something so stupid? He probably hadn't even climbed a 5.8 outdoors before, let alone a 5.9.

"Jesus, you don't have to yell at me. At least he didn't get himself killed."

I sighed. "I'm sorry, this is just a shitty situation."

We stood there silent for another five minutes or so before we heard heavy footsteps coming from the hiking trail below us. We turned around and saw a half-dozen rangers ascending toward the base of the climb. That's when we knew the situation was serious.

Without skipping a beat, two of the rangers began to free solo the class 3 ramp that I had roped up for earlier. They were still in their boots and didn't even bother putting climbing shoes on. A few minutes later, they arrived at the tree that we were anchored on.

"Are you Curtis's friends?" One of the rangers asked.

"Yeah, he's up there and doesn't look too good," I said worriedly.

"If you guys don't mind, could you rappel down?"

"Not a problem. Thank you for all you do," Randy responded.

Once we reached the bottom, we scoped out the yellow cam that initially set off signals to us that something was wrong. It was surprisingly still in good shape, despite a few dinks here and there.

"Hey, at least the cam is okay," Randy joked, attempting to bring light to a tense situation.

* * *

The rescue effort would take over two hours. There were over a dozen volunteers on site, most of them rangers, but a few volunteers from YOSAR—Yosemite Search And Rescue, we found out—as well. First, they hauled a bulky litter up a series of ropes that they had rigged to the route. After we observed that process for over an hour from the base of the cliff, we watched as they lowered Curtis down the rope system. The litter made crashing sounds as it banged against the rock on the way down, but it was clear that this was one of the burliest pieces of rescue gear available. Not only did it have to stabilize Curtis's back and spine, but it also had to withstand blow after blow from a hard granite surface.

When the contraption reached the bottom, the rescuers grabbed Curtis's litter and placed it on a specially designed tire. It was one of the largest I had ever seen, and I figured it was much needed. It was evident that we were going to wheel him down to the parking lot.

"How you doing, buddy?" Randy asked.

"I'm okay," Curtis weakly responded.

To our surprise, the rescuers asked Randy and I to join them in wheeling him out. It wasn't an easy task, as we had to maneuver over and around giant boulders for a half mile or so, but eventually our group succeeded in transporting him down to the parking lot where an ambulance was waiting.

The paramedics were careful to make sure his body was as stable as possible while they transferred him from the litter onto their stretcher. Only then did it dawn on me that this was real. No more of the fairy tale bullshit we had experienced during our travels up until then. I was petrified at what might happen. I heard one of the EMTs mutter the word *paralysis*.

But Curtis made sure to slip us one last statement that settled our nerves before the ambulance doors shut.

"Make sure you get my gear before you meet me at the hospital."

Typical climber.

Chapter 21

*"I felt my lungs inflate with the onrush of scenery—
air, mountains, trees, people. I thought, 'This is what
it is to be happy'"*

—Sylvia Plath, *The Bell Jar*

* * *

Life is a game of inches, much like climbing. You get a speeding ticket because you hit the brakes too late even though you know that there's always a cop behind those bushes. You pass a test by less than a point because at the last second you switched your answer to question 4 from D to B. You sink the half-court game-winner as it hits the top of the backboard and by some miracle bounces back toward the rim and in the net. Luck is an inextricable part of life. Some call it fate, others call it fortune. Wherever it derives from, luck can get you out of a lot of jams. Curtis knows this best.

He could have died. And then all of this—all of what we had built—would have been obsolete. I've played the scenario in my head many times, and many times the outcome was a whole lot grimmer. Five more feet of the rope, and we could have been following a hearse instead of an ambulance. Fortune is forgiving sometimes, albeit utterly unpredictable. Yet it continues to work in our favor—for now, at least.

When I heard the EMT spurt out the word *paralysis*, the dream world in which I had been residing for far too long dissolved in front of my eyes. Climbing was supposed to be a safe pastime, and the accidents and fatalities were reserved for free soloists and gumbies. Not us. Certainly not us. But that's the thing. We *were* gumbies.

My gut told me that Curtis was okay. How could he not be? Everything had gone right thus far. But as my mind raced on the way to the hospital, reality kicked in. No, not the faux-paradise reality that we had crafted ourselves over the course of the last two road trips. This was a much simpler reality—life or death.

When we saw Curtis at the hospital for the first time, we still didn't know the extent of his injuries. The doctor suspected that he had a severely bruised back and a possible broken tailbone. But his head seemed to be the biggest problem, and the doctor had no idea what kind of injury he may have suffered.

As we sat at there and he told us the story, I couldn't help but think just how damn lucky he really was. Instead of going up the planned 5.6 route, he started climbing the 5.9 variation just to the left. Realizing his mistake, he decided to keep going instead of retreating.

When he got about two-thirds up the pitch, his arms were practically dead. He told us that he tried to place a piece of gear at some point mid-climb but was physically unable to. Again, instead of backing off, he decided to keep going. At this point, he intended to keep climbing toward the top without protecting his fall with gear.

Near the apex of the climb, he was having a hard time topping out. He needed to perform a big push on his triceps to propel himself to the end, and his arms were too shot to do it. It was at this point that he started freaking out. He quickly reached for his harness and pulled out a yellow cam, which is one of the bigger ones that a climber carries. As soon as he went to place it, he lost his grip, and it went flying down the cliff. Not long after, his other arm failed, and he fell an estimated thirty to forty feet.

No one witnessed it, so we'll never actually know the distance. Nor will we know what happened to him after that. The shock of the fall was so overwhelming for him that he couldn't even remember what occurred after gravity took over. I suspect that it wasn't only the shock, but a brutal concussion.

What I think happened, based on the pull of the rope, is that he didn't free-fall though the air. Had he, the force on the rope would have been much greater, and I likely would have been pulled. Instead, he likely bounced off the rock a few times on his way down, which slowed his fall considerably.

As he reached the bottom of the wind tunnel, the rope took all his weight because the one piece of gear that he did place held. If it hadn't, he probably would have been dead—or at least a lot more injured than he was. Once the rope caught all the force, he then hit the ground and landed on his back. He also presumably hit his head, causing a concussion. But I'm still just guessing.

We can speculate what happened for eternity, but the fact is, he screwed up, big time. He made a horrible decision to take the 5.9 variation route. His experience level was there—but his stamina and endurance were not. He knew how to climb the route; he just didn't have the strength to finish it off. Certainly, if he had placed more gear and taken more frequent rests, he probably could have made it. But his boldness blinded him and caused him to make reckless decisions. At least that's my opinion. He'll probably tell you otherwise.

We all knew the trip was over for Curtis at this point. To make him as comfortable as possible, we decided to drive to a hostel in nearby Mammoth Springs and book a three-person room for the night. That way, he could attempt to heal up while we tried to figure out what our next step was. We were across the country with a lime green SUV and a very injured back. There was no way he would make it back home in a car. Before getting injured, Curtis planned to fly home from Nevada because he had purchased a ticket to the Burning Man festival. It was just over a week away, and we knew he couldn't go. He didn't.

It was a restful evening for Randy and me. Curtis, on the other hand, was moaning in pain for much of the night. At some point I decided it was time to put earplugs in, but I was genuinely concerned. There was no telling what kind of damage he had done to his head, especially since the doctor didn't even do any imaging.

"How are you feeling?" Randy had gotten up early to eat breakfast with the other hostel guests. But sleeping is my modus operandi, and I happily chose to do so.

"I'm better than yesterday, but not good." Curtis replied.

"Go get yourself some pancakes from the kitchen." He pulled the covers off Curtis. "Wakey wakey!"

We reluctantly rose and headed over to the kitchen down the stairs. Curtis had a lot of trouble getting down them without wincing in pain. It was even worse than his infected toe, which in hindsight, looked like a broken nail in comparison. When we arrived at the kitchen, a bubbly brunette welcomed us. Her name was Carly, and simply from her demeanor, we could tell she was a regular.

"Welcome to the party gentlemen!" She poured some instant pancake mix into a pan and promptly placed it on the stove.

We learned from our conversations with Carly that she was a ski bum. She lived in the hostel full time and worked in Mammoth year-round, bouncing between odd jobs. In the winter, she rode. At the time, ski culture was as elusive to me as morning coffee, but when you realize the quickest way down a snowy mountain isn't with snowshoes, you learn a new hobby.

Carly was as gracious a hostess as any. She treated Curtis better than we do. Well, I guess that isn't saying a lot. But truthfully, she made sure to welcome us to the hostel as if it was our home away from home. She fixed up pancakes for us, and asked questions. She was honestly curious about who we were and what we were doing out in Mammoth. Of course, when we told her what happened to Curtis, she immediately expressed her concerns.

"Dude, you need to rest up here for a few days. You can hang out with me and my friends. It will be a grand old time." She shoveled the last pancake onto Curtis's plate and threw the pan in the sink.

"What about you guys? What's your plan for the day?"

"We haven't really thought about it yet," I replied. Despite what had happened to Curtis the day before, I felt pulled to the cliffs. Randy had the same epiphany.

"Maybe we can do some climbing. I mean, we're only going to be here a few more days. Might as well make the most out of it."

I resisted the urge to tell him that it was a bad idea. I think we were both still traumatized from what had happened, but it was as if we needed to get back out there and prove something to ourselves. I can't really explain it. But the call of the rock was alluring, and our hands craved its texture. The best mountaineers have the worst memories, as they say. I think that's what Boldickey told us, right?

What did I have left to prove? I had overcome overwhelming odds to summit the Maroon Bells just a few days after coming down with horrible altitude sickness. And somehow, I climbed to the saddle of Capitol Peak while afflicted with that very sickness. Frankly, I think I was so affected by what happened to Curtis that I wanted to assure myself that this dangerous hobby of mine was something I wanted to keep doing.

Even more significant was the fact that this would be the first climb I would do without Curtis during our trips. For two summers, we spent nearly every waking moment together. Though at times it didn't seem like it, we looked after each other. There was Longs Peak, the Grand Canyon, Mount Whitney, Shasta, Rainier, and—who could forget—Grand Teton. Despite the hazards and challenges that confronted us, we prevailed, however gracelessly, in each instance.

Now, it was Randy and me. It didn't have the same flair to it. I love Randy to death, but he knows as much as I do just how inseparable Curtis and I were. Even when we got on each other's nerves. Which happened a lot, I guess. But where the players would be different, the setting would remain the same. Me and the mountains. Where I belong.

Chapter 22

"Jumping from boulder to boulder and never falling, with a heavy pack, is easier than it sounds: you just can't fall when you get into the rhythm of the dance."

—Jack Kerouac, *The Dharma Bums*

* * *

It was nearly 12:30 p.m. when Randy and I arrived at the trailhead for Cathedral Peak. We had to pass by the site of Curtis's accident on the way, and it didn't do much to settle my anxiety. Truth is, I was terrified about what we were getting ourselves into. Firstly, we weren't going to start climbing until after 2 p.m. at the earliest. If anything went wrong, we would be stuck suspended to a several-hundred-foot cliff in the pitch black. At the time, my qualifications were essentially nonexistent, and Randy's weren't much better. Even with another year under my belt, the most ambitious climb I had done to date was on the Grand Teton. And Dorian practically guided us up. Unprepared hardly describes that day.

"Forgetting something?" I said to Randy as he shut the trunk. I knocked on my brain bucket and gave him a smirk.

"Shit, have you seen it?" He panicked.

"Yep, front seat, right where you left it."

He dropped his overstuffed backpack pretty much in the middle of the road and retrieved his helmet from the front seat.

"Hey, you know there are cars trying to get by your massive backpack?" I dragged it away from the road and leaned it up on the left rear quarter of Mindy. "What the hell is in here anyway? It's not like we're camping out there."

He returned to his bag and secured the helmet to the outside using a carabiner. "Can never be too prepared!"

No doubt, Randy was the safer climber of the two of us. I hadn't fully processed Curtis's near-death experience, and I was still just as oblivious as I was when I left last summer on the voyage of a lifetime. Except now, I had bigger biceps and more expensive gear. False sense of security much?

We started up the trail, weaving through massive pines along an easy series of switchbacks. The hike up was therapeutic, but only delayed the inevitable. Once we spotted our cathedral, all we could do was pray for salvation. And by God, I was ready to be saved.

The trees gave way to a wide-open paradise. An arrowhead-shaped granite monolith jabbed straight into the sky like a thumbs-up from God. Its name was about as fitting as any, resembling a twelfth-century house of worship as if it was indeed a cathedral. And we sought to attend its services.

Just over an hour after commencing our hike, we were at the base of the tower. Six pitches of impeccable 5.6 climbing separated us from the apex. Anxiety was swapped for admiration, but admiration quickly turned to impatience.

"Is that rope flaked yet?" I said to Randy as I slipped on my climbing shoes.

"Getting there!"

He spent the next five minutes getting knots out of our poorly tied rope. When he finally finished, I secured myself to the rope and began my pilgrimage to the top.

As the cliché goes, all good things must come to an end. So too, would our second road trip—but in a dramatically different fashion than we had imagined. When Curtis and I left the previous year for Washington, D.C., we never could have predicted where we would end up. But no matter the situation, we always expected to be there for each other. We spent several years in college scheming for adventure. I fondly remember sitting with him in my apartment kitchen just six months prior to leaving. We were using my laptop to map out our trip itinerary. It was a particularly trying time in my life. I was depressed and directionless, and it seemed as if I had been waiting an eternity to leave my familiar home. I had never been anywhere west of upstate New York to that point in my life except for a weekend trip to Chicago for a school conference. My entire life to date had practically been spent within a three-hundred-mile radius, and that, coupled with my benign suburban upbringing, meant my life experiences were effectively nonexistent.

But our yearning for knowledge and experience allowed Curtis and I to feed off each other's desire to travel. College only satiated our curiosity so much. It was the road though, that brought our dreams into a self-designed reality. One that we had been building up in our heads for many years. And one that could not have developed any more seamlessly. Until Curtis fell, that is.

As I clambered up perfect rock and set up my first belay overlooking Tuolumne Meadows, I couldn't help but imagine what I could have done differently. No doubt, my best friend had gotten a little overzealous while climbing, but I should have been more perceptive of the situation. If only our communication had been better. Would he have been right there with me on Cathedral Peak, relishing the divine views? Instead, we had reached the end of an era. And it ended with a nearly forty-foot whipper and a whimper from Curtis.

Before I could stew any longer, I heard Randy yell, "YOU'RE OFF BELAY!"

* * *

Unless you're experienced enough, it doesn't make sense to commence a climb in late afternoon. At the first belay, we had maybe three hours of good daylight left. And we still had five full pitches of climbing to go. To expedite the process, I told Randy that I would lead the second pitch as well. It went quickly, but as soon as I delicately lifted myself onto the next ledge, I noticed that another group had already taken refuge there. As a result, I had to find a spot to set up an anchor so I wouldn't get in their way.

I watched in agony as the party ahead of us took a good fifteen minutes to ascend ten feet. We were going to get stuck behind them in the pitch black if we didn't figure out a plan. Rappelling down the first two pitches would have been a valid option, but we eagerly sought to keep going. Spirits were high, and we weren't going to let impending darkness ruin our redemptive climb.

"For Curtis," we chanted, as Randy began the third pitch.

We let the party in front of us get a little ahead before we started the pitch. Randy sluggishly inched up the route, placing gear every few feet until he had gone through much of his rack. His pitch took longer than both of my first two combined, and I began to worry. The sun had already begun to descend rapidly as 5:30 p.m. rolled around.

When I got up to Randy's anchor, it was obvious that the other party was going nowhere slowly on the renowned 5.6 Chimney Pitch. I decided that I would take the 5.7 variation to our left so that we could pass them. At the time, it was the hardest pitch I had led before, but I felt as if I had something to prove to myself. Not to mention I wasn't interested in finding our way back home in the darkness.

I clambered to the left and around a corner out of Randy's sight much like Curtis had done the day before. It didn't dawn on me that I was being as foolhardy as he had been. You never really realize it when you're dialed in.

As I emerged onto the face, I put my right index and middle fingers on a thin knob the size of a car stereo dial. It was sharp and sticky despite its miniature size, and I felt confident getting my left hand on another dial-sized feature. I looked up and took a deep breath. Twenty feet stood between me and the next ledge, and I saw a small crack where I could get some finnicky gear in. I placed my first piece into it and prayed it was good. No calculations had gone into my decision. Just instinct.

I made the next series of vertical movements toward my destination and breathed a labored breath. My left leg started to shake uncontrollably as I pulled out another cam to place in the crack. We climbers call this phenomenon the Elvis leg. All I could think about in that moment was "You ain't nothin' but a hound dog" and "Oh god, I hope I don't fall and die."

I got a third cam in just above my previous one as my arms tightened up and began to exhaust. Both legs started to do a little dance as I peeked my head above the ledge I had spotted and realized I was only halfway there.

I vigorously shook out my right arm as I clung to a peanut-sized hold with my left.

"Shit, shit, shit," I mumbled, as I fumbled through my harness for a nut. I had never placed one in a high-stress situation before, but there was no way I was going to fit even my smallest cam into the crack. A nut works much differently than a cam: instead of pulling a spring-loaded mechanism and slipping the device into a crack, a nut is slotted into a crack, typically from the top to the bottom. The idea is that you stick a nut into an area of the crack where it will fit and lower it down to a spot where the crack gets narrower. That way, if you fall, the nut won't rip out of the wall and take you with it.

I slotted the nut into a thin crack and pulled it downward until I was convinced it would never, ever fall out. I didn't even care if it was stuck. Above me, I located better holds that trended toward the right, bypassing the chimney pitch entirely. At this point I felt confident enough to continue effortlessly up the wall as the slope angle tapered off a bit. I plugged in a few more pieces of gear on my way up to the next belay station.

"OFF BELAY, RANDY!" I screamed over the ledge and started to pull the rope up toward me until I heard Randy's cue.

"THAT'S ME!"

I fumbled through my disorganized harness for my belay device only to realize I had left it with Randy. If I had remembered what I had learned in my crevasse rescue class from the previous year, I would have realized I could simply tie a Munter hitch.

"Dammit!" I yelled to myself. I schemed about what I could do to safely get my friend up to me, but nothing was coming to me.

That is, until I heard the din of jingling gear coming from the summit just above me.

"HEY!"

No answer.

"HEY GUYS ON THE SUMMIT!"

Crickets.

"HELP!!!!"

Two heads poked up over the summit toward me. That's one way to get someone's attention.

"WHAT'S GOING ON BUDDY?" One of the heads yelled.

"I FORGOT MY BELAY DEVICE. DOWN THERE. WITH MY BELAYER." I pointed over the edge, feeling like a true gumby.

"THAT SUCKS," he replied, indifferently.

"WHAT SHOULD . . . I DO?" I hesitantly yelled back.

Randy's voice from some hundred feet below entered the conversation.

"WHAT'S GOING ON?"

I ignored him and perked my ears up toward the guys above me.

"TIE A MUNTER. TAKE YOUR ROPE, MAKE TWO LOOPS, FACING AWAY FROM EACH OTHER, AND PUT IT IN YOUR LOCKER!"

"OKAY!" I yelled upwards as I followed the guy's instructions as best I could. Well, let's hope he doesn't fall.

"RANDY, YOU'RE ON BELAY . . . I guess."

As he began his climb, I slid the rope through the locking carabiner, thinking that if Randy was to fall, I would probably have to catch his entire body weight with just my right hand. I envisioned him plummeting perilously to his demise as he screamed my name and I couldn't help him.

I looked over the edge for what seemed like forever as I continued to pull more and more rope. That is, until I couldn't pull it anymore. Several minutes passed without any movement and I wondered what was going on. Did I wonder though? Or did I know exactly what it was?

"JUSTIN! YOUR NUT IS STUCK!"

I laughed to myself until I realized Randy had been right around the crux of the pitch. I remembered that I had no idea if he would survive a fall.

"LEAVE IT!"

"YOU SURE?"

"ABSOLUTELY."

The remainder of the climb went without a hiccup, and Randy was by my side before I knew it. I breathed a sigh of relief as he pulled himself up over my ledge.

He started to pull gear from his harness and put it on the ground in front of me for the last pitch. Until he came across my belay device.

"What's this doing here?" He glanced at my belay apparatus and stood silent for a few seconds. "Nice Munter!"

I smirked to myself as I began to clip on the gear he had left for me on the ground.

Only one pitch stood between us and the apex. I was surprised we had made it this far unscathed. As I chalked up and began the ascent, I looked up to the summit, happy to be there and happy to be alive. I scrambled quickly to the top, a kitchen table-sized ledge with barely enough room to maneuver. Ironically, I later learned that at least a dozen people have been up there simultaneously.

After putting him on a real belay this time around, Randy followed me to the top.

On our platform atop the cathedral, we witnessed only holiness. The world stopped. Beauty took over while we caught our breath, having lost it due to a combination of strain and fear. Surrounding us were several free-standing, finger-like spires that were even narrower than our haven. Beyond these formations were sweeping vistas of lakes and forests bordered by familiar domes. I surmised that we were two of only a few thousand people or fewer who had seen this view in a park that sees millions of visitors a year. It was a special moment for me, insofar as it was the first time that I had taken the lead on an ambitious rock climb and made it to the top. Before, I had always relied on others to get me from point A to point B. It was empowering. Where it signified an end of my travels with Curtis, it also commemorated a beginning.

As I sat on a precarious rocky platform several hundred feet above the ground, feet dangling off the edge, I realized just how important these mountains were to me. Before, I needed the camaraderie of others to prosper in these hills. But achieving great heights using my own common sense and determination reminded me of my quest for meaning in life. It is so important to share your experiences with others and to make sure you surround yourselves with great people to supplement the places that you go. But to truly achieve eternal happiness, you must find peace and tranquility by yourself as well. Sure, Randy was there with me every step of the way, but his presence was nothing like that of Curtis's, whom I always felt was the other half to my adventures.

Our quest was far from over, though. And danger still lurked. There wasn't an easy way down, and complete darkness was maybe an hour away. From the summit, the most efficient descent isn't to rappel. Rather, a short downclimb leads to moderate class 3 and 4 climbing around the back of the peak. But to get there, you must descend highly exposed, low class 5 terrain. Due to the exposure, we decided to rope up, just in case.

Randy led the "pitch" down to the bottom where he set up a belay for me. As Randy led, if he had fallen, I would've been able to catch him from the top. Unlike Randy's low consequences, if I fell, nothing was going to stop my fall except for the three cams that he had placed on the way down. I carefully untied from the anchor atop the summit and began my downclimb. As I stepped over the ledge, I saw hundreds of feet of nothing below me. I was in the zone, and it didn't faze me the least bit. I clambered down carefully, removing gear from the wall as I descended further toward Randy. When I reached him, we untied from the rope and coiled it up. The worst was behind us. Or so we thought.

From our vantage, we could see our desired location. We were supposed to descend and traverse over toward a gully. But the traverse was still quite exposed, and a fall here could spell doom. I took the lead, fearlessly. We had changed out of our climbing shoes into our approach shoes, so the traction wasn't nearly as good. But I felt comfortable making my way through the maze of slabby ledges as we neared the gully.

I hopped down gleefully to a ledge with a large bush as I reflected on our achievement of reaching the top. What a day it had been. Especially after what happened to Curtis. I thought back to the moments and hours after his fall. Thinking that I would never climb again. Feeling terrified. What were we doing? Climbing a goddamn wall. It clearly wasn't worth sacrificing everything for.

As my thoughts continued to wander, I heard a loud thump and a scream from behind me. I spun around to see Randy careening down toward me.

Everything went into slow motion, and I stood like a statue. The time to act was waning, and I momentarily lost control of my thoughts. Instinctively, I grabbed onto the bush and watched as Randy barreled right toward me. He must have rolled a good ten feet before skidding directly in front of me and coming to a halt.

"Jesus are you okay?" I blurted out apprehensively.

"HOLY SHHHH-SHH-SHIT!" He screamed with a tremble in his voice.

I let go of the tree and stood over Randy as he picked himself up off the ground. He looked past the bush to see what was below. Had he continued his tumble, he would have kept going for hundreds of feet.

"Dude, get the rope out," he asserted.

"Randy, it's okay, you're fine."

"I'm not going anywhere without the rope out."

"But it's easy from here, the hard parts are over . . . and it's getting dark."

"Not dark enough to get the rope out."

I raised my voice in typical fashion.

"RANDY, we don't have TIME for this."

"I ALMOST DIED, JUST LET ME GET ON THE ROPE."

I traversed the length of the sketchy section toward the gully with the rope trailing behind me. Reaching a comfortable spot, I set an anchor for Randy, who followed me on the rope, effortlessly.

"You okay?" I asked, genuinely concerned.

"Yeah. Just got a little psyched out."

The sun had fully set, and we didn't have time to lose. We found the descent gully and scurried down to the base of the mountain. I snapped a picture of the now shadowed mountain. The angle made it look like the peak was a series of jutting fingers, and as I looked closer at it, I could see the tabletop summit plateau, a mere speck on the rocky cathedral.

"Man, we were up there," I remarked, as I sipped water from my hose. Empty.

"It's crazy, huh? A little scary too."

"You almost ate shit back there."

"I did eat shit. And it tasted like pebbles and dirt."

"You hurt at all?"

"Naw. I'm good. A little freaked out though." Randy popped open his backpack and let me drink some of his water. I gulped as much as I could before he noticed.

"Hey, leave some for me!"

Though it was dark, we could still see jagged mountains illuminated in front of us as we began our hike down. They captured a reddish-orange and purple hue and lit up the valley like an uncontrolled blaze. Pines and scree straddled their slopes, which were capped by a blackening blue sky. It was an elusive display of majesty reserved for us and us alone. While the Valley slept, we whispered sweet somethings to the cool mountain air. This was paradise.

I am not a religious man by any stretch of the phrase, but it was in the mountains that I learned to embrace spirituality where nihilism once reigned. My bizarre obsession with long drives and my adolescent yearning for the road were the precursors to this lust. But it was only through my mountain travels with my best friend Curtis that I could have reached this point. It took almost a quarter-century, but I think I had finally found my purpose in life on that vibrant, sunny day at the cathedral. This was my religion. Except my church didn't have doors.

Epilogue

"There is nothing like returning to a place that remains un-changed to find the ways in which you yourself have altered."
—Nelson Mandela

* * *

When I was a kid, we had an indoor cat named Simba. Simba's favorite hobby was to jump onto the windowsill that overlooked our forested suburban yard. Often, he would claw at the screen, surely with the intent to break loose from the restraints of his cage. Seldom did he succeed in his efforts, but every once in a while we would notice the screen pushed out of the window. The rescue efforts would take anywhere from a few minutes to a few hours. Sometimes we would spot him fighting with another neighborhood cat. Other times he would emerge from the woods covered in dirt and brush. But we always found him. Even if he didn't want to be found.

As Simba got older, he would escape more often. Any time a door was accidentally left ajar, he was gone. He forced his way through the window screen more often. It was as if he recognized our negligent patterns and adapted to them.

On one occasion shortly before he died, Simba got out and *really* didn't want to come back in. Each time we attempted to corral him, he would hiss like a snake and bare his teeth at us. He lunged at my mom and scratched her up good. As I tried to reel him in with a bath towel, he dug his claws into my right arm and left a gruesome wound. Somehow, we were able to get him back inside, and he calmed down once he got in front of a bowl of food. But the scar that he imprinted on me remains to this day.

* * *

We all want change, but so many of us get settled into our daily routine—and we don't realize it until it's too late. But in a day and age where "civilization" is an integral part to the human experience, routine is becoming far less attractive. There are those who continue to abide by the notion of settling, and those who attempt to veer as far away from it as possible.

Our two road trips fostered in Curtis and me an appreciation for discomfort and insecurity—two ideas opposed to the very core of settling. We were so strangely attracted to the prospect of altering our mundane suburban lives, and travel gave us a reason to seek challenges in a life that had yet to challenge us. We'd bullshitted our way through school and mooched off everyone. We'd never had to worry about not having enough.

A million times I have attempted to explain why we wanted to escape what others would call a perfect existence. A million times I have failed to describe it without conjuring up one particular word: selfishness. We had this grand idea that what we were doing would improve our lives. But our lives were nothing short of great. We had little debt. We had college degrees. We had guaranteed jobs lined up if we wanted to take them. We had a roof over our heads. Our parents did our laundry and made us dinner nearly every night. Undeniably, we had everything.

What I've learned since I first took to the road is that having everything isn't *having everything*. We humans have created an illusory societal construct that having everything will make you happy.

Companies pay billions of dollars a year to sell their products to unsuspecting patrons. Possessions and affluence have risen to the forefront of human desire. As if we weren't indoctrinated enough, the media has crafted and pushed the shoddy narrative that having a lot of things will lead you toward contentment.

After so many years of living it, of getting everything we ever wanted, we were tired of the same old, same old. We had become lemmings in the corporatocracy, and we needed to escape. We needed to be selfish. And we needed the road. It gave us perspective and experience where we never had any before. Excessive possessions and money could never bring us happiness—at least, not long-term happiness. That was the first revelation that came upon us when we got home from our inaugural trip. It became increasingly apparent that our connection with the world around us was the starting point toward eternal satisfaction. Specifically, our appreciation of the simplest of features: dirt, sky, rocks, trees, water, flora, and fauna, to name a few.

In the 1960s, a French climber named Lionel Terray coined the term "conquerors of the useless." This phrase was later used by Yvon Chouinard of Patagonia and Black Diamond fame to describe mountaineering. It is a nihilistic perspective on an otherwise rewarding hobby, but a realistic one nonetheless. What were we accomplishing by going up and down a hill? Some people will never understand our lust for the mountains. The pure satisfaction of gripping a sharp rock in your hands as you hoist yourself up a vertical cliff. The elation that you get from the most basic of human movements—one foot in front of the other. It is so visceral and so ordinary, but so gratifying. Yet it is considered so unproductive and futile in our "civilized" society. Hence, we are conquerors of the useless.

Meaning, though, is what you make of it. Whether it's religion, philanthropy, education, or profession, your purpose in life is yours to discover. Even if others designate your path as meaningless, you are the arbiter of your own existence. Whether we were conquering something or nothing was nobody's business but our own. It gave us purpose. It made us happy.

*   *   *

A lot has changed since our first trip, though. I'm a licensed full-time lawyer in the state of Massachusetts. I practice property and criminal law among other things. The bulk of my work is in the capacity of a public defender, which is where my grandfather, Milty, commenced his legal career.

As I look back on my first road trip six years later, I realize just how naïve I was. We wanted perspective. And we got perspective. But perspective is not a one-size-fits-all concept. It is also a human construct. It is a word that simply means how we see the world and how we see others. And it is deeply personal. To me, gaining perspective requires that you embrace an open mind. While our road trips began to open my eyes, being a lawyer has further enhanced this open-mindedness. Most of my clients are near or below the poverty line. They scrape by paycheck to paycheck, if that. Many are victims and/or perpetrators of trauma. They grew up in a world where having things was a luxury, not an expectation. I never knew such a life and never knew anyone who lived one.

Growing up in suburbia distances you from reality. You reside in a separate world, much like that of college or that of the road.

Which is why I think I wanted the road so badly. I wanted to breach the unreal bubble that we have developed through geography and gentrification. We have built both visible and invisible barriers to the rest of society, much like we have built artificial borders to separate ourselves from those who live and speak differently than us. Politicians peddle hostility toward other countries whose ideas we disagree with. And we buy it thanks to corporate media.

Another experience that fueled my desire to take to the road was my abstinence from alcohol in college. It was a seemingly innocuous catalyst toward a monumental result. I was so resistant to the culture that it prompted me to want to change my life. Though I've since acquiesced to the reality of moderate alcohol consumption, my teetotalism was a huge part of who I was in college. I thought I was better than everyone, yet I had the hardest of times just making friends.

Why do I bring up my college days again? Because it reminds me how close-minded I once was. My attitude towards people who thought differently than I did was vitriolic. When I didn't understand why people acted certain ways or did certain things, I became hostile and agitated. This isn't uncommon—so many people act that same way, and their behaviors are encouraged in some circles. But if I only learned one thing from the road, it was that life is too short to worry about what other people think or do. And that I should be the best person I can be.

As for Curtis, well, he was never the same climber after his fall. Where he once had confidence on the cliffs, fear and anxiety took its stead. On multiple occasions since his injury, he has needed to back down from a climb, either from panic or pain. His headaches have returned on numerous occasions, sometimes with the same